Scattered Among the Nations

Documents Affecting Jewish History
49 to 1975

And the Lord shall scatter you among the peoples, and ye shall be left few in number among the nations, whither the Lord shall lead you away.

Deuteronomy 4:27 The Holy Scriptures according to the Masoretic Text

---

To the students who inspired this book, especially Becky Marr, Shayna Lutzker and Danya Joseph. They heed the past and look hopefully to the future.

Scattered Among the Nations

Documents Affecting Jewish History
49 to 1975

Alexis P. Rubin,
Editor

Wall & Emerson, Inc.
Toronto, Ontario • Dayton, Ohio

Requests for permission to make copies of any part of this work should be sent to: Wall & Emerson, Inc., Six O'Connor Drive, Toronto, Ontario, Canada M4K 2K1

Orders for this book may be directed to:

Wall & Emerson, Inc.	*or*	Wall & Emerson, Inc.
Six O'Connor Drive		8701 Slagle Rd.
Toronto, Ontario, Canada		Dayton, Ohio 45458
M4K 2K1		

Or by telephone or facsimile:

Telephone: (416) 467-8685 Fax: (416) 696-2460

Canadian Cataloguing in Publication Data

Main entry under title:

Scattered among the nations : documents affecting
    Jewish history 49 to 1975

Includes bibliographical references and index.
ISBN 1-895131-10-3

1. Jews - History - Sources. 2. Jewish diaspora.
I. Rubin. Alexis P.

DS102.S25 1993   909'.04924   C93-093216-1

ISBN 1-895131-10-3
Printed in Canada.

1 2 3 4 5 6   97 96 95 94 93

Table of Contents

Section Three

Section Four

List of Illustrations

Preface

The historical documents in this collection cover a time span of almost two thousand years, beginning in the early Christian era and concluding in the latter half of the twentieth century. They consist, for the most part, of laws, commentaries, and observations written by Christian religious and secular leaders. The forces both reflected and put into motion by these writings had a major impact on Jewish lives over the last two milennia. In a very real way, modern Jewish life is still shaped by them.

Scattered Among the Nations is a source book and text for one aspect of Jewish history: Christian-Jewish relations. In a sense *Scattered* presents the equivalent of a diplomatic history, with the exception that the nation in question—the Jewish people—had no territory of its own, no officially recognized ambassadors, could offer little or no protection to its "nationals," and had no army to pursue its goals. The Jews, for most of the time period in this book, lived entirely within the boundaries of other countries.

Yet the Jews scattered throughout Europe were similar to a national entity in a number of ways. They had a common language—Yiddish—derived from German (*Note:* Jews from Spain spoke Ladino, a language based on Spanish) and shared customs and beliefs which differed from the people among whom they lived. Most importantly, until Jewish emancipation in the modern era, the nations in which Jews resided viewed them as permanent aliens. Many of the authors of the documents in this book considered the Jewish people a distinctly separate nation. This concept of a permanent "alien" status is critical to understanding not only the documentary material in this collection, but also the general flow of Jewish history in Europe.

I selected the specific documents that appear in this collection because each deals with a major event or turning point in Jewish history. Gathered together, they show an evolving relationship between Christians and Jews from the viewpoint of the Christian participants, whose words speak for themselves. The book is not meant to be a detailed history of anti-Semitism. I made no attempt to concentrate solely on the issues of prejudice and persecution, nor do I claim that prejudice and persecution were the only reactions Christians had to Jews. It is true that most of the documents presented in this book reflect highly anti-Jewish feelings and describe much anti-Jewish persecution. The reader must remember, however, that like men and women today, people in the past had a tendency to dwell on and record the lurid, the senational, the unusual. Placid, everyday events often went by unnoticed. The fact that the Jewish people still exist today proves that there were many extended periods of peace and at least surface amity to offset times of ill will and physical danger.

The introductions and notes of *Scattered Among the Nations* are intended to put the documents into their historical context and explain how these writings affected Jewish life. Within the documents themselves, parentheses indicate words written by the documents' authors; brackets enclose my additional explanations.

The book's overall organization is chronological and according to topic. Within each topic, I have arranged the materials by country of origin. The documents were originally written in Greek, Latin, French, German, Spanish, English, Polish, Russian, and Italian. The English translations found in this book came from over fifty different sources, compiled and translated by both Christian and Jewish historians. I located some of the more recent material, including United Nations, British, and United States documents, in official publications and archival material. These needed no translation.

Many of the original documents were lengthy, and a number of the previous editors and translators condensed material. I have made further deletions to cut repetitious information, but kept the historically relevant passages intact. Where there are deletions, I have inserted ellipses, indicated by three dots (...).

The reader may be unfamiliar with the use of C.E. and B.C.E. Jewish historians often use these designations in lieu of A.D. (Anno Domini—in the year of our Lord) and B.C. (before Christ). C.E. stands for "Common Era" and B.C.E. for "before the Common Era." Whether one uses A.D. or C.E., B.C. or B.C.E., the years given are the same.

Acknowledgments

This book represents five years of research, writing, and "test marketing" on my students. It could not have been compiled and written without the help of many people, including mentors and colleagues.

I am deeply indebted to three people who carefully read my manuscript and offered many valuable suggestions: Dr. Aaron Goldman, Professor of History at San Jose State University; Dr. Egon Schwarz, Rosa May Distinguished University Professor in the Humanities, Washington University in St. Louis; and Dorothy Miller, Jewish educator and Hebrew High School principal, Saratoga and Los Altos, California.

Also I want to express a few words of appreciation to Dr. Charles Burdick, retired head of the School of Social Sciences at San Jose State University. His graduate classes instilled a deep love of history and a respect for historical scholarship and writing. His encouragement concerning this manuscript was most welcome.

I am grateful to Byron Wall, my publisher, and Martha Wall, my editor, for believing in this manuscript. They helped turn it into a book which I hope will both interest and inspire students of Jewish history.

The documents in this book came from many different sources. I wish to thank the librarians and staff of the following institutions for helping me locate the material I needed: the San Jose State University Library; the Saratoga, Cupertino, Santa Clara and Sunnyvale Public Libraries; the Jonnsen Library of Public Documents, the Cecil Green Graduate Library, and the Hoover Institution Library at Stanford University; the Franklin D. Roosevelt Library in Hyde Park; the National Archives; and the unseen staff of many inter-library loan departments throughout the United States.

Above all, a sincere thank you to my daughter, Miri, who undertook the arduous task of proofreading the original manuscript and to my husband, Michael, and my son, Jay, for their constant support and encouragement.

Alexis P. Rubin
Saratoga, California
September, 1992

The Exodus.

Introduction

The Foundations of an Enduring People

The Jewish people trace their history back to a Mesopotamian shepherd named Abraham. Sometime around 2000 B.C.E., he rejected the practice of polytheism and idol worship. Instead, during his wanderings through the Fertile Crescent, he adopted the belief in one, all-powerful, all-encompassing, all-knowing, and invisible God. Abraham's faith stood in striking contrast to the other religions of his time. Not only was his concept of the one God unique, but so also was his agreement with that God, an agreement that was intended to be binding on all of Abraham's descendants.

This agreement or "Covenant" very much represented a business contract. Abraham, for himself, and as a representative of his descendants, promised to worship only the one God and to live faithfully by God's laws. In return for this promise, God would choose, cherish, and keep Abraham and his descendants as a holy, "Chosen" people. This was not to be an honorific—in name only—title. The term "Chosen People" actually conferred an extra burden—that of becoming a vehicle for spreading God's message and laws to the other peoples of the earth.

To be true and faithful messengers, and to be more perfect living examples of God's law, Abraham's descendants were zealously to guard their cultural and religious identity by remaining a separate people. The sign of this perpetual covenant would be the circumcision—a visible, physical reminder that these people were distinct from all others. To close the negotiations God promised Abraham and his descendants the land between the Jordan River and the Mediterranean as their home forever.

Abraham, his son Isaac, and his grandson Jacob dwelt in this "Promised Land" and are known as the patriarchs, or fathers, who laid down the basic tenets of the Jewish faith. A drought and famine, however, forced Jacob's children to leave this land and settle in Egypt. As the generations passed, Egyptian leaders viewed the separateness of Jacob's descendants as a threat. The pharaohs impoverished and enslaved the Israelites, as they were now called, for fear that they would join with Egypt's enemies to overthrow the kingdom. Unsuccessful in overworking and starving them out, the pharaoh ordered the slaying of each newborn male Israelite.

As the story of the Exodus relates, one of the sons who escaped this mass slaughter grew up to lead the Israelites to freedom. Moses, placed in a basket to float down the Nile, was rescued by the pharaoh's sister, who raised him as her own. Later, discovering his real parentage, Moses left the royal palace, incurred pharaoh's wrath, and fled to the desert. Here, as a result of his encounter with God, Moses became the instrument for liberating the Israelites and reviving the Covenant.

Moses returned to Egypt to meet with the new pharaoh and demand the release of his people. After several acrimonious encounters, not to mention a host of plagues, including one which killed the pharaoh's oldest son and all other first-born Egyptian sons, the Israelites left Egypt. Where they had entered Egypt small in number, they left the kingdom by the Nile a numerous, rag-tag horde, gathered into twelve tribes—the descendants of Abraham's twelve great-grandsons.

The Israelites' long sojourn in Egypt brought them into intimate contact with another culture and dimmed their own concept of being a holy nation. To correct this situation, Moses delivered God's Ten Commandments, which reestablished monotheism, rejected idol worship, and set rules for the Israelites to follow in order to live peacefully with one another. Indeed, the Ten Commandments formed the basis for both a civil and a religious constitution for the Jewish people to which they still adhere today.

Egyptian slavery and forty subsequent years of wandering in the desert between Egypt and Canaan left the Israelites indelibly marked as a unique, separate people with a common goal and an uncommon destiny. Part of that destiny, they believed, was the conquering of Canaan—the Promised Land—a fertile area that lay on a natural trade and invasion route. It had been settled by many different peoples who were not willing to give up their lands without a struggle. Many years of fighting followed as the twelve tribes consolidated their holdings, settled down, and began lives as farmers, artisans, and shepherds. At the same time, the Israelites struggled to live up to their covenant with God through a process of trial and error, which helped the Jews reach an ever greater understanding and fulfilment of God's laws. Of inestimable help in this process were men of vision, called prophets, who, when the Jews strayed, called them back to God's laws.

In effect, the prophets were Israel's conscience. Surrounded by pagans, the Hebrews were at times tempted to adopt some of their neighbors' ways. But the prophets always reminded them of their duty. Needless to say, the prophets' words made many people uncomfortable. As a result, being a prophet was not always the safest calling! But, although some received rough treatment, the Hebrews eventually heeded their prophets' warnings. Ultimately, the institution of prophesy became so respected among the Jews that the prophets could chastise kings like David and Solomon for their moral lapses without fearing for their lives.

About 1000 B.C.E., King Solomon oversaw the building of a Temple to house the Ark of the Covenant containing the Ten Commandments. Solomon's Temple provided a central focus for the Hebrew religion and a visible symbol, not only of the greatness of the one God, but also the strength and vitality of the Jewish people.

When Solomon died, his sons quarreled over the succession, and around 950 B.C.E. they split the kingdom between themselves. The northern area became the kingdom of Israel, with its capital at Samaria. Judah, the southern kingdom, retained the capital at Jerusalem. Assyria, a new force from the east, conquered and annexed Israel in 722 B.C.E. Taken into captivity, the inhabitants of Israel disappeared as a group. Their uniqueness and tradition of separation were not sufficiently ingrained and the religious institutions were not well developed enough to allow for cultural and religious survival away from the Promised Land. It was a lesson many in the southern kingdom took to heart.

Judah's turn came a little over a century later. This time, Babylon, under Nebuchadnezzar, attacked Jerusalem and utterly destroyed Solomon's Temple. The conquerors removed a large segment of the population to Babylon, one of the most beautiful and cosmopolitan cities of the ancient world. Here the Jews were expected to mingle with the Babylonians and other captive people, become prosperous, and, ultimately, disappear into the surrounding population.

But Judah's Jews did not assimilate; they did not disappear as a people as had the Jews from Israel over a century earlier. Instead, they maintained their cultural ties by gathering together on holy days, such as the Sabbath, days of celebration, and days of fasting. While thus assembled, the Jews sang the songs they remembered the priest intoning during the animal sacrifices at the Temple. Sages constantly reminded them of their history and common heritage. Prophets told them what God expected of them and how, soon, they would return to the Promised Land. Of equal significance, men called scribes wrote down what was said at these assemblies and laid the foundation for the written tradition—the Bible.

In 538 B.C.E., the Persian leader, Cyrus, conquered the Babylonian Empire. Unlike Nebuchadnezzar, he chose to win the loyalty of the captive nations by letting them return to their homelands. So, in what seemed to be fulfilment of prophesy, a group of idealistic Jews left the easy life of Babylonia behind and returned to Jerusalem. They found the city and countryside in shambles. Other groups had moved in during the Jews' captivity in Babylon. The Jewish population which hadn't been carried off had sunk into poverty and mingled with the surrounding peoples, and were close to forgetting their destiny as the Chosen People. Despite these problems, or perhaps spurred on because of them, the Jews rebuilt their house of worship in Jerusalem. They dedicated the Second Temple in 516 B.C.E. to serve again as Judaism's focal point.

Religious leaders again became fearful concerning the long-term continuation of the Jewish people. Hebrew men were marrying pagan women who brought their idols into Judean homes. To post-exilic Jews, tolerance of pagan cultures led directly to absorption and disappearance. Encouraged by Ezra and Nehemiah, they adopted religious and secular reforms designed to separate them from their pagan neighbors and, above all, to ensure the continuance of a unique people living to serve God. So, dedicated as a holy nation, new laws and customs especially forbad marriages between Jews and pagans. To keep Jews from temptation, certain foods or combinations of foods which were common in their neighbors' diets were proscsribed. Since eating has always been part of most social activity, this rule effectively kept Jews socially separate.

Jews also had to maintain a strict Sabbath, a day of rest and religious reflection that became the focus of each week. At this time, somewhere around 450 B.C.E., secular and religious leaders declared the Torah (the Five Books of Moses) the holy and immutable word of God. Each week on the Sabbath, the people gathered to hear a portion of the Torah read and its significance discussed. These developments securely tied the Jews to the practice of their religion, and, of no less importance to the future, made religious rites less dependent on Temple sacrifice.

The Jews, with religiously sanctioned social separation, a written holy scripture, and religious rites not tied to Temple sacrifice, were now prepared to survive as Jews no matter what history had in store for them. This separateness, however, had its negative side. Other groups saw the Jews not as people heroically and steadfastly clinging to their traditions, but as a people who were stubborn, stiffnecked, exclusive, and intolerant. These negative views persistently followed the Jews during their sojourn through time and history. Individuals and communities suffered and died because of the prejudices spawned by these attitudes, but the Jewish people, as a whole, survived.

The expansion of Greek civilization, led by Alexander the Great around 325 B.C.E., however, sent cultural shock waves through Judea. Cosmopolitan and idealistic, the Greek conqueror made no attempt to interfere with local religious practice or to enforce the worship of the Greek gods. He let Greek knowledge, philosophy, and love of sports win over the conquered peoples. Alexander's success was astounding. While centralized Greek political domination did not survive his short reign, Greek cultural influence became widespread and deeply ingrained as it meshed with local tradition to form classical Hellenism.

Judean aristocracy was also lured by Greek culture. The upper classes soon spoke and read Greek and gave their children Greek names. Jews split between those who wished to accept those parts of Hellenism which they felt were compatible with Judaism and those who rejected any form of assimilation.

Alexander's successors complicated the issue. Following his death in 323 B.C.E., two of his generals, Seleucid and Ptolemy, took over Alexander's territories outside of Greece. After 125 years of warfare between the heirs of these two men, the Seleucid dynasty, based in Syria, took control of Judea. Much to the Jews' consternation these Syrian-Greeks, under their leader Antiochus Epiphanes, began to insist that the Jews give up their own God and customs, and begin worshipping and living according to Hellenic custom. In the manner dictated by their religious beliefs and cultural traditions, the Jews refused.

The account of Antiochus' attempt to wipe out Jewish religion and culture is retold every year in the Chanukah story. It is sufficient here to mention that the Jews, under the leadership of Judah the Maccabee (the Hammerer) and his brothers, carried out a successful revolt against Antiochus' army. The Jews again won their freedom from foreign control, and in 142 B.C.E. the surviving Maccabbee brother, Simon, became the head priest and ruler of Judea.

Simon and his heirs, called the Hasmonean dynasty, led Judea through 79 years of independence before the next great Mediterranean power, Rome, overwhelmed them. This interregnum was a stormy one, crowned by bloody struggles for the throne and religious and political friction between the aristocratic, Temple-based Sadducee party and the popularly supported, Synagogue-based Pharisees.

By 63 B.C.E., the Romans, intent upon conquering the known world, saw an opening through which they could gain mastery over Judea. In the guise of peacemaker and arbitrator, the Roman general Pompey ended Jewish independence and set the stage for the fateful scattering of the Jews among the nations and peoples of the earth.

Rome entered Judea through the back door. When the Hasmonean Queen Salome Alexandra died, her two sons claimed the throne. As Judea had had a treaty of friendship with Rome since 163 B.C.E., Salome Alexandra's sons appealed to a Roman general, Pompey, to arbitrate the situation.

Pompey, competing with Julius Caesar for popularity and power, saw his chance to win Judea for Roman glory and his own personal advancement. On the pretext of settling the dynastic quarrel, he marched his army to Jerusalem and laid siege to the city. In 63 B.C.E., the Romans broke through Jerusalem's fortifications, slaughtering Jews and laying waste to the city as they advanced to the Temple. Placing the weaker of the two Hasmonean brothers on the throne, Pompey then divided Judea into five administrative districts and made them a part of the Roman province of Syria.

A little over twenty years later, Marc Antony deposed the last Hasmonean king and replaced him with the strongly pro-Roman Herod, who was of Idumean ancestry. The people of Idumea only recently had converted to Judaism and, as a result, Herod did not truly understand Jewish customs and sensibilities. Dissatisfied with Herod's reign and Roman overlordship, many Judeans formed clandestine organizations to fight anew for Jewish independence. These groups were the progenitors of the Zealots who, in 66 C.E., led an open revolt against Rome.

Jews before the Christian era had not resided exclusively in Judea. Many had been living outside the Promised Land since the Assyrian and Babylonian conquests. As early as 700 B.C.E., these diaspora Jews had settled in Asia Minor and along the Tigris and Euphrates rivers. By the time Rome began to expand her rule, Jewish communities existed in Greece and Italia, and in Egypt along the Nile delta and the Mediterranean coast. Here, Jews made a living as merchants, traders, artisans, wine-makers, and olive growers.

The diaspora or "dispersed" Jews practised a synagogue-based Judaism, although they continued to send yearly contributions or taxes for the maintenance of the Temple in Jerusalem. They worshipped their invisible God, kept the Sabbath and holy days, maintained kashrut—the dietary laws—and married only among themselves. In outward ways, however, they were indistinguishable from their neighbors since they spoke the native languages and dressed according to local custom. The Roman emperors looked upon them favorably as law-abiding members of the empire and granted them the legal right to practice their religion.

The Hellenized pagans had mixed feelings about the diaspora Jews. The Jews' self-imposed separation and strange religious practices mystified and angered many of them. Both groups adamantly claimed their culture and religion to be the most advanced. As a result, there were deeply felt animosities between gentiles and Jews. Fueling the tensions was the fact that some gentiles were attracted to the moral and spiritual values of Judaism. Those who converted joined the Jewish community and were permanently separated from their families and friends. Others who were attracted to the faith of Moses did not take the final step to conversion but remained "fellow travelers" who admired Judaism.

Some Roman writers ridiculed Judaism because its adherents practiced a religion so different from the worship of the Roman gods. They also mistook the Jews' reluctance to mix socially and intermarry with gentiles as evidence that Jews hated all non-Jews and, therefore, hated all of mankind. It is difficult to gauge how well these writers represented public opinion. Their true significance lay in their influence on later Christian writers who stressed many of the same themes.

Jesus appears before Pontius Pilate, who "washes his hands" of the case.

Section One

The Genesis of Christian Attitudes toward Jews

As an imperial province, Judea was administered solely for the benefit of Rome. Few procurators and other officials understood or respected Jewish moral and religious traditions. Judea was a country seething with political discontent, conflicting ideologies, religious disputes, and economic hardships. During times of difficulty, deeply religious men, such as the prophets, had always come forward to offer words of comfort, visions of a better future, or dire warnings of disaster if the Jews did not mend their ways. This also happened in Roman-occupied Judea.

While some were preparing for open rebellion against Rome, other men counseled the Jews to look within themselves and turn back to God and His laws. While there were probably many such reformers, the teachings of one particular man came to have worldwide significance as a result of the actions of his followers.

This man was an itinerant carpenter from Galilee named Joshua, the son of Joseph. In his wanderings he saw his peoples' suffering and believed their salvation would come when they turned fully to God, repented their sins, and stressed love in their lives rather than hate. Relying on basic Jewish values and advocating a simple religion that all could practice, he attracted a group of devoted followers in Galilee. Joshua (known in Greek as Jesus) then decided to bring his teachings to the people in Jerusalem. But in the cosmopolitan center of Judea, the situation was quite different from that in rural Galilee.

Jerusalem's priests disagreed with Jesus' views concerning a simply practised religion. Christian writings indicate they were jealous of Jesus' popularity among the masses. The Romans, too, feared his influence on the common people. They interpreted his preaching concerning Judaism as a threat to Roman rule. With the encouragement of the priests, the Romans arrested and brought Jesus before Pontius Pilate, the Roman procurator. Pilate charged him with sedition and carried out the sentence of slow death by crucifixion, a common method of Roman execution.

Jesus' memory so impressed his Jewish followers that they began preaching not only his words and the story of his life, but also the idea that he was the long-expected Messiah. This the majority of Jews refused to believe since the true Messiah was supposed to be triumphant over Judaism's enemies. Jesus, they held, had suffered an ignominious death at the hands of the Romans.

One of those who ridiculed Jesus' messiahship was a Hellenized Jew from Tarsus named Saul. One fateful day, however, he had a vision which left him an ardent believer in Jesus and prompted him to preach Jesus' words wherever he went.

When the Jews refused to listen to him and even persecuted him, he took Jesus' message to the Hellenized pagans. Many of these people eagerly listened and accepted Saul's words as new guidelines for their lives.

The religion based on Jesus' teachings and reports of the miracles attributed to him began to spread. Paul, as he now called himself, exempted Jesus' gentile followers from many of Judaism's more stringent rules, including circumcision and strict dietary requirements. He stated that for them salvation would come through faith, not through strict adherence to Jewish religious laws. He, in effect, offered them the best of Judaism without many of its more exacting practices. It was an enormously successful combination.

To most people at the time, including the early Christians themselves, the religion of Jesus' followers was merely a variant sect of Judaism. The Jewish rebellion against Rome, however, created tensions which eventually led to the complete separation of Christianity from its mother-religion, Judaism.

In 66 C.E., the Jews of Judea began a long and tragic struggle to free themselves from Roman rule. They looked to the Maccabbee's successful fight against Antiochus and the Syrians, but failed to understand that the Roman Empire was a far more powerful enemy than Syria had been. The Roman army slaughtered the Jews mercilessly, devastated the countryside, razed Jerusalem, and utterly destroyed the Temple. The conquerors sent many of the surviving Jews to Rome as slaves. The Zealots who led the rebellion fled to the desert fortress of Masada where, in the end, they chose mass suicide rather than capitulation to Rome.

The Jews resented the fact that Jesus' followers did not help them during the rebellion. In turn, the Jews often refused to help the Christians when they were being persecuted by the Romans. In addition, the Christians began to interpret the defeat of the Jews and the destruction of the Temple as signs of God's wrath against the Jews for refusing to accept Jesus as the Messiah.

There were also other factors which drove the Jews and Christians apart. One was the traditional animosity that many Hellenized gentiles had harbored against the Jews since Ptolemy's and Selucid's time. Most of the early Christians were from these groups of people. Second, it was to the benefit of the early Christians to distance themselves from the Jewish rebellion. Rome, which recognized the practice of Judaism, ruled that Christianity was an outlawed cult. The Christians were eager to make themselves acceptable to the Romans in order to ensure the survival of the new religion. Consequently, it was politically astute of them to retell the story of Jesus' death, assigning blame to the Jews rather than to the Romans. The Gospels of Matthew, Mark, Luke, and John clearly portray Pilate as almost an innocent victim of the Jews' wrath as he bent to their will and condemned Jesus.

In the year 135 C.E., the last Jewish uprising against Rome—the Bar Kochba Rebellion—left Judea in complete shambles. The Romans had had enough of rebellion. They forbad the Jews, upon pain of death, to set foot in Jerusalem. The Romans even changed the area's name from Judea to Palestine, the home of the Philistines.

Roman soldiers carrying off the menorah from the temple in Jerusalem, which they destroyed in putting down the Great Revolt of 66 - 70 C.E.

Paul disputing with Jews.

Chapter I

The New Testament References to Jews

The Christian Testament consists of twenty-seven books. The Gospels or "good-tidings" of Matthew, Mark, Luke, and John tell about Jesus' life and death. The Acts of the Apostles discuss the spread of early Christianity. The next twenty-one books are letters written mostly by Paul to Christian communities in the Greco-Roman world and were meant to serve as guidelines on how to practice the new faith. The last book, Revelation, is a highly symbolic and surrealistic description of the climatic battle between the forces of good and evil.

The writings of the New Testament had deep and long-range effects on Christian attitudes toward Jews. The term "NEW Testament" itself refers to the idea that, with the coming of Jesus, God abandoned the Jews as the Chosen People and made a new and irrevocable covenant with the Christians.

We are concerned in this chapter with these earliest of Christian writings and how they affected relations with Jews for the next two millennia. Christian scholars assert that all the books of the New Testament were written in the century following Jesus' death. The Jewish revolts against Rome, the destruction of Jerusalem and the Temple, and the Bar Kochba Rebellion had already occurred when these books were compiled and edited around 140 C.E. by men, such as Marcion, who were known to be highly inimical to Judaism.

Unlike the order in which these books appear in the Christian Testament, the material in this chapter is presented in chronological order. In this manner the reader will be better able to discern how these writings provided the basis for Christianity's growing anti-Jewish attitudes.

Paul's letters send somewhat mixed messages on his attitude toward Jews. He clearly resented the fact that the Jews rejected his preaching concerning Jesus as the Messiah, and he described in detail how he was persecuted for his belief in Jesus. In the First Letter of Paul to the Thessalonians, one of the most vitriolic passages in the New Testament, he calls Jews the enemies of the whole human race. In spite of this, Paul believed the Jews would not be abandoned by God forever; they would eventually turn to Jesus and be saved along with all the other peoples of the earth. Both these attitudes became major factors in the Catholic Church's dealings with the Jews.

In the selections from Matthew, Mark, Luke, and John, we shall concentrate on their descriptions of the crucifixion and how, although they were not present in Jerusalem at the time, they blamed the Jews for Jesus' death. Since these writers were living in the Greco-Roman world, it was politic for them to disavow any relationship with the rebellious Jews and to show their own unswerving loyalty to the Empire. The accounts of Jesus' death cannot be understood historically without keeping this in mind.

1. The First Letter of Paul to the

Thessalonians 2:14–16

(c. 49 C.E.)

Source: The Holy Bible, Douay-Rheims Version (Rockford, Illinois: Tan Books and Publishers, Inc., 1899). This is a version of the Christian Bible used by Roman Catholics.

[In this oldest of the New Testament books, Paul writes to the gentile-Christians (those of pagan birth and background) in Thessalonica, sympathizing with their persecution at the hands of the pagans. He compares their plight to the Jewish attacks on Jewish-Christians (those of Jewish birth and background who accepted Jesus as the Messiah) in Judea. Paul then bitterly charges the Jews—his own people—with killing Jesus, driving out his followers, and preventing them from preaching Jesus' message of salvation to the gentiles. In relating this, Paul repeats a common Hellenic defamation that Jews are "adversaries to all men" or, more commonly termed, "enemies of the human race."]

For you, brethren, are become followers of the churches of God which are in Judea, in Christ Jesus: for you also have suffered the same things from your own countrymen, even as they have from the Jews, Who both killed the Lord Jesus, and the prophets, and have persecuted us, and please not God, and are adversaries to all men; Prohibiting us to speak to the Gentiles, that they may be saved, to fill up their sins always: for the wrath of God is come upon them to the end.

2.   *Mark 15: 6–15*

(c. 68 C.E.)

Source: The Bible. James Moffatt (New York: Harper and Brothers Publishers, 1935.) This is a version of the Bible used by Protestants.

[The Gospel According to Mark is the oldest and therefore the earliest narration extant of Jesus' life and death. While his description of Jesus' trial and execution is the simplest of the four Gospels, it still portrays the Jews demanding Jesus' death. Pilate, the Roman representative, innocently questions why the execution is necessary, but carries out the sentence to please the crowd. Note that Mark emphasizes the Jews' preference for Barabbas, a criminal, rather than Jesus. This left future Christian generations with no doubt as to the Jews' deep hatred for Jesus.]

At festival time he used to release for them some prisoner whom they begged from him. (There was a man called Bar-Abbas in prison, among the rioters who had committed murder during the insurrection.) So the crowd pressed up and started to ask him for his usual boon. Pilate replied, "Would you like me to release the king of the Jews for you?" (For he knew that the high priests had handed him over out of envy.) But the high priests stirred up the crowd to get him to release Bar-Abbas for them instead. Pilate asked them again, "And what am I to do with your so-called king of the Jews?" Whereupon they shouted again, "Crucify him." "Why," said Pilate, "what has he done wrong?" But they shouted more fiercely than ever, "Crucify him!" So, as Pilate wanted to satisfy the crowd, he released Bar-Abbas for them; Jesus he handed over to be crucified, after he had scourged him.

3.   *Luke 23: 13–25*

(c. 85–95 C.E.)

Source: The Bible, Moffatt.

[Luke elaborated on Jesus' trial and crucifixion, adding the presence of King Herod and a general agreement that Jesus did not deserve execution. The Jews in this Gospel are even more insistent that the carpenter from Galilee had to die.]

Then summoning the high priests and rulers and the people, Pilate said to them, "You brought me this man as being an inciter to rebellion among the people. I have examined him before you and found nothing criminal about him, for all your accusations against him. No, nor has Herod, for he has remitted him to us. He has done nothing, you see, that calls for death; so I shall release him with a whipping." But they shouted one and all, "Away with him! Release Bar-Abbas for us!" (This was a man who had been put into prison on account of a riot which had taken place in the city, and also on a charge of murder.) Again Pilate addressed them, for he wanted to release Jesus; but they roared, "To the cross, to the cross with him!" He asked them a third time, "But what crime has he committed? I have found nothing about him that deserves death; so I shall release him with a whipping." But they loudly urged their demand that he should be crucified and their shouts carried the day. Pilate gave sentence that their demand was to be carried out; he released the man they wanted, the man who had been imprisoned for riot and murder, and Jesus he handed over to their will.

4.　*Matthew 27: 15–26*

(c. 100 C.E.)

Source: The Bible, Moffatt.

[Matthew's account of Jesus' trial and execution exonerates the Romans and depicts the Jews so intent on killing Jesus that they accept his blood (the guilt for his death) not only upon themselves, but upon all their future generations. This continued to be Christianity's official position until the 1960s, when Pope John XXIII and the Vatican Council II decreed that the sin belonged solely to those Jews who actually committed the crime. Most Protestants also agree with this newer interpretation.]

At festival time the governor was in the habit of releasing any one prisoner whom the crowd chose. At that time they had a notorious prisoner called Bar-Abbas; so, when they had gathered, Pilate said to them, "Who do you want released? Jesus Bar-Abbas or Jesus the so-called 'Christ'?" (He knew quite well that Jesus had been delivered up out of envy. Besides, when he was seated on the tribunal, his wife had sent to tell him, "Let that innocent man alone, for I have suffered greatly to-day in a dream about him.") But the high priests and elders persuaded the crowds to ask Bar-Abbas and to have Jesus killed. The governor said to them, "Which of the two do you want me to release for you?" "Bar-Abbas," they said. Pilate said, "Then what am I to do with Jesus the so-called 'Christ'?" They all said, "Have him crucified!" "Why," said the governor, "what has he done wrong?" But they shouted on, more fiercely than ever, "Have him crucified!" Now when Pilate saw that, instead of him doing any good, a riot was rising, he took some water and washed his hands in presence of the crowd, saying, "I am innocent of this good man's blood. It is your affair!" To this all the people replied, "His blood be on us and on our children!" Then he released Bar-Abbas for them; Jesus he scourged and handed over to be crucified.

5.   *John 8: 44–45*

(c. 100–125 C.E.)

Source: The Bible, Moffatt.

[John, the last of the Gospel writers, has Jesus accusing the Jews of being children of the devil. To its followers, Christianity now represented God and truth, while Judaism was the ultimate evil and the Jews were congenital liars and murderers. With John, the psychological break between Christianity and Judaism seems complete.]

You belong to your father the devil, and you want to do what your father desires; he was a slayer of men from the very beginning, and he has no place in the truth because there is no truth in him: when he tells a lie, he is expressing his own nature, for he is a liar and the father of lies. It is because I tell the truth, that you do not believe me.

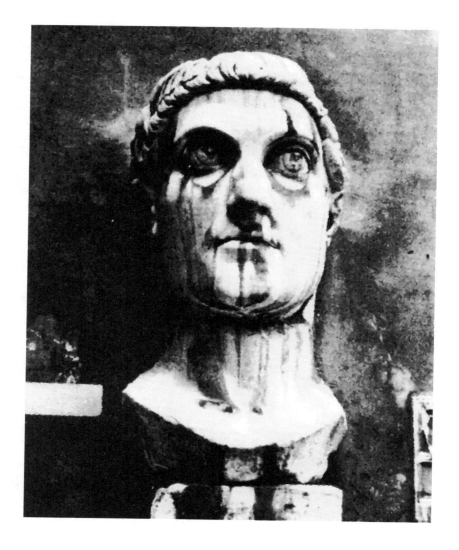

Constantine the Great.

Chapter II

Early Christian Writings Concerning Jews

The Christian religion led a precarious existence during the first two and one-half centuries following Jesus' death. The Roman Empire refused to accept the "Jesus cult" as a legally recognized religion, and many Romans cheered as Christians died in the arenas, martyrs for their faith. At the same time, Judaism competed vigorously for converts, and the traditional hostility between Hellenized gentiles and Jews in the east was strengthened by this religious competition. Two events, one a defeat and the other a victory, opened the doors for Christianity, allowing it to spread and become dominant throughout Europe.

In 135 C.E., the Jews under Bar Kochba's leadership suffered a complete and devastating defeat by the Roman Army. Banned from Jerusalem, Judaism turned inward in an attempt to survive the removal of the very heart of its faith. Christian leaders were quick to take advantage of this. They developed a theory that the Temple had been destroyed and the Jews driven from Jerusalem as divine punishment for their rejection of Jesus. The ignominious exile of the Jews was ample proof to the growing number of Christian converts of the truth of this theory.

In 311 C.E., following a military victory in which he is said to have carried a cross into battle, Emperor Constantine embraced Christianity. As a result of the Edict of Milan two years later, Christians gained the legal right to practice their faith, and Emperor Theodosius I, in 379, made Christianity the state religion of the Roman Empire. This triumph of Christianity heralded the Jews' descent into isolation and persecution as the church worked to separate the two religions firmly in the minds of the people.

Christianity's fundamental attitudes toward Jews and Judaism derived from the writings in the New Testament, which early church leaders such as Origen of Alexandria, Gregory of Nyssa, and John Chrysostom developed into a religiously inspired theory, condemning Jews in the most vicious terms. Imperial edicts and Church councils enacted laws which reinforced these anti-Jewish attitudes. In this way, theological rhetoric was transformed into a rationale for universal hatred and prejudice as the Christian population of Europe internalized the Church's teachings and put them into practice.

Theory

The New Testament writings served as the theoretical base upon which the early Christian church developed its philosophy concerning Jews. According to the Church's evolving beliefs, the destruction of the Temple and the exile from Jerusalem were divine punishments for the Jewish conspiracy against Jesus. For refusing to accept the Messiah, the Jews lost their Chosen People status and were forever damned as wanton, immoral, and murderous enemies of the whole human race.

In seeming contradiction to this attitude, the Church insisted that the Jewish people not be completely destroyed since they were destined to serve as witnesses to the Old Testament prophecies concerning Jesus' coming. The Jews were to live in servitude among Christians as befit their status as an accursed people and, at the end of time, those Jews who were left would finally convert to Christianity. This would herald Jesus' return to reign over the earth.

6.   Origen of Alexandria

Most Abominable of Crimes

(b.185–d.254 C.E.)

Source: Leon Poliakov, *The History of Anti-Semitism*, Vol. I: From the Time of Christ to the Court Jews (New York: Vanguard Press, Inc. 1965), p. 23.

[Origen was an ecclesiastical writer and teacher who contributed to the early formation of Christian doctrines. He was especially influential in developing beliefs which emphasized Jesus' divine rather than human nature.]

We may thus assert in utter confidence that the Jews will not return to their earlier situation, for they have committed the most abominable of crimes, in forming this conspiracy against the Saviour of the human race... Hence the city where Jesus suffered was necessarily destroyed, the Jewish nation was driven from its country, and another people was called by God to the blessed election.

7.   Gregory of Nyssa

Murderers, Assassins...

(b.331–d.394 C.E.)

Source: Poliakov, p. 25.

[Gregory of Nyssa was a Saint and a father of the Eastern Orthodox Church. As a theologian, he supported Origen's views and was famed for his persuasive writing. His harsh beliefs concerning Jews had a great influence on the Byzantine-Eastern Orthodox tradition which, in turn, imprinted anti-Jewish attitudes on Russian Orthodox Christianity.]

Murderers of the Lord, assassins of the prophets, rebels and detesters of God, they outrage the law, resist grace, repudiate the faith of their fathers. Companions of the devil, race of vipers, informers, calumniators, darkeners of the mind, pharisaic leaven, Sanhedrin of demons, accursed, detested, lapidators [people who throw stones at others?, people who stone others to death?], enemies of all that is beautiful...

8.   John Chrysostom

Anti-Jewish View

(b.344–d.407 C.E.)

Source: Poliakov, p. 25.

[John "Chrysostom" (from the Greek chrysostomos—"goldenmouthed"), a missionary preacher famous for his sermons and addresses, was a Saint and a father of the Eastern Orthodox Church. Practicing a life of self-denial, he was extremely critical of wealth and ostentation which he believed led eventually to social upheaval and moral disintegration. His attacks on the Jews reveal his ascetic distaste for what he perceived as their sumptuous life styles.]

Brothel and theater, the synagogue is also a cave of pirates and the lair of wild beasts... Living for their belly, mouth forever gaping, the Jews behave no better than hogs and goats in their lewd grossness and the excesses of their gluttony. They can do one thing only: gorge themselves with food and drink...

Laws

Even before Christianity became the established religion in the Roman Empire, church and state leaders began translating theory concerning Jews into ecclesiastical and secular laws which defined the Jewish peoples' place in Christian society. The major thrust of these laws was the social and religious separation of Jews from Christians. Jews were forbidden to hold public office in which they could exercise any control over Christians. They could not testify in court against members of the Christian faith. There could be no intermarriage between the two groups. Jews could not possess Christian slaves, nor could they circumcise or convert pagan ones. Jews could not prevent other Jews from converting to Christianity, and the church forbade Jews to accept proselytes from any group. They could repair old synagogues but build no new ones.

While this legislation was highly restrictive, the early popes and Christian emperors insisted that the Jews not be forcibly baptized and that they should be safe from physical violence. The Jewish people could retain all the traditional freedoms and rights which they had possessed up to that time, but could acquire no new ones.

Interestingly, one of the earliest church councils, held at Elvira in 304 C.E., decreed that Jews could not bless Christian fields and Christians could not eat with

Jews. The historian must assume these were still common practices and that the Church worked energetically in the early years to convince ordinary Christians that it was necessary to separate themselves from their Jewish neighbors. Judaism also preached the separation of Jews from gentiles and so, in this instance, both religions had a common goal.

---

9.   Council of Elvira

Laws Relating to Jews

(304 C.E.)

Source: E. H. Lindo, *The History of the Jews of Spain and Portugal* (New York: Burt Franklin, 1848; reprinted, 1970), p. 10.

[The Council of Elvira, held near Granada in Spain, was one of the earliest gatherings of Church leaders convened to give definitive answers concerning Christian religious beliefs and Church policy. It met nine years before Emperor Constantine issued the Edict of Milan, legalizing the practice of Christianity in the Roman Empire. Although concerned with the Church in Spain, four of the Council's 81 canons or laws set precedents on how the separation of Christians and Jews would be enforced in Christian society soon to spread throughout Europe.]

Canon 16

The daughters of Catholics shall not be given in marriage to heretics, unless they submit themselves to the Catholic Church; the same is also ordained for Jews and schismatics. Parents who transgress this order shall be excommunicated for five years.

Canon 49

Landholders are to be admonished not to permit the produce they thankfully receive from God to be blessed by the Jews, lest our benediction be rendered invalid and unprofitable. Should any person presume to do so after this interdiction, let him be entirely rejected from the church.

Canon 50

If any person, whether clerical or one of the faithful, shall take food with Jews, he is to abstain from our communion, that he may learn to amend.

Canon 78

If one of the faithful, having a wife, commit adultery with a Jewess or Pagan, he is to be ejected from our communion.

10.   Constantine the Great

Laws Concerning Jews, Heaven-Worshippers, and Samaritans

(October 18, 315 C.E.)

Source: Jacob R. Marcus, *The Jew in the Medieval World*, (Cleveland: World Publishing Company, 1961. Orig. copyright 1938) p. 4.

[Within two years of the legalization of Christianity, Constantine made it a capital crime for Jews to seek out new converts. The Church continued this policy, and Judaism's ability to grow by missionary action all but disappeared.]

We wish to make it known to the Jews and their elders and their patriarchs that if, after the enactment of this law, any one of them dares to attack with stones or some other manifestation of anger another who has fled their dangerous sect and attached himself to the worship of God *[Christianity]*, he must speedily be given to the flames and burnt together with all his accomplices.

Moreover, if any one of the population should join their abominable sect and attend their meetings, he will bear with them the deserved penalties.

11.   Theodosius II, Roman Emperor in the East

Treatment of Jews

(412 or 418 C.E.)

Source: Edward A. Synan, *The Popes and the Jews in the Middle Ages* (New York, The Macmillan Company, 1965), p. 30.

[Widespread attacks on Jewish communities in the Eastern Roman Empire, fueled by religious tensions and long-standing animosities, led Emperor Theodosius II to issue orders protecting the Jews. This was later included in the Code of Justinian.]

Let no one who has done no harm be molested on the ground that he is a Jew, nor let any aspect of his religion result in his exposure to contumely; in no place are their synagogues or dwellings to be set afire, or wantonly damaged, for, even if the case be otherwise and some one of them is implicated in criminal activities, obviously it is for precisely this that the vigor of the judiciary and the protection of public law have been instituted among us: That no one should have the right to permit himself private vengeance. But, just as it is Our will that this be the provision for those persons who are Jews, so too do We judge it opportune to warn the Jews that, elated, it may be, by their security, they must not become insolent and admit anything which is opposed to the reverence due to Christian worship.

12. Theodosius II

Novella III: *Concerning Jews, Samaritans, Heretics, and Pagans*

(January 31, 439 C.E.)

Source: Marcus, pp. 5–6.

No Jew—or no Samaritan who subscribes to neither *[the Jewish nor the Christian]* religion—shall obtain offices and dignities; to none shall the administration of city service be permitted; nor shall any one…fortified by the authority of the acquired rank…have the power to judge or decide as they wish against Christians, yes, frequently even over bishops of our holy religion themselves, and thus, as it were, insult our faith.

Moreover, for the same reason, we forbid that any synagogue shall rise as a new building. However, the propping up of old synagogues which are now threatened with imminent ruin is permitted…

13. Pope Gregory I (the Great)

How to Deal with the Jews

(June, 591 C.E.)

Source: Marcus, p. 111.

[Gregory I may well have been the most important and influential pope in the history of the Catholic Church. He developed and enforced Church liturgy, doctrine, discipline, and organization. While he worked vigorously to convert all pagans to Christianity, he steadfastly spoke out against forcing Jews to accept baptism and insisted that no one should deprive them of their traditional freedoms.]

Very many, though indeed of the Jewish religion, resident in this province *[Rome]*, and from time to time traveling for various matters of business to the regions of Marseilles, have apprised us that many of the Jews settled in those parts have been brought to the font of baptism more by force than by preaching. Now I consider the intention in such cases to be worthy of praise, and allow that it proceeds from the love of our Lord. But I fear lest this same intention, unless adequate justification from *[a verse of]* Holy Scripture accompany it, should either have no profitable effect; or there will ensue further (God forbid) the loss of the very souls which we wish to save.

For, when any one is brought to the font of baptism, not by the sweetness of preaching but by compulsion, he returns to his former superstition, and dies the worse for having been born again.

Let, therefore, your Fraternity stir up such men by frequent preaching, to the end that through the sweetness of their teacher they may desire the more to change their old life. For so our purpose is rightly accomplished and the mind of the convert returns not again to his former vomit. *[Note: Here, Gregory I is referring to a quote from the New Testament (2 Peter 2:22) which in turn comes from Proverbs 26:11: "As a dog that returneth to his vomit, so is a fool that repeateth his folly." This expression was often borrowed by future popes when referring to baptized Jews who returned to Judaism.]*

14. Pope Gregory I

Jewish Rights

(c. 600 C.E.)

Source: Bernard S. Bachrach, *Early Medieval Jewish Policy in Western Europe* (Minneapolis: University of Minnesota Press, 1977), p. 35.

Just as no freedom may be granted to the Jews in their communities to exceed the limits legally established for them, so too in no way should they suffer a violation of their rights.

15. Pope Stephen IV

Epistle on Error of Granting Land in Christian Territories to Jews

(768 C.E.)

Source: Synan, p. 62.

[Visigoths ruled Southern France after the collapse of the Roman Empire. These people practiced Arianism, a form of Christianity which worshipped Jesus, but claimed he was not divine and was not co-equal with God. This belief was at odds with the Roman Catholic rite followed by other Christians. Unlike Catholicism, Arianism was not anti-Jewish in its views and, consequently, the Jews fared well under the early Visigothic rulers.

Visigoths allowed Jews to own land and enjoy freedoms that would have been unprecedented in areas controlled by Catholics. Even when the Franks took Gaul from the Visigoths in 507, Jews continued to own hereditary estates. The following letter from Pope Stephen IV bitterly complained that Jesus' enemies had no right to own fields and vineyards.

As Europe entered the Medieval era, several factors combined to force Jews off the land. The first was direct pressure from the Church decrying Jewish land-ownership. The second factor was secular and Church prohibition of Jews owning slaves or hiring Christian servants. Without access to this manpower, farming large estates was all but impossible. Finally, with the spread of feudalism, land ownership required swearing a Christian oath of fealty to the local noble or king. Jews, unable and unwilling to take those oaths, became landless wanderers driven from one kingdom to another as it pleased the kings' whims.]

For this reason are We touched by sorrow, anxious even unto death, since We have known through you that the Jewish people, ever rebellious against God and derogatory of our rites, within the frontiers and territories of the Franks, own hereditary estates in the villages and suburbs, as if they were Christian residents; for they are the Lord's enemies... Christian men cultivate their vines and fields, and Christian men and women, living with those same deceivers both in town and out of town, are day and night strained by expressions of blasphemy... What was sworn to and handed over to those unbelievers by the Lord himself...has been taken away deservedly, in vengeance for the crucified Savior.

Practice

Several hundred years of theologically inspired anti-Judaism had its effect on the Christian population of Europe. We have documentary evidence that even before the Crusades, Jewish communities in Europe suffered periodic attacks by Christian mobs. Pope Gregory I, later sainted by the Church, warned against plans to annihilate the Jewish people as early as 600 C.E. Theory that the Jews were the enemies of the Christians and laws reinforcing separation between the two groups resulted in a growing fear and hatred of the Jewish people. Prejudice and persecution followed.

---

16. Pope Alexander II

Warning against Violence toward the Jews

(c. 1060)

Source: Robert Chazan, *Church, State and Jew in the Middle Ages* (New York: Behrman House, Inc., 1980) pp. 99–100.

[About the year 1060, Spanish fighters, pledged to push the Moslems out of their country, attacked Jewish communities not only to kill those whom they considered infidels, but also to steal what money and supplies the Jews possessed. These

anti-Jewish actions served as a prologue to the Crusading era when hundreds of Jewish communities suffered and disappeared as Christian soldiers made their way to the Holy Land to fight the Saracens.]

Pope Alexander to all the Bishops of Spain:

We are pleased by the report which we have heard concerning you, that you have protected the Jews living among you, lest they be slain by those who set out to war against the Saracens in Spain. These warriors, moved surely by foolish ignorance and strongly by blind cupidity, wished to bring about the slaughter of those whom divine charity has perhaps predestined for salvation. In the same manner Saint Gregory also admonished those agitated *[agitating?]* for annihilating them, indicating that it is impious to wish to annihilate those who are protected by the mercy of God, so that, with homeland and liberty lost, in everlasting penitence, damned by the guilt of their ancestors for spilling the blood of the Savior, they live dispersed throughout the various areas of the world. The situation of the Jews is surely different from that of the Saracens. Against the latter, who persecute Christians and drive them out of their cities and homes, one may properly fight; the former, however, are prepared to live in servitude.

17.   Pope Gregory VII

Letter to Alphonso VI, King of Spain
Synagogue of Satan

(1081)

Source: Synan, p. 65.

[This letter from Pope Gregory VII shows how the Jews' fate was often tied to which man sat on the Throne of Saint Peter. Some popes, although always making clear they rejected the Jewish faith, protected Jews and their rights in Christian lands. Other popes, using highly emotional anti-Jewish rhetoric, inflamed Christian populations with increased hatred and prejudice.]

We are compelled out of duty to warn Your Affection, that you ought not permit Jews in your land to be lords over Christians, or to wield power over them any longer. For what is it to set Christians beneath Jews, and to make the former subject to the judgment of the latter, except to oppress the Church and to exalt the Synagogue of Satan, and, while you desire to please the enemies of Christ, to condemn Christ himself?

18. Henry IV, Holy Roman Emperor

Settlement Charter in the German States

(February 19, 1090)

Source: Chazan, *Church, State and Jew in the Middle Ages*, pp. 60–63.

[Emperor Henry IV's settlement charter gave asylum to Jews who had been attacked and, in some cases, tortured, where they had previously resided. It offered them physical protection and the right to carry on trade and business without restriction. Two provisions differed markedly from common practice in dealing with Jews. Contrary to custom in other countries, where Jews were forbidden to disinherit converts, Henry IV's charter ordered apostate Jews to leave their possessions behind. He also allowed Jews to own pagan slaves, a practice which the Church frowned upon since these pagans might easily be persuaded to accept Judaism.

This charter, unfortunately, provided only a temporary haven. In 1096, Crusaders viciously attacked and slaughtered entire Jewish communities along the Rhine River, including Speyer, Mainz, Worms, and Cologne. Only those Jews who accepted baptism survived. When the crusading fever cooled, Henry IV, again contrary to Church policy, allowed the forcibly baptized Jews to return to their ancestral faith.]

In the name of the Holy and undivided Trinity, Henry, by divine mercy third august emperor of the Romans, to all the bishops, abbots, dukes, counts, and all subjects of the laws of our kingdom:

Let it be known that certain Jews, Judah b. Kalonymus, David b. Meshullam, Moses b. Yekutiel, and their associated, came before us at Speyer and requested that we take and hold them under our protection, along with their descendants and all those who seem to hope for security through them. May all our faithful know that this has been done. Therefore through the intervention and petition of Huozmann, bishop of Speyer, we have ordered that this authoritative writ of ours be granted and given to them. Hence by the royal declaration of our majesty, we order and command that:

1. Henceforth no one who is invested in our kingdom with any dignity or power, neither small nor great, neither free man nor serf, shall presume to attack or assail them on any illicit grounds.

2. Nor shall anyone dare to take from them any of their property, which they possess by hereditary right, whether in land or in houses or in gardens or in vineyards or in fields or in slaves or in other property both movable and immovable. If indeed anyone shall perpetrate violence against them in disregard of this edict, he shall be forced to pay to the treasury of the bishop one pound of gold; also he shall repay doubly the item which he took from them.

3. They may have the free right to exchange their goods in just trading with all men and to travel freely and peacefully within the bounds of our kingdom in order to carry on their business and trade, to buy, and to sell. No one may exact from them tolls or demand any public or private levy.

4. Guests are not to be lodged in their homes without their consent. No one may requisition from them a horse for a royal or episcopal journey or for the service of a royal expedition.

5. If a stolen item be found in their possession and if the Jew claims that he bought it, he shall substantiate by an oath according to his law how much he paid and how much he would accept, and in that way he shall return the item to him to whom it belonged.

6. No one shall presume to baptize their sons or daughters against their will. If anyone baptize them against their will or when they have been carried off by stealth or seized forcibly, he shall pay twelve pounds to the royal or episcopal treasury. If certain of them wish freely to be baptized, they shall be held three days, so that it be clearly known if indeed they repudiate their law because of Christian faith or by virtue of some injury which they have suffered. Just as they leave behind their ancestral law, so also are they to leave behind their possessions.

7. No one shall divert their pagan slaves from their service, baptizing them under the pretext of Christian faith. If anyone does this, he shall pay a ban, i.e., three pounds of silver, enforced by the judicial authority. Moreover he shall return the slave to his master without delay. The slave must abide by all the commands of his master, except for the observance of the Christian faith, with whose sacraments he has been imbued.

8. It is permissible to have Christians do their work, except on festivals and Sundays.

9. It is not, however, permissible for them to buy a Christian slave.

10. If a Christian has a dispute or contention against a Jew concerning any matter or vice versa, each may carry out justice and prove his case according to his law.

11. No one may force a Jew to judgment by hot irons or boiling water or frigid water or turn them over for stripes or place them in prison. Rather he shall swear by his law after forty days. Nor may he be convicted by any witnesses on any issue. Anyone who wishes so to force them against this edict shall be forced to pay a ban, i.e., three pounds of silver.

12. If anyone shall wound a Jew, but not mortally, he shall pay one pound of gold. If it be a slave that killed or wounded him, his master shall both pay the impost stipulated and shall hand over the slave for punishment. If, suffering from indigence, he be unable to pay the prescribed amount, the same penalty will be levied by means of which the assassin of the Jew Vivus was punished at the time of Emperor Henry my father, viz., his eyes will be put out and his right hand cut off.

13. If the Jews have a dispute or a case among themselves to be decided, they shall be judged and convicted by their peers and by none other. If any wicked one among them wishes to hide the truth of an internal affair, he shall be forced, according to their law, by him who stands in charge of the synagogue by appointment of the bishop to confess the truth of the matter in question. If difficult issues or disputes are raised among them or against them, they shall be referred to the presence of the bishop—their peace being preserved in the meantime—so that they might be settled by his judgment.

14. Moreover, they may have the right to sell their wine and their dyes and their medicines to Christians. As we have stated, no one shall demand from them a money levy or transport services or any exaction public or private.

In order that the authority of this concession remain inviolate for all times, we have ordered that this charter be written and sealed with the impression of our seal.

The Altneuschul in Prague. The eighteenth century clock on the tower has Roman numerals and runs clockwise. The lower clock on the sixteenth century dormer has Hebrew characters and runs counterclockwise.

Section Two

The Jewish Middle Ages

In European history, the term "Middle Ages" encompasses the time span between the fall of the Roman Empire and the flowering of the Renaissance, approximately 500 to 1450 C.E. The Middle Ages for Christian Europe was a time of retrenchment when the Church filled in the vacuum left by the decay of Roman power and control. Religion—specifically, Roman Catholicism—provided a needed barrier against the uncertainties of the world and gave its followers a definite place in the universal "scheme of things." The Church, in trying to bring order out of early medieval chaos, insisted on strict submission to its authority and did its best to discourage innovation and questioning.

While Europe's Jews lived through that continent's medieval era, they also endured a Middle Ages of their own. This Jewish "Middle Ages" likewise represented an era of hardship, restricted world view, and economic and political decline. Medieval Europe's sufferings—political disintegration, social upheaval, unending warfare, and years of bubonic plague—visited double hardships on the Jews. In addition to sharing all their neighbors' miseries, Jews had to endure being blamed for those miseries. Beginning with the Crusades and not lessening until the Napoleonic era, persecution, prejudice, and social isolation followed Europe's Jews wherever they settled.

To a great extent, the Church's negative view of the Jews was the major factor behind the centuries of hostility and hardship. Religious leaders taught the populace that Jews killed Jesus and were forever enemies of the Christians. This encouraged the crusaders' slaughter of Jewish settlements, the almost continuous expulsions from one kingdom to another, the charge that Jews murdered Christians for their blood, and the incarceration of Jews in squalid, spirit-numbing ghettoes.

The Jewish people survived their "Middle Ages" in Europe partly because they refused to change and partly because they were marvelously adaptable. On the one hand, they adamantly clung to their religious beliefs, which, during the worst times, gave them a buffer against the terrors and uncertainties of the real world. On the other hand, Jews learned to make the best of all situations and honed their survival techniques to perfection. For the most part, they did not fight back against persecution and slaughter since armed resistance on the part of such a small minority would have been disastrous. Instead they learned the skills of relocation and negotiation: move to someplace new, offer its leaders something they needed, and negotiate protection and, hopefully, better conditions. The Jews' continued existence through the Middle Ages into the modern world offers ample proof of their ability to adapt to new conditions and their unshakable desire to endure as a people.

Expelled Jews on the move to a new home.

Constantinople under attack during a Crusade.

Chapter III

The Crusades and the Jews

By the year 1000 C.E., the unity of the Roman Empire was but a distant memory. Europe consisted of small kingdoms steeped in the medieval feudal tradition of constant petty warfare. The Roman Catholic Church was the only institution to which all Christian Europeans, at least spiritually, owed allegiance. As supreme leaders of that church, the Medieval popes worked ceaselessly to expand their control into the temporal, non-religious, world.

In 1095, the Byzantine Emperor, Alexius, appealed for help to defend his empire and the Holy Land against the Moslem Seljuk Turks. Pope Urban II responded in a speech at Clermont in France by calling for a holy crusade to drive the infidel Turks out of Jerusalem and to crush finally the Moslem threat to Christianity. In launching the crusading movement, Urban also hoped to strengthen the power of the papacy and to unite the warring factions in Europe behind the conquering cross.

The pope assumed his call for a holy war against the Saracens, as Christians called the Moslems, would be carried out by the strongest feudal nobles in an organized manner. His call, however, struck a deeply responsive chord in the minds of the common people. The thrill of participating in such an undertaking, not to mention spiritual and possible monetary rewards, was too strong for many poor peasants and artisans to wait for organized leadership. Lured by dreams of fame, fortune, and adventure, and forgiven their sins and debts by the pope, the crusaders set off in unruly throngs toward the Holy Land. Their leaders were unscrupulous men who retained control by keeping the peasants' passions and hatreds stirred.

Given this situation, Jews provided the perfect targets for these rapacious mobs. There, right in their midst, were the people the Crusaders believed to be the enemies of Christ. The peasants' leaders told them, in effect: Slay the Jews, avenge Jesus' death, and all that is theirs will be rightfully yours. It was a powerful argument for the superstitious, the illiterate, and the poor. For Jewish communities, particularly those along the Rhine, the Crusaders' attacks were devastating. Where once they had tended their vineyards, sold their goods, and existed, for the most part, peacefully with their Christian neighbors, now whole communities perished by the Crusaders' swords.

When Pope Eugenius III called for the Second Crusade in 1145, the Church took steps to make sure the crusaders were responsibly led. Bernard of Clairvaux, one of the most respected religious leaders of his time, preached widely against anti-Jewish violence. His admonitions had only a temporary effect.

Jewish life in Western Europe was almost extinguished during the eight crusades which lasted from 1095 to 1270. Growing Christian "nationalism" during this era permanently branded the Jew as an alien, an eternal enemy, and an implacable foe. Accusations of ritual murder, host desecration, and well poisoning, causing the Black Death, which we shall discuss later in this section, were direct outcomes of the new anti-Jewish animus.

---

19.   *Report of Attack on the Jewry of Mainz during the First Crusade*

(1096)

Source: August Krey (ed.) *The First Crusade; The Accounts of Eye-Witnesses and Participants* (Gloucester, Mass.: Peter Smith, 1958), pp. 54–56.

[As earlier documents in this collection make clear, a strong anti-Jewish attitude appeared very early in the development of Christianity. Traditional animosities between Jewish and Hellenic communities—now mostly Christian—fueled the problem, as did the Jews' continued refusal to accept "one of their own" as the promised Messiah and the son of God. Church teachings put Jews in a unique situation: they were to be degraded, detested, reviled, shunned, and harangued, but they were also to be allowed to survive and to practice Judaism, albeit, in a humble manner. Theologically, the Church insisted, the Jews were the slaves of Christians, damned for rejecting Jesus and deserving only of eking out a barely minimal existence. The fact that many Jews were successful at their trades and managed to live comfortable, if not sumptuous, lives only deepened Christian enmity. In retrospect, it seems

surprising that the popes reacted with amazement when centuries of vituperation from the pulpit erupted into anti-Jewish violence.

With Urban II's call for a holy Crusade, the nurtured hatred and jealousy which simmered just below the surface exploded violently throughout Christendom. As they faced the furious onslaughts, motivated primarily by "greed of money" and secondarily by blind religious fervor, the Jews soon realized they could depend on no one. Neighbors, who at first promised support, and local leaders all failed to help them. They desperately tried to defend themselves, but with no outside aid and facing a vastly superior force in both numbers and weapons, the Jews' resistance was futile.

A Jewish report of events at this time is revealing: "Then they [the Jews] *all approached the gate to do battle against the Crusaders and burghers (businessmen in the towns who viewed the Jews as their major economic competition). One side fought against the other at the gate. But, as a result of our sins, the enemy triumphed and captured the gate…" (Chazan, European Jewry and the First Crusade, p. 139.) The lament that defeat came as a result of Jewish "sins" is an interesting comment.*

The Jews tended to view their dispersion in somewhat the same way as the Christians did: they had lost Jerusalem and were consequently spread over the face of the earth because they had sinned. Christians and Jews, however, had a different concept of what that "sin" was. The Christian teaching was quite specific: the Jews denied Jesus and murdered him. The Jews' rationale for their dispersion was rarely specific. Somehow they were not fulfilling God's laws and commandments with sufficient vigor. With the memory of Masada as a precedent, this feeling that they had somehow failed God led many besieged Jews to slay their loved ones and then kill themselves. It was a way of not only avoiding slaughter at the hands of the Christians, but also of dying for Kiddush Ha-Shem, *the sanctification of God's name.*

Christians were appalled by suicide, which was strictly forbidden by Church teachings. They added this enigmatic behavior to the catalogue of strange practices which they used as a rationale for hating the Jews.]

At the beginning of summer in the same year in which Peter and Gottschalk, after collecting an army, had set out, there assembled in like fashion a large and innumerable host of Christians from diverse kingdoms and lands; namely, from the realms of France, England, Flanders, and Lorraine… I know not whether by a judgment of the Lord, or by some error of mind, they rose in a spirit of cruelty against the Jewish people scattered throughout these cities and slaughtered them without mercy, especially in the Kingdom of Lorraine, asserting it to be the beginning of their expedition and their duty against the enemies of the Christian faith. This slaughter of Jews was done first by citizens of Cologne. These suddenly fell upon a small band of Jews and severely wounded and killed many; they destroyed the houses and synagogues of the Jews and divided among themselves a very large amount of money. When the Jews saw this cruelty, about two hundred in the silence of the night began flight by boat to Neuss. The pilgrims and crusaders discovered them, and after taking away all their possessions, inflicted on them similar slaughter, leaving not even one alive.

Not long after this, they started upon their journey, as they had vowed, and arrived in a great multitude at the city of Mainz. There Count Emico, a nobleman, a very mighty man in this region, was awaiting, with a large band of Teutons, the arrival of the pilgrims who were coming thither from diverse lands by the King's highway.

The Jews of this city, knowing of the slaughter of their brethren, and aware that they themselves could not escape the hands of so many, fled in hope of safety to Bishop Rothard. They put an infinite treasure in his guard and trust, having much faith in his protection, because he was Bishop of the city. Then that excellent Bishop of the city cautiously set aside the incredible amount of money received from them. He placed the Jews in the very spacious hall of his own house, away from the sight of Count Emico and his followers, that they might remain safe and sound in a very secure and strong place.

But Emico and the rest of his band held a council and, after sunrise, attacked the Jews in the hall with arrows and lances. Breaking the bolts and doors, they killed the Jews, about seven hundred in number, who in vain resisted the force and attack of so many thousands. They killed the women also, and with their swords pierced tender children of whatever age and sex. The Jews, seeing that their Christian enemies were attacking them and their children and that they were sparing no age, likewise fell upon one another, brother, children, wives, and sisters, and thus they perished at each other's hands. Horrible to say mothers cut the throats of nursing children with knives and stabbed others, preferring them to perish thus by their own hands rather than to be killed by the weapons of the uncircumcised.

From this cruel slaughter of the Jews a few escaped; and a few because of fear, rather than because of love of the Christian faith, were baptized. With very great spoils taken from these people, Count Emico, Clarebold, Thomas, and all that intolerable company of men and women then continued on their way to Jerusalem, directing their course toward the Kingdom of Hungary, where passing along the royal highway was usually not denied the pilgrims… *[Note: Along the way, they also slaughtered numerous Christians and were forced to flee for their lives.]*

Emico and some of his followers continued in their flight along the way by which they had come. Thomas, Clarebold, and several of their men escaped in flight toward Carinthia and Italy. So the hand of the Lord is believed to have been against the pilgrims, who had sinned by excessive impurity and fornication, and who had slaughtered the exiled Jews through greed of money, rather than for the sake of God's justice, although the Jews were opposed to Christ. The Lord is a just judge and orders no one unwillingly, or under compulsion, to come under the yoke of the Catholic faith.

20. Bernard of Clairvaux

Better to Convert than to Kill the Jews

(1146)

Source: Chazan, *Church, State and Jew in the Middle Ages*, p. 105. From Bruno James (trans.), The Letters of St. Bernard of Clairvaux, London, 1953, pp. 465–466.

[While telling the mobs not to kill Jews to prove their love of Jesus, Bernard tried to persuade them that it was far better to save Jewish souls through conversion.]

...Is it not a far better triumph for the Church to convince and convert the Jews than to put them all to the sword? Has that prayer which the Church offers for the Jews, from the rising up of the sun to the going down thereof, that the veil may be taken from their hearts so they may be led from the darkness of error into the light of truth, been instituted in vain? If she did not hope that they would believe and be converted, it would seem useless and vain for her to pray for them. But with the eye of mercy she considers how the Lord regards with favor him who renders good for evil and love for hatred. Otherwise where does that saying come in, "Not for their destruction I pray," and "When the fullness of the Gentiles shall have come in, then all Israel will be saved," and "The Lord is rebuilding Jerusalem, calling the banished sons of Israel home"?

21. *Some Reasons for Anti-Jewish Actions in England during the Crusades*

(1189)

Source: Robert Chazan, *European Jewry and the First Crusade*, (Berkeley: University of California Press, 1987), pp. 189–190. From William of Newburgh recording the Chronicles of the Reign of Stephen, Henry II, and Richard I, ed. Richard Howlett, 4 vols, (London, 1884–1889, I, 294–312, 313–314.)

[Christians first began attacking Jewish "usury" at the beginning of the Third Crusade. At that time, usury meant interest paid on a loan no matter what the rate. The question of usury was one of concern even during biblical times. Exodus 22:24 states: "If thou lend money to any of My people, even to the poor with thee, thou shalt not be to him as a creditor; neither shall ye lay upon him interest." Jews

dispersed in Christian lands tended to interpret this passage in two ways. First, "My people" referred to the Jews, and, second, interest-free loans were meant only for the poor. The Christian Church took this passage literally and forbad Christians to lend money at any interest. The Church ruling, however, did not eliminate the need for people to borrow money and the Jews moved in to fill the vacuum.

Just before the First Crusade, the famed Jewish scholar and teacher, Rabbi Solomon ben Isaac, known by the acronym Rashi, warned his fellow Jews: "He who loans money at interest to a foreigner will be destroyed." A century later, other rabbis agreed that gentiles should not be charged interest on loans. However, since Jews could not own land and were barred from so many ways of earning a living, charging interest on loans to Christians was necessary for survival and had to be allowed.

From the late 12th century on, attacks on Jewish usury filled both public and private documents and the public imagination. Shakespeare's Shylock in The Merchant of Venice *merely reflected the deeply held belief that Jews were evil money-lenders ever intent upon destroying Christians by stealing their money or by demanding their "pound of flesh."*

The reason behind the sudden interest in and condemnation of usury was purely economic. Waging almost continuous war was costly business and many noblemen (kings included!), as well as peasants, were deeply in debt to Jews. Branding them with the "sin" of usury was useful in many ways. Kings and princes used usury as an excuse to expel Jews from their territories. They also canceled their debts to those Jews and promptly seized all the Jews' assets. The same rapacious logic motivated the crusading peasants who attacked and plundered Jewish communities. The fact that the Church promised to forgive the sins and debts of all the men who swore upon the cross to defend the Holy Land as soldiers for Christ only encouraged their boldness. The following document by William of Newburgh, written at the beginning of the Third Crusade, gives a clear account of these anti-Jewish attacks and the reasons behind them.]

After these events, the fury of a new storm against the Jews developed at Stamford. At that place fairs were held during the solemnities of Lent. A multitude of young men from different areas who had accepted the sign of the Lord and were about to set out for Jerusalem arrived there. They were indignant that the enemies of the cross of Christ who lived there should possess so much, while they themselves had so little for the expenses of so great a journey. They thought they would extort from the Jews, as unjust possessors, that which they could apply to the needs of the pilgrimage which they had undertaken. Thinking therefore that they would render service to Christ by attacking his enemies, whose goods they desired to possess, they violently attacked them. None of the inhabitants of the place or those who had come to the fairs opposed such efforts; some even cooperated with them. Several of the Jews were killed, and the rest, who escaped with difficulty, were received within the castle. Their houses, however, were plundered, and a great quantity of money was seized. The plunderers left with the reward of their labor; and no one was questioned on account of this affair, out of a concern for public order...

Now the king, after the tumult at London, had enacted a law for the peace of the Jews and had acted in good faith towards the rest of the Jews throughout England, according to the ancient custom. Yet, when the king was afterwards resident in areas beyond the sea, many in the county of York took an oath together against the Jews, being unable to bear their opulence while they themselves were in want. Without any scruple of Christian conscience, they thirsted for their *[the Jews']* perfidious blood, aroused by desire of plunder. Those who urged them on to dare these measures were certain persons of higher rank, who were indebted for large sums to those impious usurers. Some of these, who had pledged their estates to them for sums received, were overwhelmed by great poverty. Others, who were obligated by their own bonds, were pressured by the tax-gatherers to satisfy the royal usurers. Some also of those who had accepted the sign of the Lord and were now in readiness to set out for Jerusalem could more easily be impelled to aid the expenses of a journey undertaken for the Lord out of the plunder of his enemies, because they had very little reason to fear that any question would arise on this account after they had begun their journey.

A street in the Roman ghetto.

Chapter IV

The Road to the Ghetto

When Catholic Church leaders laid down the ground rules for Christian-Jewish relations, Christianity was a religion struggling to establish itself and expand. Judaism posed a risk to this process since it was Christianity's major rival for the same potential converts. In addition, as the "mother religion," Judaism seemed more legitimate to many pagans. Much of early Christian legislation and teaching concerning Jews was meant to counter these threats. Thus, the early Church taught that the Jews hated God and his Covenant, and they expressed that hatred when they spurned Jesus as the Messiah and insisted that Pilate crucify him. As a result of these actions, the writers of the New Testament claimed that God allowed the Romans to destroy Jerusalem and drive the Jews into exile. Here, they were to suffer continual punishment until they repented their sins and accepted Jesus. Christians claimed their faith was the new instrument for delivering God's message to humanity and they were the new Elect or Chosen People.

By 1000 C.E., Christianity, firmly established in southern and western Europe, was no longer in any real peril from Jewish competition. Yet the Church perceived Judaism as more dangerous than ever. With the nettlesome Moslem occupation confined to Spain and the Balkans, and the Scandinavians and Slavs about to enter the fold, only the Jews were left as the major non-Catholic, alien element in Europe. Soon, Christian perception of Jewish power was exaggerated completely out of proportion to the Jews' numbers and actual influence. The belief that Jews were permanent aliens became a self-fulfilling prophecy. The longer the Jews were so reviled, the more they withdrew among themselves and the greater the differences between Jews and Christians became.

The popes did occasionally respond to Jewish pleas for protection, but new prejudices and restrictions added to the perilousness of Jewish life, while all the previous prejudicial beliefs and laws remained in force. Church and secular leadership grew increasingly concerned with usury—the taking of interest on a loan—during this time. Borrowing from Moslem practice, the Church encouraged princes and local officials to force the Jews to wear special identifying badges. Around 1200, the popes became aware of the written compilation of Jewish Oral Tradition known as the Talmud. Believing it to be anti-Christian and not inspired by God, the papacy condemned it. The popes also backed forced Jewish attendance at Christian sermons and the use of the Inquisition to ferret out baptized Jews who secretly continued to practice their ancient faith. As a last attempt to control what it deemed Jewish "perfidy," the papacy called for restricting Jews to ghettos and also gave its blessings to princes who wished to expel them permanently. Thus the final process in separating Jews from the Christian community, begun as early as the Council of Elvira in 304 C.E., reached its ultimate conclusion with the establishment of the ghetto and the 1492 expulsion of the Sephardic Jews from Spain.

---

22.   Pope Innocent III

Constitutio Pro Judeis—*An Edict in Favor of the Jews*

(September 15, 1199)

Source: Solomon Grayzel, *The Church and the Jews in the XIII Century* (New York: Hermon Press, 1966), pp. 93, 95.

[Beginning with the papacy of Calixtus II in 1119, Jews requested protection and a written declaration of their basic rights when each new pope ascended the Throne of Saint Peter. The contents of these edicts followed the same formula outlined by Pope Gregory in 591: Jews had the right to life, they could continue to practice Judaism, and they could not be forcibly baptized. Those popes who chose to issue the edict made no effort to enforce the protection they offered. Therefore, it was up to the Jews themselves to present this statement to the local religious and civil authorities with the hope they would honor its provisions for enforcement.

The Latin term "constitutio" was not a constitution in the modern sense, but a letter to the Catholic faithful which dealt with matters of religion and discipline. The pope's granting of the Constitutio Pro Judeis *in no way implied that the Church looked favorably upon Jews or their religion.]*

Although the Jewish perfidy is in every way worthy of condemnation, nevertheless, because through them the truth of our own Faith is proved, they are not to be severely oppressed by the faithful. Thus the Prophet says, "Thou shalt not kill them, lest at any time they forget thy law," or more clearly stated, thou shalt not destroy the Jews completely, so that the Christians should never by any chance be able to forget Thy Law, which, though they themselves fail to understand it, they display in their book to those who do understand.

Therefore, just as license ought not to be granted the Jews to presume to do in their synagogues more than the law permits them, just so ought they not to suffer curtailment in those (privileges) which have been conceded them. That is why, although they prefer to remain hardened in their obstinacy rather then acknowledge the prophetic words and the eternal secrets of their own scriptures, that they might thus arrive at the understanding of Christianity and Salvation, nevertheless, in view of the fact that they begged for our protection and our aid, and in accordance with the clemency that Christian piety imposes, we, following in the footsteps of our predecessors of happy memory, the popes Calixtus, Eugene, Alexander, Clement, and Coelestine, grant their petition and offer them the shield of our protection.

We decree that no Christian shall use violence to force them to be baptized as long as they are unwilling and refuse, but that if anyone of them seeks refuge among the Christians of his own free will and by reason of his faith, (only then,) after his willingness has become quite clear, shall he be made a Christian without subjecting himself to any calumny. For surely none can be believed to possess the true faith of a Christian who is known to have come to Christian baptism not willingly, and even against his wishes.

Moreover, without the judgment of the authority of the land, no Christian shall presume to wound their persons, or kill (them) or rob them of their money, or change the good customs which they have thus far enjoyed in the place where they live. Furthermore, while they celebrate their festivals, no one shall disturb them in any way by means of sticks and stones, nor exact from any of them forced service, except that which they have been accustomed to perform from ancient times. In opposition to the wickedness and avarice of evil men in these matters, we decree that no one shall presume to desecrate or reduce the cemetery of the Jews, or, with the object of extorting money to exhume bodies there buried. If any one, however, after being acquainted with the contents of this decree, should presume to act in defiance of it (which God forbid), he shall suffer loss of honor and office, or he shall be restrained by the penalty of excommunication, unless he shall have made proper amends for his presumption.

We wish, however, to place under the protection of this decree only those (Jews) who have not presumed to plot against the Christian Faith.

23.   Pope Innocent III

Papal Bull—On Forced Baptisms

(September, 1201)

Source: Poliakov, footnote page 47.

Pope Innocent III.

[The first recorded instances of forced conversions of Jews occurred in the Spanish Balearic Islands in 418 C.E. For more than a millennium after that date, European Jewry lived with the fear of forced baptism. The Church taught that the Sacrament of Baptism, whether administered to a consenting adult or to an infant who was unable to give consent, was legal and binding for the rest of the person's life. The question often arose whether the baptism of a Jew whose life was being threatened to encourage the conversion was truly valid. Innocent III in this 1201 papal bull chose to deal with the issue by defining the term "forced" to mean the Jew who loudly and repeatedly refused baptism, but was, nevertheless, sprinkled with the holy water. In that case only, Innocent ruled, would the baptism not be valid. In all other cases, even when threatened with torture and execution, the Jew who mutely accepted baptism had indeed become a Christian. Innocent conveniently overlooked the fact that the protesting Jew soon became the dead Jew, and so, in reality, the Church considered all baptisms valid.

Note: The word "bull" comes from the official seal (Latin bullum*) used on these papal letters.]*

Assuredly, it is contrary to the Christian faith that one who is unwilling and totally opposed to it *[baptism]* be constrained to adopt and observe Christianity. For this reason, some make a distinction, which is valid, between those who are unwilling and those who are constrained. It is thus that he who is led to Christianity by violence, by fear, and by torture, and who receives the sacrament of baptism to avoid harm (even as he who comes falsely to baptism), receives indeed the stamp of Christianity and can be obliged to observe the Christian faith, even as he who expresses a conditional will, although in absolute terms he is unwilling. It is in this fashion that the decree of the Council of Toledo must be understood, which stated that those who previously had been forced to become Christians, as was done in the time of the most pious Prince Sisebut, and their association with the divine sacraments having been established, by the grace of the baptism received, they themselves having been anointed by the holy oil and having participated in the body of the Lord, must be duly constrained to abide by the faith they had accepted by force. However, he who has never consented, but has altogether opposed it, has received neither the stamp nor the purpose, for it is better to object expressly than to manifest the slightest consent...

24. Fourth Lateran Council

Church Laws Concerning Jews

(November 11, 1215)

Source: Grayzel, pp. 307, 309, 311, 313.

[Throughout the history of the Roman Catholic Church, bishops, abbots, and priors met on an irregular basis to determine the state of the Church and to set policies for the future. In 1215, churchmen convened for the fourth time at the Basilica of St. John Lateran in Rome to make needed reforms within the Church, suppress heresies, clarify the concept of the Trinity, and to send out a proclamation for a fifth crusade. A small number of the Council's decrees dealt with regulating Jews and defining their place in Christian society, a process begun as early in Christian history as the 304 C.E. Council of Elvira. The Fourth Lateran Council's concluding decrees condemned usury (especially "heavy or immoderate" interest rates), reiterated that Jews should hold no public offices, urged Church leaders to compel baptized Jews to remain Christians, and ordered Jews (and Saracens residing in Christian-controlled Europe) to wear special identifying badges.

The Council's decree on usury was repeated to underscore the opposition of the Church to money lending at interest. Since the Church's main enforcement tool was excommunication, it was not possible to compel the Jews directly to give up usury. The Council found another means to accomplish the same end: the Church declared it would excommunicate any Christians who did business with Jews who practiced usury. This indirect censure was often referred to as the "judgement of the Jews."

Pope Innocent III was the moving force behind the Fourth Lateran Council, and, without a doubt, much of its anti-Jewish legislation was the result of his endeavors.]

Usury

67. The more the Christian religion refrains from the exaction of usury, the more does the Jewish perfidy *[non-belief]* become used to this practice, so that in a short time the Jews exhaust the financial strength of Christians. Therefore, in our desire to protect Christians in this matter, that they should not be excessively oppressed by the Jews, we order by a decree of this Synod that when in the future, a Jew, under any pretext, extort heavy and immoderate usury from a Christian, all relationship with Christians shall therefore be denied him until he shall have made sufficient amends for his exorbitant exactions. The Christians, moreover, if need be, shall be compelled by ecclesiastical punishment without appeal, to abstain from such commerce. We also impose this upon the princes, not to be aroused against the Christians because of this, but rather to try to keep the Jews from this practice.

We decree that by means of the same punishment the Jews shall be compelled to offer satisfaction to the churches for the tithes and offerings due them and which these churches were wont to receive from the houses and possessions of Christians before these properties had under some title or other passed into Jewish hands. Thus shall this property be conserved to the Church without any loss.

Jewish Badges

68. Whereas in certain provinces of the Church the difference in their clothes sets the Jews and Saracens apart from the Christians, in certain other lands there has arisen such confusion that no differences are noticeable. Thus it sometimes happens that by mistake Christians have intercourse with Jewish or Saracen women, and Jews or Saracens with Christian women. Therefore, lest these people, under the cover of an error, find an excuse for the grave sin of such intercourse, we decree that these people (Jews and Saracens) of either sex, and in all Christians lands, and at all times, shall easily be distinguishable from the rest of the populations by the quality of their clothes; especially since such legislation is imposed upon them also by Moses.

Moreover, they shall not walk out in public on the Days of Lamentation or the Sunday of Easter; for as we have heard, certain ones among them do not blush to go out on such days more than usually ornamented, and do not fear to poke fun at the Christians who display signs of grief at the memory of the most holy Passion.

We most especially forbid anyone to dare to break forth into insults against the Redeemer. Since we cannot shut our eyes to insults heaped upon Him who washed away our sins, we decree that such presumptuous persons shall be duly restrained by fitting punishment meted out by the secular rulers, so that none dare blaspheme against Him Who was crucified for our sake.

Regarding Jews in Public Office

69. Since it is quite absurd that any who blaspheme against Christ should have power over Christians, we, on account of the boldness of the transgressors, renew what the Council of Toledo *[Fourth Council of Toledo—Canon 65, 633]* already has legislated with regard to this. We forbid that Jews be given preferment in public office since this offers them the pretext to vent their wrath against the Christians. Should anyone entrust them with an office of this kind, he shall be restrained from so doing by the Council of the Province (which we order to be held every year). Due warning having been given him, he shall be restrained (therefrom) by such means as the Council deems fit. These officials themselves, moreover, shall suffer until they shall have turned for the use of poor Christians in accordance with the dispositions of the bishop of the diocese, all that they may have earned from the Christians through the office they had undertaken. Disgraced, they shall lose the office which they had so irreverently assumed. This shall apply also to pagans.

"Backsliding" after Baptism

70. We have heard that certain ones who had voluntarily approached the baptismal font, have not completely driven out the old self in order the more perfectly to bring in the new. Since they retain remnants of their former faith, they tarnish the beauty of the Christian Religion by such a mixture. For it is written "Cursed be he who walks the earth in two ways," and even in wearing a garment one may not mix linen and wool. We decree, therefore, that such people shall in every possible manner be restrained by the prelates of the churches, from observing their old rites, so that those whom their free will brought to the Christian religion shall be held to its observance by compulsion, that they may be saved. For there is less evil in not recognizing the way of the Lord than in backsliding after having recognized it.

More on Usury

[Note: Some historians speculate that the popes' growing concern with usury during the 11th and 12th centuries stemmed from the desire to encourage men to enlist in the Crusades. When the Church promised that interest on debts would be suspended or forgiven to all who signed up to fight for the Holy Land, peasants and noblemen, deeply in debt as a result of money borrowed from Jews, gladly accepted the offer. To keep faith with these Crusaders, the Church must have felt it needed to eliminate usury altogether.]

We order that the secular powers shall compel the Jews to remit their usury, and until the Jews have done so they shall be denied commercial intercourse with Christians, the latter being forced to do so under pain of excommunication. Moreover, for those who are unable at the present time to pay their debts to the Jews *[this refers to the crusaders]*, the princes shall procure the needed moratorium, so that, until their death or return be definitely established, they shall not suffer any inconvenience of accruing interest. The Jews shall be compelled to count into the capital, the income from the gage, minus the cost of maintenance, which it will yield in the meantime...

The Controversy over the Talmud

From the time it was codified around 400 B.C.E., the Torah, or Five Books of Moses, has served as the foundation for Jewish law, much as written constitutions form the basis for laws of states and nations. Like constitutional law, Jewish law, based on passages in the Torah, developed in response to contemporary legal and ethical problems. Since times and situations change, the answers to these problems were not always found in the exact words of the Torah: learned men had to interpret those words to make meaningful applications of Torah law. These legal decisions and interpretive commentary were called "Oral Law." Since Judaism is a cultural tradition as well as a religion, "Oral Law" allowed Judaism to grow, change, and remain relevant to the Jewish people. This proved to be crucial to Jewish survival in the Diaspora. Around 200 C.E., Judah ha-Nasi, a well-known and highly respected scholar, completed a written compilation of this Oral Law. It is known as the Mishnah or "study by repetition." Following the Mishnah's codification, many generations of scholars, called the Amoraim, further explained and commented upon Judah ha-Nasi's work. These writings became known as the Gemarah. Scholars in Palestine and Babylonia, working independently, each developed their own Gemarah. In the long run, the Babylonian Gemarah, finished around 500 C.E., was a more complete and definitive work, and Jews preferred it over its Palestinian counterpart.

The Mishnah plus the Babylonian Gemarah combine to form what Jews call the Talmud. It applies the laws and customs of the Jewish tradition to every aspect of a Jew's life. By the time of the First Crusade, the Talmud, which served as a guide for personal and religious stability, supplanted the Bible as the major object of detailed Jewish study.

Christianity remained ignorant of the Talmud until an apostate named Nicholas Donin denounced it to Pope Gregory IX in 1239. It was not uncommon for Jewish converts to Christianity to attack their former faith. Donin, however, took special delight in criticizing the Talmud. This has led some Jewish historians to speculate that he was a Karaite.

[*Note:* Karaism was a movement within Judaism, begun around 760 C.E., which denied the authoritativeness of the Talmud and stressed that the Bible was the sole guide for Jewish life. Karaites believed that through repeated interpretation and the creation of vast numbers of minute laws, the original meaning of the Bible had been lost. Each Jew, they claimed, had the right and the ability to interpret the Bible according to individual conscience. Jews who believed in the Oral Tradition as codified in the Talmud denied the Karaite claims. They looked upon the movement as a dangerous heresy which could destroy the unity and stability the Jewish people needed to survive in Christian and Moslem lands.]

---

25.   Pope Gregory IX

Attacking the Talmud

(1239)

Source: Grayzel, p. 243.

[Nicholas Donin reported to the pope that Jews believed God gave Moses the Oral Law (Talmud) along with the Torah. Therefore, it was already "holy" when it was finally put into written form. Gregory IX rejected this interpretation and claimed the Talmud was a purely human invention. The Church condemned it as profane and credited it with blinding the Jews to the truth of Christianity. Gregory ordered the Talmud to be burnt at the stake in the same way the Church put heretics to death.]

...to the Bishop and the Prior of the Dominicans, and the Minister of the Franciscan Friars, in Paris:...

If what is said about the Jews of France and of the other lands is true, no punishment would be sufficiently great or sufficiently worthy of their crime. For they, so we have heard, are not content with the Old Law which God gave to Moses in writing: they even ignore it completely, and affirm that God set forth another law which is called "Talmud," that is "Teaching," handed down to Moses orally. Falsely they allege that it was implanted within their minds and, unwritten, was there preserved until certain men came, whom they call "Sages" and "Scribes," who, fearing that this Law might be lost from the minds of men through forgetfulness, reduced it to writing, and the volume of this by far exceeds the text of the Bible. In this is contained matter so abusive and so unspeakable that it arouses shame in those who mention it and horror in those who hear it.

Wherefore, since this is said to be the most important reason why the Jews remain obstinate in their perfidy, we, through Apostolic Letters, order Your Discretion to have the Jews who live in the Kingdoms of France, England, Aragon, Navarre, Castile, Leon and Portugal forced by the secular arm to give up their books. Those books, in which you will find errors of this sort, you shall cause to be burned at the stake. By Apostolic Power, and through use of ecclesiastical censure, you will silence all opponents. You will also report to us faithfully what you have done in the matter. But, should all of you be unable to be present at the fulfillment of these instructions, someone of you, nonetheless, shall carry out its execution.

26.   Pope Innocent IV

Attack on the Talmud

(May 9, 1244)

Source: Grayzel, pp. 251, 253.

[By the papacy of Innocent IV, Church leaders believed that the Talmud, written in Hebrew, which they were unable to read, and interpreted for them by apostates who were hostile to Judaism, contained numerous blasphemies against God and attacks on Jesus and Mary.]

...to the King of France...

The wicked perfidy of the Jews, from whose hearts our Redeemer has not removed the veil of blindness because of the enormity of their crime, but has so far permitted to remain in blindness such as in a measure covers Israel, does not heed, as it should, the fact that Christian piety received them and patiently allows them to live among them through pity only. Instead, it (the perfidy) commits such enormities as are stupifying to those who hear them, and horrible to those who tell them. For, ungrateful to the Lord Jesus Christ, who, in the abundance of His kindliness, patiently expects their conversion, they, displaying no shame for their guilt nor reverence for the honor of the Christian Faith, throw away and despise the Law of Moses and the prophets, and follow some tradition of their elders. On account of these same traditions the Lord reproves them in the Gospel saying: "Wherefore do you transgress the law of God, and render it void because of your traditions, teaching doctrines and commands of men?" *[Paraphrase of Matthew 15:3]*

In traditions of this sort they rear and nurture their children, which traditions, are called "Talmud" in Hebrew. It is a big book and among them, exceeding in size the text of the Bible. In it are found blasphemies against God and His Christ, and obviously entangled fables about the Blessed Virgin, and abusive errors, and unheard of follies. But of the law and doctrines of the prophets they make their sons altogether ignorant. They fear that if the forbidden truth, which is found in the Law and the Prophets, be understood, and the testimony concerning the only-begotten Son of God that He appeared in the flesh, be furnished, these (children) would be converted to the Faith and humbly return to their Redeemer...

27. John I of Castile

Establishment of a "Ghetto"

(1412)

Source: Salo Wittmayer Baron, *A Social and Religious History of the Jews*, volume XI (New York: Columbia University Press, 1967), p. 90.

[Since people often desire to live amongst others like themselves, Jewish residential sections in European towns existed from early Roman times. This social separation was especially important for the Jews whose customs (e.g., kashrut, Sabbath observance, and non-intermarriage) required proximity to others of their faith. With the disintegration of Roman law in the early Middle Ages, Jews and their secular protectors built walls around the Jewish quarter to shield them from the occasional ravages of their Christian neighbors. Here the gates remained open except in times of severe unrest.

One of the earliest mentions of enforced residential confinement appears in a ruling by John I of Castile in Spain. He ordered Jews and Moors (Moslems) to live apart from Christians in an area surrounded by a wall, and accessible by only one gate. The actual term "Ghetto" would not be used to describe this separate area for at least another 150 years.

Psychologically, there is a great difference between voluntarily residing in a certain section of a town and being required by law to do so. Walls to keep Jews in and specifically to enforce separation from the Christian population eventually became a mental as well as a physical barrier. These walls increased the sense of the leper-like existence of the Jews, indelibly marking them as pariahs.]

In the first place from now on all Jews and Jewesses, Moors and Moorish women of My kingdoms and dominions shall be and live apart from the Christian men and women in a section or part of the city or village or any place where they have resided. It shall be surrounded by a wall and have but one gate through which one could enter it. All Jews and Jewesses, Moors and Moorish women shall live in the said enclosure thus assigned to them and in no other place or house outside it. They shall begin to move thereto within eight days after these places are assigned to them. And if some Jews or Jewesses, Moors or Moorish women should stay outside the said enclosure, he or she shall by that very fact lose all his or her possessions. The body of such a Jew or Jewess, Moor or Moorish woman shall likewise be at My mercy to impose upon him or her any corporal punishment according to my discretion.

28.   Pope Benedict XIII

Laws Regarding Jews

(May 11, 1415)

Source: Lindo, pp. 213–215.

[Benedict III's bull of 1415 contained numerous provisions for restrictions on Jewish life and contributed to a movement during the Renaissance to impoverish, uproot, and isolate the Jews. This movement reflected the declining economic importance of European Jewry, the growth of nation-state nationalism, and the appearance of the Protestant Reformation, which the Church blamed partially on Jewish influence. Benedict's bull covered almost all aspects of Jewish life. It repeated the Church's condemnation of the Talmud and usury. It restricted the professions Jews could enter, decreed separate residence, and required the wearing of identifying badges. It also limited the number and size of synagogues and called for the forced attendance of Jews at sermons meant to win them over to Christianity.]

1. To prohibit generally all persons, without distinction, publicly or privately, to hear, read, or teach the doctrines of the Talmud; ordering that within one month there be collected in the cathedral of every diocese, all copies that can be found of the Talmud, its glossaries, summaries, compendiums, notes, and every other writing that has directly or indirectly any relation to such doctrine; and the diocesans and inquisitors are to watch over the observance of this decree, visiting the Jews personally or by others, within their jurisdictions every two years, and punishing severely every delinquent.

2. That no Jew be permitted to possess, read, or hear read a book entitled "Mar Mar Jesu," it being full of blasphemies against our Redeemer Jesus Christ; nor any other book or writing that may be injurious to Christians, or that speaks against any of its dogmas, or the rights of the church, in any language in which it may be written: the contravener of this decree is to be punished as a blasphemer.

3. That no Jew may make, repair, or under any pretence have in his possession any crucifix, chalices, or sacred vessels, nor bind Christians' books in which the name of Jesus Christ or the most Holy Virgin Mary is written. Christians who give any of these articles to Jews, from any cause whatever, are to be excommunicated.

4. No Jew may exercise the office of judge, even in causes that may occur among his people.

5. All synagogues recently built or repaired, are to be closed. Where there is but one, it may remain, provided it is not sumptuous; and should there be two or more, one of the smallest only is to be left open; but should it be proved that any one of the said synagogues has at any time been a church, it is immediately to be closed.

6. No Jew may be physician, surgeon, druggist, shopkeeper, provision dealer, or marriage maker, or hold any other office, whereby he has to interfere in Christians' affairs; nor may Jewesses be midwives, or have Christian nurses; nor Jews have Christians to serve them, or sell to, or buy provisions of them, or join them at any banquet, or bathe in the same bath, or be stewards or agents to Christians, or learn any science, art, or trade in their schools.

7. That in every city, town, or village where there are Jews, barriers shall be appointed for their residence apart from Christians.

8. That all Jews or Jewesses shall wear on their clothes a certain red and yellow sign, of the size and shape designated in the bull,—men on the breast of the outward garment, and women in front.

9. That no Jew may trade, or make any contract; thus to avoid the frauds they practise, and the usuries they charge to Christians.

10. That all Jews and Jewesses converted to the Catholic faith, and all Christians generally who are related by consanguinity to Jews, may inherit from their unconverted parents and relatives; declaring null any testament, codicil, last-will, or donation INTER VIVO they may make to prevent any of their property devolving to Christians.

11. That in all cities, towns, and villages, where there may be the number of Jews the diocesan may deem sufficient, three public sermons are to be preached annually: one on the second Sunday in Advent; one on the festival of the Resurrection; and the other on the Sunday when the Gospel, "And Jesus approached Jerusalem," is chanted. All Jews above twelve years of age shall be compelled to attend to hear these sermons. The subjects are to be the first to shew them that the true Messiah has already come, quoting the passages of the Holy Scripture and the Talmud that were argued in the disputation of Jerome of Santa Fé; the second to make them see that the heresies, vanities and errors of the Talmud, prevent their knowing the truth; and the third, explaining to them the destruction of the Temple and the city of Jerusalem, and the perpetuity of their captivity, as our Lord Jesus Christ and the other prophets had prophesied. And at the end of these sermons this bull is to be read, that the Jews may not be ignorant of any of its decrees.

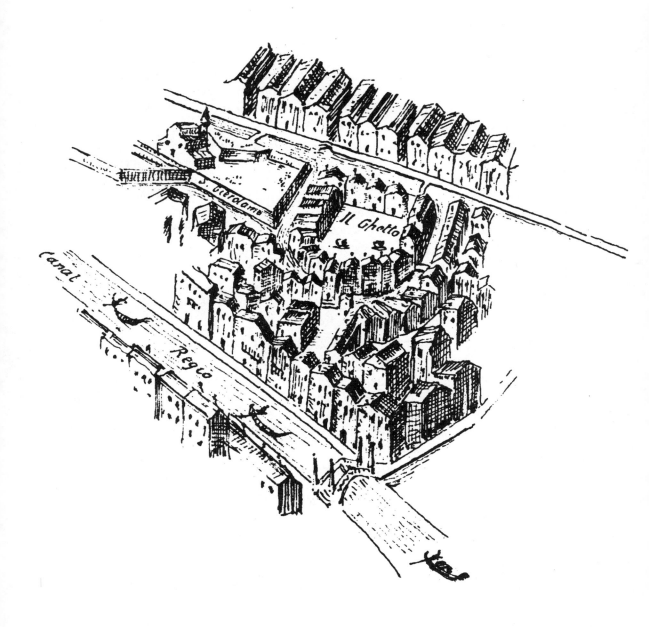

The Ghetto of Venice.

29.   Venetian Senate

Establishing a Ghetto

(1516)

Source: Baron, volume XI, p. 93.

[This decree by the Senate in Venice officially began the age of the Ghetto. During the Middle Ages, Jews provided Christian Europe with necessary banking, loan, and financial services. When Renaissance Italian banking houses finally helped persuade the Church to accept usury practiced by Christians, Jewish usefulness was at an end. Venice's middle class now looked upon Jews as unwanted competitors and searched for a way to control and isolate them. They ordered the Jews to move to two islands called geto nuevo and geto vecchio. The term "ghetto" came from the Italian word geto, which meant "[iron]-foundry." After being forced into the geto, the Venetian Jewish community eked out an existence by buying and selling used merchandise.]

...all Jews who at present are found residing in the various streets of this Our city, as well as those who might come from elsewhere, shall, until it will be differently decided in accordance with the exigencies of the time, be obligated to proceed to dwell together in the kind of houses located in the *geto* next to the Church of St. Jerome.

30.   Pope Paul IV

Cum nimis absurdum—*Sweeping Restrictions on Jews*

(July 12, 1555)

Source: Poul Borchensius, *Behind the Wall; The Story of the Ghetto* (London: George Allen and Unwin, 1964), p. 93.

[The 16th-century Church was besieged on all sides by Italian Renaissance secularism, Northern European Humanism, and the Protestant Reformation. Catholic leaders blamed these movements, at least partly, on the Jews, claiming they lured Christians away from the true faith. Recognizing the rapid decline of the Jews' economic importance in Europe, the Church decided the time had come to finally deal with the Jewish "menace." In 1555, Pope Paul IV issued the bull Cum nimis absurdum *which contained anti-Jewish restrictions so complete that, for all practical purposes, Jewish participation in European life ended.]*

Whereas it seemeth absurd and outrageous that Jews, being by God condemned for their guilt to everlasting slavery, should enjoy our Christian love and tolerance and, rewarding this our indulgence with ingratitude, instead of submission should aggressively seek power; and whereas we are informed that such is their shameless-ness that in Rome, as elsewhere within the domains of the Holy Roman Church, they take up their abode among Christians, and indeed in the immediate proximity of the churches without outward sign of their identity, and that they also rent houses on respectable streets, purchase and acquire property, keep Christian servants and nurses in their houses, and in other ways trample Christian honour under foot; be it known that we find ourselves compelled to have recourse to the undermentioned measures…

[The papal bull then listed the following physical, economic, social, and relig-ious sanctions:

All Jews were to be confined to ghettos surrounded by walls to be built "at great speed" and to be paid for by the Jews themselves. The ghetto wall would contain one gate which would be opened and closed at prescribed times.

Jews had to immediately sell all their real property and even had to rent their homes in the ghetto from Christians. Jewish doctors could not treat Christian patients. Jews could not have Christian servants and could have no further dealings with Christians in general. They could not trade in grain or other necessary goods. Jews would henceforth be restricted to buying and selling old clothes and other second-hand goods.

Jewish men could not be addressed by the courteous title, "Signor." They had to wear easily identifiable saffron-yellow hats, and their women could not go out in public without veils. The Church abolished all Jewish local and personal privileges.

The Jews could have only one synagogue per town. All others would be torn down, but the Jews had to continue to pay taxes on them. Each ghetto had to contain a Casa Dei Catacumeni—*maintained from Jewish coffers—where they would be forced to hear Christian sermons and where they could be converted to Christianity.]*

Interior of the Altneu Synagogue in Prague.

Jews on a march out of Vienna during a temporary expulsion.

Chapter V

Settlement, Restriction, and Expulsion

Jews during the Middle Ages were not able to establish firm, lasting roots in individual Western European countries. They were allowed to settle in a particular area only when their presence was deemed useful to the state and the monarch's treasury. Christian princes, ever eager to expand their wealth, invited Jews to settle where they could develop commerce and new trades. Considered in perpetual servitude to Christianity in the theological sense, Jews soon became *Servi Camerae,* servants of the imperial chamber, which meant that they and all their possessions belonged to the crown. As mercenary as this policy sounds, it actually afforded the Jews a reasonable measure of protection against attack by local peasants and jealous burghers. Princes would not tolerate any destruction of their "property."

Sometimes other factors overcame the monarch's long-term economic self-interest. Often he needed the support of zealous noblemen and bishops who were offended by the Jews' presence in a good Christian land. At other times the prince might be heavily indebted to Jews for loans of money. He might choose to wipe out these debts by expelling the Jews, seizing their property, and eliminating the necessity of repayment.

In all this the Jews were pawns, essentially powerless creatures, buffeted by the winds of ambition, greed, and religious prejudice. In the process, Jews learned to deal from a position of physical weakness and vulnerability. They learned that negotiation (often translated by their enemies as "manipulation") and their ability to provide needed goods and services could insure their survival. They purchased protection with these talents and won rights to settle in exchange for payments of special taxes, levies, and tolls.

During prosperous and peaceful times, Jews went about proudly, dressed in their richest finery, holding their heads high. During dark times, they hid themselves away and, when they had to, walked softly, carrying not a big stick, but a humble, beseeching manner. When even this did not work and they received the official order for their expulsion, they tried to salvage what they could and went in search of another, safer place to settle.

The documents presented in this chapter follow the fortunes of Jews in the German states, France, England, Spain, and Poland from the 12th to the 16th centuries. They show settlement charters, edicts restricting freedoms, and decrees for expulsion. For the most part, however, these legal papers offer only a narrow glimpse of what daily life was like for most Jews during this era. Rulers often found reasons for, and ways to get around, harsh official ordinances. In this way, Jews could lead safe and peaceful lives for several generations. On the other hand, rulers could apply both secular and ecclesiastical laws strictly, resulting in a much more precarious existence. Often noblemen, peasants, and burghers carried out anti-Jewish actions with complete disregard of the laws listed in some of these documents.

Just as today when the unusual makes the headlines, it is probable that it was the unusual event that made document "news." Medieval chroniclers, Christian and Jewish, may not have considered periods of peace and co-operation newsworthy items, and thus they were rarely mentioned.

The German and Austrian States or the Holy Roman Empire and the Jews

Charlemagne, in 800, tried to create an empire that would recapture the grandeur of Rome and be dedicated to the service of God through the Catholic Church. Because of his own personal strength and perseverance, his "Roman" Empire extended from the North Sea to the Pyrenees and just south of Rome, and from the Atlantic coast to the Oder River on the east. After his death, Charlemagne's sons fought bitterly for control, and finally, in 843, the Treaty of Verdun divided this vast territory into three parts. The western third consisted of what we now call France.

Lorraine, Burgundy, the Lowlands, and Northern Italy made up the middle third, and the eastern third later formed present-day Germany and Austria. Each section went its own way and developed independently. About a hundred years later, Otto I revived the concept of a "Holy Roman" Empire in hopes of uniting the many small German states. In reality, as many historians have observed, this government was neither "holy" nor "Roman" nor in any real sense an "empire."

Otto I created an interesting and potentially troublesome situation when he made Catholic bishops and abbots land-owning nobles. This policy proved troublesome because it opened the way for interference from the pope in Rome, and, from the Jewish point of view, it put Catholic ecclesiastical leaders in direct secular charge of an area's Jewish population. In addition to this confusing situation, the Holy Roman Emperor was elected by the three ecclesiastical princes of Mainz, Trier, and Cologne, and four secular princes—the king of Bohemia, the duke of Saxony, the margrave of Brandenburg, and the count Palatine. Later, the princes of Bavaria, Hesse, and Hannover also became imperial electors.

Each of these princes was jealous of the prerogatives and strengths of the others, and all worked to reduce the effectiveness of the emperor they were responsible for electing. Soon the emperor's power and influence depended only on how much territory he owned personally, and, as a result, his main efforts went to expanding his own possessions. He cared little for national welfare or unity. These conditions produced grave consequences for the extensive Jewish communities residing here in the Middle Ages. Since Jews were "servants of the imperial chamber," their welfare depended directly on the strength and commitment of the Holy Roman Emperor.

Jews, unable to own land, settled almost exclusively in cities and towns. Here, too, the weakness of the imperial system affected them directly. There were two types of cities in the German states: the "free" cities, which were independent of local princely control, and the "imperial" cities, which were under the "protection" of the Holy Roman emperor. As city dwellers, Jews made their living as merchants, tradesmen, and moneylenders. The Christian burghers resented their competition, their protected status with the emperor, and the fact that Jewish taxes went directly into the imperial treasury and not into the city's coffers. As a result, free cities dealt cruelly with the Jews, expelling them or refusing to let them settle in the first place. Imperial city burghers, although they resented the Jews, had to be somewhat more careful.

German disunity and imperial weakness, plus the Church's desire to influence secular government, led to general chaos, degradation of the peasant class, and the use of Jews as "scapegoats." Since the Jews belonged to the emperor, anti-Judaism became a way for princes, townspeople, peasants, and the Church to resist any attempt by an emperor to extend his control.

---

31.   Duke Frederick of Austria

Jewish Charter

(July 1, 1244)

Source: Marcus, pp. 29–32.

[Duke Frederick of Austria (who was also Holy Roman Emperor Frederick III) was primarily concerned with expanding the wealth and influence of the Hapsburg dynasty. Making use of the Jews' ability to generate revenue for the crown was part of this process. This extremely favorable charter of 1244 protected the Jews as imperial property from attacks by Christians. It also tried to eliminate the possibility of anyone other than the duke exercising control over the Jews. Sections IX and XI provided an effective deterrent and monetary reimbursement in the event of such attacks. Jews were to receive "compensatory" damages in silver, and the duke was to be paid much larger "punitive" damages in gold.]

I. We decree, therefore, first, that in cases involving money, or immóvable property, or a criminal complaint touching the person or property of a Jew, no Christian shall be admitted as a witness against a Jew unless there is a Jewish witness together with the Christian...

V. Likewise, a Jew is allowed to receive all things as pledges which may be pawned with him—no matter what they are called—without making any investigation about them, except bloody and wet clothes which he shall under no circumstances accept...

VIII. Likewise, if the Jews engage in quarreling or actually fight among themselves, the judge of our city shall claim no jurisdiction over them; only the Duke alone or the chief official of his land shall exercise jurisdiction. If, however, the accusation touches the person, this case shall be reserved for the Duke alone for judgment.

IX. Likewise, if a Christian should inflict any sort of a wound upon a Jew, the accused shall pay to the Duke twelve marks of gold which are to be turned in to the treasury. He must also pay to the person who has been injured twelve marks of silver and the expenses incurred for the medicine needed in his cure.

X. Likewise, if a Christian kill a Jew, he shall be punished with the proper sentence, death, and all his movable and immovable property shall pass into the power of the duke.

XI. Likewise, if a Christian strike a Jew, without, however, having spilt his blood, he shall pay to the Duke four marks of gold, and to the man he struck four marks of silver. If he has no money, he shall offer satisfaction for the crime committed by the loss of his hand...

XII. Likewise, wherever a Jew shall pass through our territory no one shall offer any hindrance to him or molest or trouble him. If, however, he should be carrying any goods or other things for which he must pay duty at all custom offices, he shall pay only the prescribed duty which a citizen of that town, in which the Jew is then dwelling, pays.

XIII. Likewise, if the Jews, as is their custom, should transport any of their dead either from city to city, or from province to province, or from one Austrian land to another, we do not wish anything to be demanded of them by our customs officers. If, however, a customs officer should extort anything, then he is to be punished for *praedatio mortui*, which means, in common language, robbery of the dead.

XIV. Likewise, if a Christian, moved by insolence, shall break into or devastate the cemetery of the Jews, he shall die, as the court determines, and all his property, whatever it may be, shall be forfeited to the treasury of the Duke...

XV. Likewise, if any one wickedly throw something at the synagogues of the Jews we order that he pay two talents to the judge of the Jews *[who is a Christian]*.

XIX. Likewise, we decree that no Jew shall take an oath on the Torah unless he has been summoned to our presence...

XXI. Likewise, if a Christian raises his hand in violence against a Jewess, we order that the hand of that person be cut off...

XXIII. Likewise, if a Christian has redeemed his pledge from a Jew but has not paid the interest, the interest due shall become compounded if it is not paid within a month...

XXVI. Likewise, if any man or woman should kidnap a Jewish child, we wish that he be punished as a thief... *[Thieves received the death penalty.]*

32. Albert III Achilles, Margrave of Brandenburg

Jewish Serfdom

(1462)

Source: Baron, *A Social and Religious History of the Jews*, volume XI, p. 5.

[The Margrave of Brandenburg (Prussia) was both a prince and an elector of the Holy Roman Empire. This pronouncement concerning Jewish serfdom theorized that the emperor owned Jewish lives so exclusively and totally that he even had the right to kill them. Fortunately for the imperial treasury, the Jews could honor a new emperor with a third of their wealth and thus avoid such an unfortunate possibility. While this short treatise was shockingly harsh, Albert's actual treatment of Brandenburg's Jews was much more moderate. Often such words were propaganda meant not only to warn the Jews not to overstep their bounds, but also to soothe pious Christian sensibilities.]

Upon his coronation each Roman king or emperor may take away from the Jews throughout the Empire all their goods, even their lives, and kill them all, except for the few who ought to be preserved for remembrance. Hence all the Jews in the lands of the German Empire had been granted the opportunity to avoid such an eventuality by giving each new emperor a third part of their possessions, in order thus to redeem their bodies, lives and property.

33. Charles V, Holy Roman Emperor

Jewish Privileges

(April 3, 1544)

Source: Salo Wittmayer Baron, *The Social and Religious History of the Jews*, volume XIII (New York: Columbia University Press, 1969), p. 277.

[No lover of the Jewish people, Emperor Charles V nevertheless recognized the economic contribution Jews could make to his treasury. Jews who resided in the various states of the Holy Roman Empire were "servants of the imperial chamber," and thus the amount of taxes the emperor could obtain from them depended directly on how successful they were at earning a living. In this edict, Charles not only permitted usury, but also stated Jews could make larger profits than Christians would normally be allowed.]

Jews and Jewesses are subjected in many parts of the Empire to imposts and services with respect to their persons and property in a much higher degree than are the Christians; at the same time they are allowed neither to own landed estates nor to serve in public employ, hold offices, or ply handicrafts for Christian customers from which they might be able to defray such imposts and earn a living. Hence they must secure all their revenue from the utilization of their ready cash. That is why We concede to the Jews henceforth…they shall be allowed to invest and make use of their funds by lending them on interest and by making use of them in some other way at much higher rates and greater profit than is permitted to Christians.

Medieval France and the Jews

Jewish peddlers and traders followed the Roman armies as they spread through Gaul subduing the various Germanic tribes. Towns often developed around the army encampments, and Jews became early residents of those towns. Later, southeastern Gaul, peopled by the Arian Christian Visigoths, proved particularly hospitable to Jewish settlement. Here the Jews were agriculturalists—owning land which included large estates and vineyards—as well as skilled artisans. Sometime around 496 C.E., Clovis I, king of the Franks, converted to Roman Catholicism as that religion spread rapidly through central and northern Gaul. Along with the Catholic faith, the clergy also carefully taught the populace about the Jews' perfidy and the Jews' place in the Christian world. A little over a century later, King Dagobert, hoping to increase his power by winning the support of this clergy, expelled all the Jews from his territories in central Gaul. In doing so, he began a long, sad cycle of tolerance, persecution, expulsion, and re-admission that marked much of the Jews' history in France.

Some of the displaced Jews settled in towns along the Rhine River. Others moved to southeastern Gaul where, although Roman Catholicism had officially replaced Arianism, Jewish-Christian relations remained friendly and where Jews could still own land and practice skilled trades. Here, also, nourished by the tolerant atmosphere, Jewish scholarship began to develop, especially in the Provence region. The massacres of the Crusades, beginning in 1096, and the general uncertainty of Medieval times forced an untimely end to a promising center of Jewish learning.

Clovis and Dagobert tried, though unsuccessfully, to unify and centralize control of Gaul. Two hundred years later, Charlemagne temporarily achieved this goal when he accepted the crown offered by Pope Leo III in 800 C.E. and forged the Holy Roman Empire. Although interested in furthering the goals of the Christian church in Europe, Charlemagne and his immediate successors also believed in making full use of all their subjects' talents. Accordingly, they issued many charters to Jewish merchants and traders. They protected the Jews, knowing these people could help them economically.

In the century following Charlemagne's death, France was divided into many petty feudal territories. In fact, French kings controlled only the county of Paris, also known as the Ile de France. The Crusades spurred the French kings' efforts to extend their real control beyond Paris's borders. Jews played an important, if indirect, role in this unification and centralization process. Mirroring the situation in other Christian countries in the Middle Ages, Jews and everything they owned belonged first to the local lord and later to the king. Jews could not leave the lord's territory without permission and, like serfs, they became part of a lord's inheritance. Unlike serfs, however, who produced mainly agricultural products, Jews, whose money lending was heavily taxed, produced much needed currency. French kings often used Jews as economic resources to pay for their expansionist policies.

---

34. King Philip II Augustus of France

Expulsion

(1182)

Source: Chazan, *Church, State and Jew in the Middle Ages*, pp. 311–312. From Harvey Robinson, Readings in European History, V.I, pp. 427–428 (N.Y., 1904–1906).

[As king, Philip II Augustus constantly pursued two related policies: depriving the English kings of their land holdings in France and expanding the control of the French monarchy. He was successful in both areas. Through open war and behind-the-scenes intrigue, Philip won back most of the French land held by the English kings Henry II, Richard I, and John. Philip also supported and benefitted by Pope Innocent III's crusade against the heretical Albigensians in southeastern France. With the defeat of this sect, the king gained the county of Toulouse for the French crown.

Years of plotting and warfare required a great deal of money. In 1182, Philip expelled the Jews in his realm and confiscated all their land. This proved to be only a short-term economic gain, and within a few years Philip realized that he needed the revenues the crown could get by taxing Jewish money lending. He asked the Jews to come back in 1198.

Philip II Augustus' clerical biographer wrote the document shown below. He described the 1182 Jewish expulsion, giving the king's deeply felt Christian piety as the reason behind the order. The biographer does mention, however, that the king benefitted directly by the Jews' expulsion.]

In the year of our Lord's incarnation 1182, in the month of April, which is called by the Jews Nisan, an edict went forth from the most serene king, Philip Augustus, that all the Jews of his kingdom should be prepared to go forth by the coming Feast of Saint John the Baptist *[June 24]*. And then the king gave them leave to sell each his movable goods before the time fixed, that is, the Feast of Saint John the Baptist. But their real estate, that is, houses, fields, vineyards, barns, winepresses, and such like, he reserved for himself and his successors, the kings of the French.

When the faithless Jews heard this edict, some of them were born again of water and the Holy Spirit and converted to the Lord, remaining steadfast in the faith of our Lord Jesus Christ. To them the king, out of regard for the Christian religion, restored all their possessions in their entirety and gave them perpetual liberty.

Others were blinded by their ancient error and persisted in their perfidy. They sought to win with gifts and golden promises the great of the land, counts, barons, archbishops, bishops, and through their influence and advice and through the promise of infinite wealth, they might turn the king's mind from his firm intention. But the merciful and compassionate God, Who does not forsake those who put their hope in Him and Who humbles those who glory in their strength...so fortified the illustrious king that he could not be moved by prayers nor promises of temporal things...

The infidel Jews, perceiving that the great of the land, through whom they had been accustomed easily to bend the king's predecessors to their will, had suffered repulse, and astonished and stupefied by the strength of mind of Philip the king and his constance in the Lord, exclaimed "Shema Yisrael!" and prepared to sell all their household goods. The time was now at hand when the king had ordered them to leave France altogether, and it could not be in any way prolonged. Then did the Jews sell all their movable possessions in great haste, while their landed property reverted to the crown. Thus the Jews, having sold their goods and taken the price for the expenses of their journey, departed with their wives and children and all their households in the aforesaid year of the Lord 1182, in the month of July, which is called by the Jews Tamuz, in the third year of the reign of King Philip Augustus, and the seventeenth year of his life... For they left in the month of July, as has been said; there thus remained three weeks or twenty-one days to the completion of his seventeenth year...

When the expulsion of the infidel Jews and their dispersal throughout the entire world had been completed, King Philip Augustus, aware of their deeds, in 1183 A.D., at the beginning of the eighteenth year of his life, through the grace of God, finished auspiciously the effort so auspiciously begun. For all the synagogues of the Jews, which are called schools by them and where the Jews, in the name of the false faith, convene daily for the sake of feigned prayer, he ordered cleansed. Against the will of all the princes, he caused those synagogues to be dedicated to God as churches, and he ordered altars to be consecrated in these synagogues in honor of our Lord Jesus Christ and of the blessed Mother of God, Virgin Mary. Indeed he believed piously and properly that where the name of Jesus Christ of Nazareth used to be blasphemed daily, as indicated by Jerome in his commentary on Isaiah, the Lord, Who alone accomplishes great miracles, should be praised by the clergy and by the entire Christian populace.

Jews forced to attend Christian sermons in an effort to convert them.

35. Louis IX of France

Forced Attendance at Sermons

(1269)

Source: Chazan, *Church, State and Jew in the Middle Ages*, pp. 261–262.

[Paul Christian, a Jewish convert to Christianity, told Louis IX of the need to preach to the Jews in hope of their ultimate acceptance of Jesus and the Church. The pious Louis agreed and sent out a letter ordering that Jews be forced to attend conversionary sermons. Jews also had to turn over their religious books—presumably including the Talmud—for inspection. In an attempt to prove the superiority of the Christian faith, churchmen and lay leaders questioned Jews and forced them to defend their books and their religion. The outcome of these "disputations" was, of course, never in question, for the Church believed it possessed the ultimate truth. Forced sermons and disputations spread through France, Italy, Germany, and Spain.]

Since our beloved brother in Christ, Paul Christian of the Order of Preaching Brethren, the bearer of the present letter, wishes and intends, for the glory of the Divine Name, to preach to the Jews the word of light, in order, we understand, to evangelize for the exaltation of the Christian faith, we order you to force those Jews residing in your jurisdiction to present themselves to hear from him

A public disputation between Christian humanists and Jewish scholars.

without objection the word of the Lord and to present their books as the aforesaid friar shall require. You shall compel the Jews to respond fully, without calumny and subterfuge, on those matters which relate to their laws, concerning which the aforesaid friar might interrogate them, whether in sermons in their synagogues or elsewhere. You shall provide, moreover, for the protection and safety of the aforesaid friar as he shall require of you, so that no violence or injury or impediment be inflicted upon him or his circle.

This letter shall be valid for as long as it pleases our will.

[Before Louis IX left for the Crusades, he is said to have ordered the Jews out of his kingdom. The order was not carried out. His grandson, Philip the Fair, however, did expel the French Jews in 1306. He charged them with ruthlessly oppressing Christians by means of high interest rates on loans. He confiscated the Jews' properties, including homes, synagogues, and cemeteries, and then required his oppressed subjects to pay him, in full, the debts they had owed to the Jews. In 1315, his son, Louis X, invited the Jews back, returned their stolen property, and was happy to receive the income they produced for the crown. The Jews, however, were still not destined to live in peace. Shepherds and peasants from the countryside, unhappy over social and economic conditions, rebelled and, in their rampages, killed many Jews.

The next calamity occurred when a group of lepers "confessed" under torture that Jews and Moors from Spain had paid them to poison wells in order to kill Christians. In 1321, Philip V ordered the Jews out. A new royal invitation in 1359 asked them to come back again. Finally, King Charles VI, in 1394, ordered all Jews to leave France for good. By the French Revolution in 1789, approximately 40,000 Jews lived in Alsace-Lorraine, and a few thousand others, many descended from Marranos who fled the Spanish Inquisition, made a marginal living scattered throughout the rest of France.]

Medieval England and the Jews

Jews crossed the Channel to England following William the Conqueror's victory at the Battle of Hastings in 1066. The Norman kings of England allowed Jewish families to settle in the larger towns. Several royal charters promised them protection. The Jews paid for this privilege through exorbitantly high taxes levied on the profits of money lending, the one profession open to them.

Jews lent money on a pledge. People who wished to borrow money would bring something they owned to the moneylender. They would then receive an amount of money based on the value of this "pledge." If they failed to repay the loan plus the specified amount of interest, the moneylender would then be free to sell the pledge to make up what he lost when the borrower failed to pay him back. Today, pawnbrokers function in exactly the same manner; banks often lend money with people's homes serving as pledges.

The problem for Jews in the Middle Ages arose when, because of the high taxes the kings forced them to pay, they had to charge high interest rates on the money they loaned. The higher the interest rate, the more difficult it was to repay the loan. Peasants could lose the goods they had brought in as pledges, and wealthier people who needed larger loans faced the possible loss of their lands or estates. As a result of this process, the Christian population felt increasingly resentful toward the Jews.

Monarchs understood this situation well; in fact, it was to their advantage to have the Jews in this position. Kings made a great deal of money from the lesser nobles and peasants through the taxes Jews paid, but these people turned their resentment against the Jews instead of against the crown. Then, when the resentment grew deep enough, the king expelled the Jews, seized their wealth and property, *and* earned the thanks of the Christian population for ridding them of the Jewish scourge.

With the exception of the first appearance of a ritual murder accusation in Norwich in 1144 (see Section Three), the situation in England remained outwardly peaceful through the first and second Crusades. However, tales of crusader attacks on infidel Jews and growing indignation over usury caused emotions to seethe under the deceptively calm surface. The first real trouble occurred in 1189 during Richard I's coronation as king of England. Somehow a rumor spread through London that the new king had issued orders for an attack on the Jews. Bloody anti-Jewish riots followed. Richard immediately put these down and made it clear he would not tolerate such actions. The Jews, after all, were the king's personal property. Nevertheless, anti-Jewish slaughters, more widespread and deadly than before, broke out when Richard left England to fight in the Third Crusade. The situation did not improve when Richard's brother, John, became king after the "Lion-Heart's" death.

36. King John of England

Protecting London's Jews

(1203)

Source: Chazan, *Church, State and Jew in the Middle Ages*, pp. 122–123.

[As John's troublesome reign progressed, he squeezed the Jews continually for more taxes. This became one of the major sources of income and helped John, at least for a time, to avoid begging the Parliament for more money. The Jews tried to recoup their increasing losses by higher interest on loans, and when the borrowers defaulted on these loans, small land owners and noblemen alike lost their properties. Complaints against the Jews escalated, as did anti-Jewish attacks. King John, in the following edict, ordered London's leaders to halt the rioting immediately. Note that John made reference to "dogs," saying, in effect, Jews might be as low as dogs, but if the king wanted them protected, responsible leaders had better see to their safety.]

The king, etc., to the mayor and barons of London, etc.:

We have always loved you greatly and have caused your laws and liberties to be carefully observed. Therefore, we believe that you love us in a special way and that you freely wish to do those things that enhance our honor and the peace and tranquillity of our land. Indeed, as you know that the Jews are under our special protection, we are amazed that you permit harm to be done to the Jews residing in the city of London, since this is obviously against the peace of the kingdom and the tranquillity of our land. In fact, we are further amazed and concerned because other Jews, wherever they dwell throughout England, live in peace, except those who reside in your city. We say this not only for our Jews, but also for our peace, for if we gave our peace to a dog it should be inviolably observed. Therefore, we commit henceforth the Jews residing in the city of London to your care, so that, if anyone attempts to do them harm, you shall defend them, affording them assistance by force. We shall require their blood of your hands, if perchance, through your failure, any harm befalls them, Heaven forbid. Indeed we well know that such things happen through the fools of the city and not through its wise men. However, the wise must restrain the folly of the fools.

With myself as witness, at Montford, July 29 [1203].

37. King Henry III of England

Restricting Jewish Freedoms

(1253)

Source: Chazan, *Church, State and Jew in the Middle Ages*, pp. 188–189.

[John's son, Henry III, continued his father's rapacious taxing of the English Jews. Article 1 of this edict made clear that Jews were simply royal sources of income. By this time the Jews were close to financial exhaustion and had little more to offer the king's treasury. This may have been one of the reasons Henry issued orders enforcing Jewish separation from Christians, including requirements to wear the Jewish badge. The era of royal protection for Jews in England was near an end.]

The king has provided and ordained etc.:

1. That no Jew remain in England unless he do the king service, and that from the hour of birth every Jew, whether male or female, serve us in some way.

2. That there be no synagogues of the Jews in England, save in those places in which such synagogues were in the time of King John, the king's father.

3. That in their synagogues the Jews, one and all, subdue their voices in performing their ritual offices, that Christians may not hear them.

4. That all Jews answer to the rector of the church of the parish in which they dwell touching all parochial dues relating to their houses.

5. That no Christian man or woman serve any Jew or Jewess or eat with them or tarry in their houses.

6. That no Jew or Jewess eat or buy meat during Lent.

7. That no Jew disparage the Christian faith or publicly dispute concerning the same.

8. That no Jew have secret familiar intercourse with any Christian woman, and no Christian man with a Jewess.

9. That every Jew wear his badge conspicuously on his breast.

10. That no Jew enter any church or chapel save for the purpose of transit or linger in them in dishonor of Christ.

11. That no Jew place any hindrance in the way of another Jew desirous of turning to the Christian faith.

12. That no Jew be received in any town but by special license of the king, save only in those towns in which Jews have been wont to dwell.

The justices assigned to the custody of the Jews are commanded that they cause these provisions to be carried into effect and rigorously observed on pain of forfeiture of the chattels of the said Jews.

38. King Edward I of England

Expulsion of the Jews

(1290)

Source: Chazan, *Church, State and Jew in the Middle Ages*, pp. 318–319.

[In this letter, Edward I made reference to his expulsion of the Jews from England. He had previously ordered them to stop money lending at interest. When they did not do so, he charged them with treason and ordered them out of the country. He thereby satisfied the demands of English noblemen and peasants, his mother, the pope, and the local clergy. The true reason for the Jews' expulsion may have been that as the king's personal property, they had little more to offer him financially. Also, another group, the Lombards, had recently come to England. These people offered financial services, including money lending, to the English. Moreover, the Lombards were Christian. Edward could now get rid of the Jews with little loss to the kingdom.

King Edward I.

The subject of this letter concerned the money which Christian borrowers had owed the expelled Jews. Edward I ordered that the principal (but not the interest) be paid directly to him. So even after there were no Jews left in England, their transactions continued to be of benefit to the crown.]

Whereas in our parliament held at Westminster on the quindene of Saint Michael in the third year of our reign *[October 13, 1275]*, we, moved by solicitude for the honor of God and the well-being of the people of our realm, did ordain and decree that no Jew should thenceforth lend to any Christian at usury upon security of lands, rents, or aught else, but said Jews did thereafter wickedly conspire and contrive a new species of usury more pernicious than the old...and made use of the specious device to the abasement of our said people on every side, thereby making their last offense twice as heinous as the first; therefore we, in requital of their crimes and for the honor of the

Crucified, have banished them from our realm as traitors. We, being minded in nowise to swerve from our former intent, but rather to follow it, do hereby make totally null and void all penalties and usuries and whatsoever else in those kinds may be claimed on account of the Jewry by actions at what time soever arising against any subjects of our realm. Being minded that nothing may in any wise be claimed from the said Christians on account of the said debts except only the principal sums which they have received from the said Jews, we decree that the said Christians do verify the amount before you by the oath of three true and lawful men, by whom the truth of the matter may the better be known, and thereafter pay the amount to us at such convenient times as may be determined by you. And to that intent we command you that you cause this our grace so benevolently granted to be read, and to be enrolled in the said Exchequer, and to be strictly observed, according to the form above indicated.

Medieval Spain and the Jews

King Sisebut ordered the baptism of all Jews in Spain in 616. Those who refused conversion had to leave the country and forfeit all their properties. To avoid this, many Jews accepted baptism and continued to practice Judaism in secret. These crypto-Jews hoped that some day the king's order would be rescinded. Other Jews chose exile over feigned conversion. These people either crossed the Pyrenees into tolerant southeastern France or fled to North Africa.

The invasion and conquest of Spain by the Moors in 711 allowed the crypto-Jews to return to their ancestral faith. While Charles Martel's defeat of the Moorish forces at Tours, France, in 732, halted the spread of Islam through Western Europe, the Moors remained in Spain until 1492. With the exception of the brief and bloody invasion of the fanatical Moslem Almohades (1148), Jews lived in peace, prospered, and developed what historians today call the "Golden Age" of Spanish Jewry.

Beginning in the 11th century, Spanish Christians mounted a continuous and increasingly successful movement to reconquer Spain from the Moors. The monarchs of small feudal kingdoms that developed in the liberated areas needed and welcomed Jewish financial resources. They also used Jews as interpreters and diplomats, thereby taking advantage of the fact that the Jews spoke Arabic and understood Moorish customs. To encourage Jewish assistance in the Reconquista (reconquest of Spain from the Arabs), the kings were willing to suspend the old anti-Jewish laws.

39.   Alphonso X

Las Siete Partidas

(1261)

Source: Lindo, pp. 97–102.

[Alphonso X "El Sabio" (the Wise) was the king of Castile and Leon. Under his patronage legal scholars prepared a vast collection of laws known as Las Siete Partidas, *the Seven Sections. This code reflected traditional Roman statutes and Church "Canon" law and included most of the same restrictions on Jews which had been passed in Christian Spain since the Council of Elvira in 304 C.E. Law 11 in the section "On Jews," which ordered Jewish men and women to wear distinctive badges or signs, reflected the growing Church insistence on isolating Jews from their Christian neighbors. While this law was not consistently enforced, the trend toward Jewish separation in Spain was escalating.*

By the middle of the 13th century, the Spanish had pushed the Moors south to the Kingdom of Granada where they remained until the final reconquest in 1492. With the Moorish threat diminished, Spanish Christians not only had less need for Jewish financial and diplomatic help, but they also developed a growing distaste for Jewish participation and influence in everyday life.]

On Jews:

Jews are a description of people that will not believe in the faith of our Lord Jesus Christ; but Christian potentates have always permitted them to reside among them. Whereas, in the preceding title, we treated with diviners and other persons we shall here treat of the Jews, who contradict and deny his name, and the miraculous and holy deed he performed when he sent His son, our Lord Jesus Christ, into the world to save sinners...

Law 1. The meaning of Jew, and whence the name is derived.—Those are termed Jews who believe the Law of Moses, following it to the letter, who practise circumcision, and perform other ceremonies enjoined by their religion. The name is derived from the tribe of Judah, which was the noblest, and braver than the other tribes; it also had another pre-eminence, the king of the Jews was to be elected from it; besides, in battle that tribe was the foremost. The reason the Church, emperors, kings and princes, permitted Jews to live by themselves among Christians, is, that they might always live as in captivity, and that they may ever be a memorial to mankind, that they are from the genealogy of those who crucified our Lord Jesus Christ.

Law 2. Jews residing among Christians must live humbly, and without evil intention, observing their religion, and not speak ill of the faith of our Lord Jesus Christ, which Christians observe...

Law 3. ...The emperors, who were formerly masters of the whole world, considered it just and right, that for the treason committed in putting their Lord to death, they [the Jews] should lose the honors and prerogatives they formerly enjoyed, so that no Jew should ever hold a post of honor, or public office, by virtue of which he would have to pass sentence on Christians.

Law 4. ...A Synagogue is a place where Jews perform their devotions. In no part of our dominions without our permission, may any new one be erected; but should those they have fall into decay, they may rebuild and repair them on the same site, and in the same manner as before; but they may not enlarge, elevate, or beautify them... We...forbid Christians putting animals in or near them, or causing any molestation to Jews, while engaged at their prayers, according to their religion.

Law 5. ...Saturday is a day whereon Jews observe their Sabbath... We therefore order, that no judge shall condemn or arrest Jews on Saturdays, or bring them to judgment for debt, or seize, or do them any hurt on that day... We further command, that all demands Christians may have against Jews, or Jews against Christians, shall be heard and determined by our Judges and not by their elders... Furthermore, we forbid any Christian to dare to seize or do any injury to the person or property of a Jew; but if he has any demand against him, he is to bring it before our Judges; and should any person presume to steal, or forcibly take anything from a Jew, he shall be compelled to return double the value.

Law. 6. ...No force or compulsion is to be used to make Jews turn Christians, but by good example, kindness, and the maxims of the Holy Scriptures, should they be converted to the faith of our Lord Jesus Christ, for he neither requires nor desires compulsory service. Furthermore, should any Jew or Jewess hereafter wish to become a Christian, other Jews are in no manner whatever to prevent them, and should any of them stone, wound, or kill those that wish to become Christians, or that have been baptized, if proved, we order, that the murderers and advisers of such outrage are to be burned... We furthermore order, that all persons in our kingdom are to respect Jews that become Christians, and no one insultingly shall reproach them or their descendants with having been Jews. And they shall keep possession of their property and all belonging to them, sharing with their brothers, and inheriting from their fathers, mothers, and other relations, the same as if they were Jews; and they are to be eligible to every honour, post, and employment held by other Christians.

Law 7. ...Such evil results from Christians turning Jews, that we order, that any Christian who does shall suffer death...

Law 8. ...We forbid Jews presuming to have Christian slaves in their houses; but they may employ them as labourers and cultivators of their outdoor possessions, and to guard them when travelling on a road considered unsafe. We furthermore forbid Christians to invite any Jew or Jewess, or to accept an invitation to eat and drink wine with them, or to drink wine make by Jews. Further, we order, that no Jew is to presume to bathe in the same bath with Christians. We also prohibit Christians receiving any medicine or purges made up by Jews, nevertheless they may take it on the advise (*sic.*) of an experienced person, provided it be compounded by Christians, who know and understand the ingredients of which it is composed.

Law 9. ...It is highly disrespectful and insolent for Jews to cohabit with Christian women. We therefore order, that if it be proved of any Jew, that he has committed such an offence he shall suffer death for it...and we consider it right that a Christian woman guilty of such a crime should not go unpunished; we therefore order, whether she be a virgin, married woman, widow, or prostitute, she shall suffer the same punishment, as enacted for a Christian woman who cohabits with a Moor [Lindo: *the first time she shall lose half her property, the second time, she shall suffer death*].

Law 10. ...Jews may not purchase or possess Christian slaves, either male or female... Furthermore, we forbid any Jew presuming to make his slave a Jew or Jewess, although they are Moors or other Barbarians...

Law 11. ...Many mistakes and injurious occurrences take place between Christians and Jews and Jewesses, and Christian women, from their living and residing together in towns and dressing alike. Therefore...we order that every Jew and Jewess residing in our dominions shall wear a particular sign on their heads, that people may publicly know who are Jews and Jewesses. And we order that any Jew who appears in public without it shall be fined, for each time, ten maravedis of gold; and if he has not the means to pay the fine, he shall publicly receive ten lashes.

40. *Ordinances of Soria*

(1380)

Source: Lindo, pp. 161–163.

[Following trends in the rest of Europe, Spanish Christians began seeing Judaism as an ever-growing threat. Apostate Jews, as anxious to increase their own

positions as to advance their newly adopted faith, often made the situation worse by condemning the practices of their former religion. One such convert to Christianity named Pedro Alphonso told of certain daily prayers said by Jews that were blasphemous to Christianity. A section of the 1380 Ordinances of Soria forbad Jews to use these particular prayers.

One of the prayers "which is said standing" may refer to either the Aleynu or Amidah, or both. The Aleynu prayer predates the destruction of Solomon's Temple (c. 580 B.C.E.) and was directed against pagan idolaters. Many Churchmen, knowing Jews considered religious statues to be idolatrous, believed the following words were meant to attack Christianity:

> ...We therefore hope in Thee, Lord our God,
> Soon to behold the glory of thy might
> When Thou wilt remove idols from the earth
> And the non-gods shall be wholly destroyed...

Source: Harry Gersh, *The Sacred Books of the Jews* (New York: Stein and Day, 1968), pp. 228–229.

The Amidah is a series of benedictions praising God and asking for divine help. The controversial section dealt with a plea added in Imperial Roman times asking for God's protection against "sectaries"—Christians who tried to win Roman favor by slandering Jews. Later, at the Church's insistence, the word "slanderers" appeared in the Amidah in lieu of "sectaries."

Source: Gersh, p. 223.

The Ordinances of Soria also tried to reduce the influence of the rabbis in the Jewish community. Perhaps Christians felt that with a weaker rabbinate, Jews would be more prone to convert.]

1. Whereas we have been informed, that the Jews are commanded by their books and other writings of the Talmud, daily to say the prayer against heretics, which is said standing *[the Aleynu prayer],* wherein they curse Christians and churches, we strictly command and forbid any of them, hereafter, to say it, or have it written in their rituals or any other books; and those that have it written in the said books, are to erase and cancel it in such manner as not to be legible, which is to be done within two months after the publication hereof; and any one who says or responds to it, shall publicly receive one hundred lashes. And if it be found in his breviary or other book, he is to be fined one thousand maravedis; and if he cannot pay the fine, one hundred lashes are to be given to him. And furthermore, be it known, we shall proceed severely against them, the same as against persons that curse the Christian religion.

2. Furthermore, as the Jews have been accustomed to choose their Rabbis and other judges among themselves, empowering them to decide all causes that

come before them, whether civil or criminal, which it is a great sin to authorise and permit; for according to the words of the prophets they were deprived of all power and liberty on the coming of our Lord Jesus Christ. And as many injuries and much harm accrue to our kingdoms, and to all Christians of our dominions and the commonalty therefrom, by their Jewries generally and in particular. For this reason we ordain and command that henceforward it shall not be permitted for any Jews of our kingdoms, whether rabbis, elders, chiefs, or any other persons that now are, or shall be hereafter, to interfere to judge any criminal cause to which death, loss of limb, or banishment is attached; but they may decide all civil causes that appertain to them according to their religion. Criminal cases shall be tried by one of the Alcaldes, chosen by the Jews in the towns and places of their respective jurisdictions. But, whereas the said Jews are ours, it is our pleasure that the appeals of said criminals, whether belonging to the Seigniories or any other places whatever, shall be brought before our court. This is to be understood for those criminal cases that have hitherto been tried by the said Jews. And if any cause has been decided contrary hereto we order that the sentence be null, and that no alcalde, judge, or other person, undertake to execute it, under the penalty of six thousand maravedis each. And if any act or ordinance contain anything contrary hereto, we command that it be not executed, nor is it to be valid. And if, thereby, any penalty or fine is inflicted, we order that it be annulled.

41. Ferdinand and Isabella of Spain

Edict for the Expulsion of the Jews

(March 30, 1492)

Source: Lindo, pp. 277–280.

[With the Reconquista, Spain and its leaders had little need socially, diplomatically, or economically for the Jews. Ferdinand and Isabella, the king and queen who finally united Spain and drove the Moors out, devoted themselves to achieving one faith, one monarchy, and one nation. Their reign ended a century which witnessed thousands of Spanish or "Sephardic" Jewish conversions. Some of these Jews were threatened with death, but most converted, outwardly at least, to retain their properties and professions. A few were true converts who left their former faith and embraced Catholicism wholeheartedly. Most—derisively called Marranos—were, as historian Cecil Roth put it succinctly, "Jews in all but name, Christians in nothing but form." Because of talent, education, and family tradition, the Marranos soon achieved positions of leadership in the legal professions, the army, the universities, and in the Spanish Church itself. Eventually some even married into the nobility.

Tomás de Torquemada, Inquisitor General of Castile and Aragon, pleading with King Ferdinand and Queen Isabella to expel the Jews from their realms.

Ferdinand and Isabella were greatly disturbed that many of these new Christians dared to practice Jewish rituals in secret. Finally, in 1478, their majesties asked Pope Sixtus IV to establish a holy Inquisition in Spain to root out the unbelievers. Thus began the dreaded Spanish Inquisition. The frenzy of arrests, tortures, expropriations, and burnings, headed by the Grand Inquisitor Tomás de Torquemada, however, failed to eliminate the secret practice of Judaism. Ferdinand and Isabella then believed that openly practicing Jews, who, as non-Christians, did not fall under the Inquisition's jurisdiction, were the contamination that kept Marranos faithful to the ancient religion. They issued an order for the expulsion of all Jews from Spain by July 31, 1492. The last Jews actually set sail on August 2, the same date Christopher Columbus embarked upon his historic journey to the New World.]

Whereas, having been informed that in these our kingdoms, there were some bad Christians who judaized and apostatized from our holy Catholic faith, the chief cause of which was the communication of Jews with Christians; at the Cortes we held in the city of Toledo in the year 1480, we ordered the said Jews in all the cities, towns, and places in our kingdoms and dominions, to separate into Jewries and places apart, where they should live and reside, hoping by their separation alone to remedy the evil. Furthermore, we have sought and given orders, that inquisition should be made in our said kingdoms, which, as is known, for upwards of twelve years has been, and is done, whereby many guilty persons have been discovered, as is notorious. And as we are informed by the inquisitors, and many other religious, ecclesiastical, and secular persons, that great injury has resulted, and does result, and it is stated, and appears to be, from the participation, society, and communication they held and do hold with Jews, who it appears always endeavour in every way they can to subvert our holy Catholic faith, and to make faithful Christians withdraw and separate themselves therefrom, and attract and pervert them to their injurious opinions and belief, instructing them in the ceremonies and observances of their religion, holding meetings where they read and teach them what they are to believe and observe according to their religion; seeking to circumcise them and their children; giving them books from which they may read their prayers; and explaining to them the fasts they are to observe; assembling with them to read and to teach them the histories of their law; notifying to them the festivals previous to their occurring, and instructing them what they are to do and observe thereon; giving and carrying to them from their houses unleavened bread, and meat slaughtered with ceremonies; instructing them what they are to refrain from, as well in food as in other matters, for the due observance of their religion, and persuading them all they can to profess and keep the law of Moses; giving them to understand, that except that, there is no other law or truth, which is proved by many declarations and confessions, as well of Jews themselves as of those who have been perverted and deceived by them, which has greatly redounded to the injury, detriment, and opprobrium of our holy Catholic faith.

Notwithstanding we were informed of the major part of this before, and we knew the certain remedy for all these injuries and inconveniences was to separate the said Jews from all communication with Christians, and banish them from all our kingdoms, yet we were desirous to content ourselves by ordering them to quit all the cities, towns, and places of Andalusia, where, it appears, they had done the greatest mischief, considering that would suffice, and that those of other cities, towns and places would cease to do and commit the same.

But as we are informed that neither that, nor the execution of some of the said Jews, who have been guilty of the said crimes and offences against our holy Catholic faith, has been sufficient for a complete remedy to obviate and arrest so great an opprobrium and offence to the Catholic faith and religion.

And as it is found and appears, that the said Jews, wherever they live and congregate, daily increase in continuing their wicked and injurious purposes; to afford them no further opportunity for insulting our holy Catholic faith, and those whom until now God has been pleased to preserve, as well as those who had fallen, but have amended and are brought back to our holy mother church, which, according to the weakness of our human nature and the diabolical suggestion that continually wages war with us, may easily occur, unless the principal cause of it be removed, which is to banish the said Jews from our kingdoms.

And when any serious and detestable crime is committed by some persons of a college or university, it is right that such college or university should be dissolved and annihilated, and the lesser suffer for the greater, and one be punished for the other; and those that disturb the welfare and proper living of cities and towns, that by contagion may injure others, should be expelled therefrom, and even for lighter causes that might be injurious to the state, how much more then for the greatest, most dangerous, and contagious of crimes like this.

Therefore, we, by and with the counsel and advice of some prelates and high noblemen of our kingdoms, and other learned persons of our council, having maturely deliberated thereon, resolve to order all the said Jews and Jewesses to quit our kingdoms, and never to return or come back to them, or any of them. Therefore we command this our edict to be issued, whereby we command all Jews and Jewesses, of whatever age they may be, that live, reside, and dwell in our said kingdoms and dominions, as well natives as those who are not, who in any manner or for any cause may have come to dwell therein, that by the end of the month of July next, of the present year, 1492, they depart from all our said kingdoms and dominions, with their sons, daughters, man-servants, maid-servants, and Jewish attendants, both great and small, of whatever age they may be; and they shall not presume to return to, nor reside therein, or in any part of them, either as residents, travellers, or in any other manner whatever, under pain that if they do not perform and execute the same, and are found to reside in our said kingdoms and dominions, or should in any manner live therein, they incur the penalty of death, and confiscation of all their property to our treasury, which penalty they incur by the act itself, without further process, declaration, or sentence.

And we command and forbid any person or persons of our said kingdoms, of whatsoever rank, station, or condition they may be, that they do not presume publicly or secretly to receive, shelter, protect, or defend any Jew or Jewess, after the said term of the end of July, in their lands or houses, or in any other part of our said kingdoms and dominions, henceforward for ever and ever, under pain of losing all their property, vassals, castles, and other possessions; and furthermore forfeit to our treasury any sums they have, or receive from us.

And that the said Jews and Jewesses during the said time, until the end of the said month of July, may be the better able to dispose of themselves, their property, and estates, we hereby take and receive them under our security, protection, and royal safeguard; and insure to them and their properties, that during the said period, until the said day, the end of the said month of July, they may travel in safety, and may enter, sell, barter, and alienate all their moveable and immoveable property, and freely dispose thereof at their pleasure.

And that during the said time, no harm, injury, or wrong whatever shall be done to their persons or properties contrary to justice, under the pains those persons incur and are liable to, that violate our royal safeguard.

We likewise grant permission and authority to the said Jews and Jewesses, to export their wealth and property, by sea or land, from our said kingdoms and dominions, provided they do not take away gold, silver, money, or other articles prohibited by the laws of our kingdoms, but in merchandise and goods that are not prohibited.

And we command all the justices of our kingdoms, that they cause the whole of the above herein contained to be observed and fulfilled, and that they do not act contrary hereto; and that they afford all necessary favour, under pain of being deprived of office, and the confiscation of all their property to our exchequer.

[Note: A large number of the exiled Jews fled to Portugal where, at first, the Portuguese king, Manoel, gave them refuge. But the king was betrothed to Ferdinand and Isabella's daughter, the Infanta Isabella. The Infanta declared she would never set foot in Manoel's country as long as one Jew lived there. Her insistence forced Manoel to take action, but he did not want Portugal to suffer economically should the Jews be driven out. Instead, he ordered all the Jews to immediately become

An Auto-da-fé, or Act of Faith, carried out by the Spanish Inquisition. Two converted Jews are to be burned at the stake for being heretics.

Christian. His men forcibly separated children from their parents and baptized them. To prevent this, mothers and fathers killed their children and then committed suicide. In the end, almost all of those who remained alive became Christians. Those few who refused to convert were threatened with perpetual slavery. Manoel's program was extremely successful, and the mere handful of professing Jews remaining were expelled from Portugal in 1497.]

Poland and the Jews

Jewish traders, merchants, and artisans lived in Greece and what is now Turkey long before the Christian era. Following a campaign of persecution by the increasingly powerful Eastern Christian Church, they spread north to the Balkans and west to the area between the Black and Caspian Seas. In the latter area they converted the king and much of the nobility of the Khazar Empire to Judaism. For over three hundred years this Jewish kingdom, made up of Christians, Muslims, and pagans, as well as Jews, was an island of toleration surrounded by a sea of religious persecution. In 1016, the Muscovite Russians conquered Khazaria, dispersing many of its Jews farther north to the Kiev area. The Jews remained there until the terrors of the 1450 Tatar invasion prompted them to move west into what would eventually be part of Poland. In the west, Jews from Europe, first fleeing the Crusaders' slaughters and later escaping from ritual murder and Black Plague accusations, migrated to Poland seeking refuge. Boleslaw the Pious, ruler of Great Poland, offered both groups of Jews a highly favorable settlement charter in 1264. This marked the beginning of the great Polish-Jewish community which lasted almost 700 years.

---

42.   King Boleslaw of Kalish

A Royal Patent for the Jews

(1264)

Source: Walter Ackerman, *Out of Our People's Past* (New York: The United Synagogue Commission on Jewish Education, 1977), pp. 105–108. From Halperin, Israel. Beth Yisroel B'Polin, Jerusalem, Youth Department of the World Zionist Organization, 1954, Vol. 2, pp. 231–233.

[King Boleslaw wished to develop Poland's economy, and the Jews fleeing western Europe had the financial and mercantile skills his kingdom needed. His royal patent or charter offered them broad protections, including a stern refutation of not only the ritual murder accusations, but also many of the other persecutions Jews had

suffered in Western Europe. It also carefully regulated relations between the existing Roman Catholic Christian communities and the new Jewish settlers.]

First of all we affirm that the testimony of a Christian alone may not be admitted in any matter which concerns the money or property of a Jew... In every such instance there must be testimony from both a Christian and a Jew.

Similarly if a Christian brings a complaint charging that he gave a Jew security and the Jew denies the charge and the Christian does not accept the statement of the Jew...let the Jew take an oath on an article equal in value to the alleged security and he will be exempt...

Likewise, if a Jew should charge without producing witnesses to that effect, that he lent a certain sum to a Christian, and the Christian denies the claim, the Christian may take an oath and exempt himself.

A Jew may accept as security, without any sort of inquiry, any item which is brought to him, no matter what, with the exception of clothes which are damp or stained with blood and holy vestments; these he cannot accept under any circumstances...

In the case of strife or quarrel between one Jew and another, no matter what the cause, the local magistrate may not bring judgment. Only we, our Palatine or his court may sit in judgment in such an instance. In capital cases only the royal court may sit in judgment.

If a Christian injures a Jew in any which way, the accused shall pay a fine to the royal treasury or to our Palatine...

...If the Jew...is carrying any goods or materials he is obliged to pay duty at each custom station. The duty he is to pay shall be the same as that paid by other citizens of the city in which the Jew is resident at the time.

If the Jews should transport, as is their custom, one of their dead from one city to another, or from one district to another...we decree that our customs collectors take nothing from them...

If a Christian desecrates or defiles a Jewish cemetery in any which way, it is our wish that he be punished severely as is demanded by the laws and customs of our realm and that all his possessions be remitted to our treasury.

If anyone should intentionally throw stones at a synagogue, it is our desire that he pay our Palatine two stone-weight of pepper...

...If a Jew should do injury to another Jew, he may not refuse to pay the fine to his judge...

If a Jew be murdered in secret, in such a manner as there are no witnesses to the deed and there is no way of knowing the murderer; and if after an investigation the

Jews begin to suspect someone, we shall provide the Jews with a prosecutor against the suspect.

...If a Christian should attack a Jew, the Christian shall be punished as required by the laws of this land...

No one may be billeted in the house of a Jew...

If someone should kidnap the child of a Jew, he is to be dealt with as a thief...

It is our wish that no one coerce a Jew to redeem pledges on any of his holidays...

In keeping with the directives of the Pope and in the name of our Holy Father, we absolutely forbid anyone to accuse the Jews in our dominion of using the blood of human beings...the laws of their faith prohibit the use of any blood. And if a Jew should be accused of putting a Christian child to death, the charge must be proven by the testimony of three Christians and a like number of Jews. Only then will the charge be considered proven. Should the Jew be found guilty then he shall be punished in the manner prescribed for such a transgression. But if the Jew be found innocent of the charge, then the Christian...shall be punished in the same manner as the Jew would have been had he been found guilty...

We affirm that if any Jew cry out in the night as a result of violence done him, and his Christian neighbors fail to respond to his cries and do not bring the necessary help, they shall be fined...

We also affirm that Jews are free to buy and sell all manner of things...just as Christians. And if anyone hamper them, he shall pay a fine to our Palatine.

In order that these privileges herein noted be enforced in the days to come we do bring the testimony of witnesses...and the sign of our seal. Given this day in Kalish, September 10, 1264.

43. Sigismund II Augustus

Permission to Establish a Yeshiva in Lublin, Poland

(August 23, 1567)

Source: Ackerman, p. 109. From Halperin, pp. 239.

[The document given below is surely one of the most pro-Jewish pronouncements offered in this collection. The historian might suspect it was drawn up by one or more Jews and then signed into law by the king. Sigismundus II Augustus not only gave permission to build a Yeshiva [school of higher religious learning], but also encouraged only the most learned and prestigious Jewish scholar in the realm to become

the head [Rosh] of the new school. Students could attend tuition free AND the king exempted the Yeshiva from all taxes.]

As a result of the efforts of our advisors and in keeping with the request of the Jews of Lublin we do hereby grant permission to erect a Yeshiva…and a synagogue by its side…and to outfit the said Yeshiva with all that is required to advance learning. The administration of the Yeshiva is to be vested in a person who will be accorded authority and influence by the teachers and who will be capable of maintaining order and discipline among the students.

All the learned men and rabbis of Lublin shall come together and from among their number choose one to serve as the head of the Yeshiva. Let their choice be of a man who will magnify the Torah and bring it glory! To him shall be granted the right of supervision over teachers and students alike.

We hereby grant him the honorary title of Rosh Yeshiva and assert that he shall not be subject to the authority of the present rabbi of Lublin nor to that of those who hold that position in the future. Not only that, we do here affirm that the Rosh Yeshiva shall be the superior of all the rabbis and learned men of the city.

And inasmuch as instruction in the said Yeshiva is to be given without charge and at no cost to the student, we declare the Rosh Yeshiva to be exempt from all taxes and duties due our treasury and the treasury of the State.

[Sigismundus II Augustus died in 1572. The Jagello dynasty and the tradition of strong royal leadership died with him. Feuding nobles asserted their right to elect the king and did their best to keep him weak and dependent. Poland was defenseless when the Cossacks in the Polish-ruled Ukraine rebelled. Led by the fierce Bogdan Chmelnitzki, the Cossack hordes invaded Poland proper, slaughtering the people and laying waste to the land. Chmelnitzki's men reserved their special fury for the Jews who, as agents of absentee Polish noblemen, collected the oppressive taxes that were one reason for the Ukrainian rebellion. The Polish government was unable to stop the three-year reign of terror. Shortly thereafter, Russia and Sweden invaded Poland, taking advantage of its weakness. The country was ravaged by ten years of warfare before Poland finally pushed the invaders out. By this time, the once thriving Jewish community, along with the rest of Poland, lay in ruins.]

Title page of Luther's book,
On the Jews and their Lies.

Chapter VI

Martin Luther, the Reformation, and the Jews

Throughout Church history, many Christian free thinkers founded movements which differed from official Catholicism in doctrine and ritual practice. The Arian, Albigensian, and Hussite heresies, all ruthlessly uprooted, were the most famous. The Church by the 16th century, however, found it increasingly difficult to muzzle dissent while, at the same time, widespread Church abuses fueled ever greater dissatisfaction and finally open rebellion.

Worldly popes, born and reared in the heady atmosphere of the Italian Renaissance, led the Catholic world in the 16th century. Moral laxness pervaded the Church, and many clerics, high and low, blatantly broke their vows of poverty and chastity. Some popes even donned armor and went to war to expand papal territory and influence. The popes, as true renaissance princes, spent fortunes patronizing the arts and architecture for the greater glory of God and the beautification of the Church's home in Rome. The more grandiose the scheme, the greater the need for money and the more motivated the clergy to find creative means to raise the funds.

The Church's moral crisis caused many to desire a return to a simpler (and less corrupt) form of Christianity, closer to what they believed Jesus' early followers practiced. The key to many of these "reformed" faiths was the elimination of the clerical hierarchy and the belief that humans could communicate directly with God, without priests as intermediaries. The reformed faiths "protested" against what they considered Church abuses and thus came the term "Protestant Reformation."

Martin Luther.

Without a unified, central authority, the Protestants developed many different modes of worship, all based on different interpretations of Christian doctrine. Several of these sects seemed to have been influenced by Jewish ideas. The Antitrinitarians did not believe in the Trinity—the Christian belief that God was made up of three distinct yet united parts. The Sabbatarians moved their worship services and day of rest from Sunday to Saturday. Despite these seemingly "Jewish" traits and the Protestants' general admiration of the biblical Hebrews, they felt no kinship to, and little sympathy for, the Jews of their time.

Without a doubt, Martin Luther, an Augustinian monk, priest, teacher, and doctor of theology, became the most famous and most influential Protestant reformer. Luther began his revolt against the Church when, in 1517, he publicly posted an invitation to a scholarly debate, entitled "95 Academic Theses On the Power of Indulgences." Indulgences were religious guarantees promising a reduction in the time a dead person spent in a place called "purgatory" suffering for sins committed while alive. Sales of indulgences proved to be one of the "creative" ways devised to raise money for the pope's coffers. As a result of the "95 Theses," the Church condemned Luther and ordered him to defend himself against the charge of heresy. Luther would not recant his objection and, furthermore, told his attackers that he believed people could only be saved from the fires of hell by faith in Jesus, who would then, out of love for humanity, forgive the sinner. The Church with all its intricate doctrines and its stress on good works, he insisted, could not guarantee salvation. Luther also denied papal power and, in fact, charged that the pope was anti-Christ. The Church condemned Luther, but because of its own weakness and the continual conflicts between the Holy Roman Emperors and the papacy, it was not able to silence him nor was it able to destroy the reform movement.

The Reformation was a very difficult and dangerous time for the Jews. The Catholic Church accused the many Protestant denominations of being Judaizers and issued edicts restricting the Jews and punishing them for turning the reformers away from the true faith. Each Protestant group also called the other groups Judaizers and blamed the Jews for leading them astray. The Catholic/Protestant and Protestant/Protestant differences led to bloody massacres and the Thirty Years' War that did not leave the Jews untouched.

From the long-range point of view, however, the decentralization of Christian leadership, one of the results of the Protestant Reformation, made it more difficult to mount a concerted attack on Jews and Judaism. In addition, the Reformation also encouraged people to think for themselves and to question authority. Ultimately the development of many different Christian faiths led to toleration of other religions and ideas. Protestants and Catholics eventually extended this toleration to Judaism, and the Jewish people eventually benefitted from the seeds of tolerance sown during this era of religious revolution.

44. Martin Luther

That Jesus Christ Was Born a Jew

(1523)

Source: Mark Edwards, Jr., *Luther's Last Battles: Politics and Polemics, 1531–46* (Ithaca, New York: Cornell University Press, 1983), pp. 121–122.

[Martin Luther lived in a section of Germany where Jews had been expelled many years before. There is no historical proof that he ever personally encountered any Jewish people at all. He paid little heed to them until the 1520s when he began openly to court Jews in hopes of their eventual conversion to his new faith. At the time, he had no doubts that Jews would prefer Lutheranism, as it came to be called, to Catholicism. He believed his reformed religion better reflected both Old Testament beliefs and the original faith of the very first Christians. He wrote "That Jesus Christ Was Born a Jew" in 1523 to show his sympathy toward Jews in their long struggle with the papacy. He ridiculed how the Roman Catholic Church had handled the Jews for the past 1500 years. It may be, however, that the major reason he wrote this treatise was to continue his attack on the pope and the Church hierarchy.

Note: *The "stink" mentioned below by Luther referred to the* foetor Judaicus *or Jewish odor. Christians believed Jewish people had an inherently bad odor which could only be washed away by baptism.]*

For our fools, the popes, bishops, sophists, and monks—the gross asses' heads—have treated the Jews to date in such fashion that he who would be a good Christian might almost have to become a Jew. And if I had been a Jew and had seen such oafs and numbskulls governing and teaching the Christian faith, I would have rather become a sow than a Christian.

For they have dealt with the Jews as if they were dogs and not men. They were able to do nothing but curse them and take their goods. When they were baptized, no Christian teaching or life was demonstrated to them, rather they were only subjected to papistry and monkery. When they then saw that Judaism had such strong scriptural support and that Christianity was nothing but twaddle without any scriptural support, how could they quiet their hearts and become true good Christians? I myself have heard from pious baptized Jews that if they had not in our time heard the gospel, they would have remained life-long Jews under the Christian exterior. For they confess that they never yet have heard anything about Christ from their baptizers and masters...

Therefore, I would request and advise that one manage them decently and instruct them from the Scripture so that some of them might be brought along. But since we now drive them with force and slander them, accuse them of having Christian blood if they don't stink, and who knows what other foolishness, so that they are regarded just as dogs—what good can we expect to accomplish with them? Similarly, that we forbid them to work, do business, and have other human association with us, so that we drive them to usury—how does that help them?

If we wish to help them, we must practice on them not the papal law but rather the Christian law of love, and accept them in a friendly fashion, allowing them to work and make a living, so that they gain the reason and opportunity to be with and among us [and] to see and to hear our Christian teaching and life.

If some are obstinate, what does it matter? After all, we too are not all good Christians. Here I will let matters rest until I see what I have accomplished.

45. Martin Luther

On the Jews and their Lies

(1543)

Source: Martin Luther, *Luther's Works*, volume 47, edited by Franklin Sherman, (Philadelphia: Fortress Press, 1971), pp. 137, 156, 157, 166, 254, 267, 268+, and 292.

[When several years of kind thoughts and patient exhortation failed to convince the Jews to convert, Luther took this rejection almost as a personal insult and his previous positive feelings concerning Jews turned to pure hate. It was as if he unconsciously felt that Lutheranism (like Catholicism before it) needed Jewish conversion as proof of the ultimate truth of Christianity. He accused Jews of the most vicious crimes and repeated ritual murder accusations. He called on Christians to

destroy Jewish homes, synagogues, and sacred books. He advocated what he called a "sharp mercy" where the Jewish infection would be cut out from the heart of Christian existence. He completely ignored, in his bitterness, that he went far beyond anti-Jewish measures advocated up to that time by any of the popes.]

I had made up my mind to write no more either about the Jews or against them. But since I learned that these miserable and accursed people do not cease to lure to themselves even us, that is, the Christians, I have published this little book, so that I might be found among those who opposed such poisonous activities of the Jews, and who warned the Christians to be on their guard against them…

…It is not my purpose to quarrel with the Jews, nor to learn from them how they interpret or understand Scripture; I know all of that very well already. Much less do I propose to convert the Jews, for that is impossible…

They are real liars and bloodhounds who have not only continually perverted and falsified all of Scripture with their mendacious glosses from the beginning until the present day. Their heart's most ardent sighing and yearning and hoping is set on the day on which they can deal with us Gentiles as they did with the Gentiles in Persia at the time of Esther. Oh, how fond they are of the book of Esther, which is so beautifully attuned to their bloodthirsty, vengeful, murderous yearning and hope. The sun has never shone on a more bloodthirsty and vengeful people than they are who imagine that they are God's people who have been commissioned and commanded to murder and to slay the Gentiles. In fact, the most important thing that they expect of their Messiah is that he will murder and kill the entire world with their sword. They treated us Christians in this manner at the very beginning throughout all the world. They would still like to do this if they had the power, and often enough have made the attempt, for which they have got their snouts boxed lustily…

So it became apparent that they were a defiled bride, yes, an incorrigible whore and most evil slut with whom God ever had to wrangle, scuffle, and fight. If he chastised and struck them with his word through the prophets, they contradicted him, killed his prophets, or, like a mad dog, bit the stick with which they were struck…

I stated earlier that they corrupt their circumcision with human ordinances and ruin their heritage with their arrogance. In the same manner they also desecrate their Sabbath and all their festivals. In brief, all their life and all their deeds, whether they eat, drink, sleep, wake, stand, walk, dress, undress, fast, bathe, pray, or praise, are so sullied with rabbinical, foul ordinances and unbelief, that Moses can no longer be recognized among them. This corresponds to the situation of the papacy in our day, in which Christ and his word can hardly be recognized because of the great vermin of human ordinances…

…We do not curse them but wish them well, physically and spiritually. We lodge them, we let them eat and drink with us. We do not kidnap their children and pierce them through; we do not poison their wells; we do not thirst for their blood. How, then, do we incur such terrible anger, envy, and hatred on the part of such great and holy children of God?

There is no other explanation for this than the one cited earlier from Moses—namely, that God has struck them with "madness and blindness and confusion of mind." So we are even at fault in not avenging all this innocent blood of our Lord and of the Christians which they shed for three hundred years after the destruction of Jerusalem, and the blood of the children they have shed since then (which still shines forth from their eyes and their skin). We are at fault in not slaying them. Rather we allow them to live freely in our midst despite all their murdering, cursing, blaspheming, lying, and defaming; we protect and shield their synagogues, houses, life, and property. In this way we make them lazy and secure and encourage them to fleece us boldly of our money and goods, as well as to mock and deride us, with a view to overcoming us, killing us all for such a great sin, and robbing us of all our property (as they daily pray and hope). Now tell me whether they do not have every reason to be the enemies of us accursed Goyim, to curse us and to strive for our final, complete, and eternal ruin!...

What shall we do with this rejected and condemned people, the Jews? Since they live among us, we dare not tolerate their conduct, now that we are aware of their lying and reviling and blaspheming. If we do, we become sharers in their lies, cursing, and blasphemy. Thus we cannot extinguish the unquenchable fire of divine wrath, of which the prophets speak, nor can we convert the Jews. With prayer and the fear of God we must practice a sharp mercy to see whether we might save at least a few from the glowing flames. We dare not avenge ourselves. Vengeance a thousand times worse than we could wish them already has them by the throat.

46.   Martin Luther

On the Jews and their Lies (continued)

Source: Marcus, pp. 168–169.

First, their synagogues or churches should be set on fire, and whatever does not burn up should be covered or spread over with dirt so that no one may ever be able to see a cinder or stone of it...

Secondly, their homes should likewise be broken down and destroyed. For they perpetrate the same things there that they do in their synagogues. For this reason they ought to be put under one roof or in a stable, like gypsies, in order that they may realize that they are not master in our land, as they boast, but miserable captives, as they complain of us incessantly before God with bitter wailing.

Thirdly, they should be deprived of their prayer-books and Talmuds in which such idolatry, lies, cursing, and blasphemy are taught.

Fourthly, their rabbis must be forbidden under threat of death to teach any-more...

Fifthly, passport and traveling privileges should be absolutely forbidden to the Jews...

Sixthly, they ought to be stopped from usury. All their cash and valuables of silver and gold ought to be taken from them and put aside for safe keeping. For this reason, as said before, everything that they possess they stole and robbed from us...

Seventhly, let the young and strong Jews and Jewesses be given the flail, the ax, the hoe, the spade, the distaff, and spindle, and let them earn their bread by the sweat of their noses as is enjoined upon Adam's children...

If, however, we are afraid that they might harm us personally, or our wives, children, servants, cattle, etc. when they serve us or work for us...let us drive them out of the country for all time. For, as has been said, God's rage is so great against them that they only become worse and worse through mild mercy, and not much better through severe mercy. Therefore away with them...

I wish and ask that our rulers who have Jewish subjects exercise a sharp mercy toward these wretched people, as suggested above, to see whether this might not help (though it is doubtful)... If this does not help we must drive them out like mad dogs, so that we do not become partakers of their abominable blasphemy and all their other vices and thus merit God's wrath and be damned with them. I have done my duty. Now let everyone see to his. I am exonerated.

Finally I wish to say this for myself: If God were to give me no other Messiah than such as the Jews wish and hope for, I would much, much rather be a sow than a human being...

[Sadly, Luther's hateful diatribes against Jews, coming from the highly respected founder of Germany's major Protestant religion, had a great impact on later generations of Germans. They influenced Germany's 19th-century anti-Semitic movement and gave its advocates an air of legitimacy. Numerous books and pamphlets appeared in print detailing Martin Luther's "heroic" struggles against the Jews. In the 1930s and 1940s, Hitler's Nazi propagandists borrowed heavily from the earlier German anti-Semites and from Luther's urging "...not to suffer them, or bear with them any longer."]

The Simon of Trent blood libel.

Section Three

Ritual Murder Accusations and Other Charges

Nowhere in the annals of anti-Jewish prejudice has there been a more outrageous and defamatory assertion than that of blood libel or ritual murder. In its simplest form, Christians claimed Jews murdered Christian boys and used their blood for such religious purposes as preparing the Passover matzoh. Since Passover and Easter usually occurred near the same date, accusations of ritual murder generally appeared in the early spring. Church and secular leaders sharply denounced these defamations, but people refused to abandon this myth. The historian can only suggest some of the reasons for its continual reappearance through the Middle Ages and beyond.

Perhaps because the blood accusation was a variant on the theme of cannibalism, Christians assumed it to be evidence of the Jews' utter depravity and debasement. Human beings, literally, could sink no lower. So, to believe that Jews, whom the Church had called perfidious God-killers, would commit such crimes against society's weakest members was not beyond the imagination and credulity of the superstitious masses.

Ritual murder allegations satisfied several needs of the Medieval populace. The dead child became a martyr who was reputed to perform miracles. In this way his death supposedly proved the miraculous powers of Christianity. There were also mercenary reasons for slandering Jews as ritual murderers. Usually Christians executed large numbers of Jews for the crime, sometimes slaying the whole local Jewish population. They then confiscated Jewish property and canceled whatever debts they owed to the Jews. In addition, on the site of the child's martyrdom the faithful built a church or shrine, which contained bones or other relics for veneration. The pilgrimages made by Christians to the shrine or church contributed greatly to the local economy. Finally, the execution of the Jews found "guilty" of the crime provided exciting entertainment for people whose daily lives were tedious and difficult.

References to blood libel date back to the Greco-Roman era. Pagan groups accused each other of killing one of its members and using the victim's blood for its religious ceremonies. These same pagans claimed Jews captured Greek men in order to sacrifice them in the Temple to Judaism's invisible God. Romans charged Christians with the same crime, the last recorded accusation occurring in 416 C.E. We hear no more of ritual murder until 1144 when villagers of Norwich, England, greatly influenced by the fervor surrounding the Crusades, accused local Jews of torturing and murdering a child named William.

Ritual murder indictments against Jews spread from England to France, the German states, Poland, and Spain. Popes, kings and emperors declared that Jews, if for no other reason than their strict dietary laws banning even the smallest drop of blood in meat or poultry, were incapable of the crime. The Christian populace was not impressed. In 1385, Geoffrey Chaucer published his *Canterbury Tales* which included an account of Jews murdering a deeply pious and innocent Christian boy. Thus blood libel became a part of English literary tradition. Even Martin Luther in "On the Jews and Their Lies" made reference to his belief that Jews had committed these heinous acts.

Because Medieval Christians (and Luther as late as the Reformation) believed it would be unnatural for the Jews, who were continually persecuted, not to want revenge for their ill-treatment, they believed the Jews were always seeking new ways to destroy Christendom. They claimed Jews poisoned wells which caused the bubonic plague—the Black Death which killed a large percentage of Europe's population. In another related crime, Christians alleged Jews desecrated the "host." They claimed Jews stabbed, abused, and tortured the wafer or "host" which Catholics assert is miraculously transformed into the actual body of Jesus during the sacrament of the Holy Eucharist. With the spread of Protestant Christianity, which claimed the wafer only symbolized Jesus' body, host desecration charges slowly disappeared.

Ritual murder accusations, however, did not fade away. They lasted well into the 20th century with the 1913 trial in Russia of Mendel Beilis, attacks on Holocaust survivors in post-war Poland, and sporadic references to Jewish blood libel in the Arab press in the 1970s and 1980s. Only the future will tell if this most spurious and abhorrent of indictments has ceased to be a threat to Jewish communities in Europe and the rest of the world.

Burning of Jews by zealous Christians.

Chapter VII

The Terrible Legacy of False Accusations

47. Monk Thomas

Ritual Murder Accusation

(1144)

Source: Robert Chazan, *Church, State, and Jew in the Middle Ages*, pp. 142–145.

[This report by a monk named Thomas of Monmouth is the first record in existence of a ritual murder accusation against the Jews. As such, it is an extremely important document, but it leaves us with many questions and almost no concrete answers. The following are the basic details of the accusation. On Good Friday, March 24, 1144, a man claimed to come across a group of Jews carrying something. After touching it, he believed it to be a human body. The next morning, a forester discovered a boy's body which showed evidences of torture. He told a priest who convinced him to wait until Monday, the day after Easter, to bury the body. Rumors quickly spread, and the Christians in the area threatened to kill all the local Jews. John, the Sheriff of Norwich, protected the Jews and refused to let the situation get out of hand. The local monastery and cathedral in Norwich, previously very poor, took the child's body and soon became a great attraction for pilgrims wishing to see the remains of the martyred William of Norwich.

Two years after the supposed ritual murder, William of Turbeville, the Bishop of Norwich, asked Thomas to write down the details of what was quickly becoming a legend. The monk recorded the tale told to him by some of the local inhabitants. We do not know whether these people had actually seen the dead child's body or the Jews who were supposedly carrying it away. We do not know how Thomas knew what the Jews he claimed were involved in the crime said and did among themselves. And we do not know how much of Thomas's account was fictional narrative and supposition added to make the story more dramatic.

Was this truly the first time, as some historians claim, that Christians accused Jews of ritual murder? Careful reading of the text would seem to indicate that the villagers in and around Norwich were astonished by the crime, but that they "knew" almost instinctively that Jews were the culprits. The sentence which stated "...it could only have been the Jews who would have wrought such a deed, especially at such a time," suggests that at least some kind of rumor about Jews, ritual murder, and Easter had circulated for some time. Even more telling, Monk Thomas stated that it happened "...on a day when it was not the custom for the Jews to leave their houses." It is doubtful that the monk would have mistaken Friday, rather than Saturday, as the Jewish Sabbath and the reason Jews stayed in their homes. No Jewish holiday fell on or around this date which would have required the Jews to remain inside. We are left with the conclusion that Good Friday was the reason the Jews sequestered themselves. Yearly, during the entire week before Easter, Christians heard about Jesus' death on the cross and how the Jews betrayed and murdered him. Anti-Jewish feeling was always at its highest at this time. The Jews probably did remain behind closed doors to escape physical attacks by Christians whose passions were always stirred during Holy Week.

The Crusades themselves also created passionate excitement, engendering many attacks on Jews. In 1096, there had been a rumor that Jews murdered a crusader, immersed his body in boiling water, and proceeded to pour the resulting "broth" into drinking water in order to poison Christians. Years of escalating hate and prejudice led Christians to believe that Jews were capable of committing the most outrageous and heinous crimes. Once voiced, ritual murder accusations spread from Norwich through much of Europe, reappearing almost annually during the week before Easter.]

The morrow dawned, when everywhere the Christian religion specially celebrates a day of solemnity by reason of the sacramental rite of the Adoration of the Cross *[Good Friday]*. On that day it is the custom among all Christians with sparing diet to abstain from all amusements and pleasures and, while going around the churches of the saints, to be diligently engaged in devout attendance at the prayers. At daylight therefore on this day the Jews who had been chosen the day before, namely Eleazar and another, tied up the body of the blessed martyr William in a sack and carried it out. And when they had left the city with the body and were just entering Thorpe Wood, it chanced that a certain citizen of Norwich, one of the most eminent and richest of the citizens, met them. His Christian name was Aelward and his surname was Ded. He, after visiting all the churches in the city during the previous night, was returning from the Church of Saint Mary Magdalene, which is the church of the sick folk whose abode is near the aforesaid wood, and was making his way with a single servant to Saint Leonard's Church, along the edge of the wood. This happened by the ordaining of God's grace and in order that a lawful witness might be forthcoming, so that when the body was afterwards discovered the matter might not be concealed from the Christians. So Aelward, coming upon the Jews as they were going along, recognized them, but could not tell what it was that one of them was carrying before him on his horse's neck. However, being in doubt and considering what the passers-by were about and what it could possibly be which they were carrying with them and why they should have gone so far from home on a day when it was not the custom for the Jews to leave their houses, he halted for a moment and asked them where they were going. Then, going nearer and laying hands thereupon, he touched what they were carrying with his right hand and he found it was a human body. But they, frightened at having been discovered and in their terror not having anything to say, made off at full gallop and rushed into the thick of the wood. Whereupon a suspicion of some mischief suggested itself to the mind of Aelward; yet he recalled his thoughts to the road which he had been pursuing when he was engaged in his devotional employment.

Meanwhile the Jews, picking their way through the tangled thickets of the wood, hung the body by a thin flaxen cord to a tree and left it there and then returned home by another path. And because they were extremely terrified and conceived new fears at every meeting with anyone that they saw, I conjecture that there occurred with them that which usually happens with very timid people who are conscious of guilt. For they who are in such a case look with suspicion at everybody that comes in their way, and they see pitfalls everywhere, and they suppose that the stones and trees in the distance are men. At any rate the Jews, when they got back, told the others the mishap that had occurred to them on the road.

The enemies of the Christians, being very much alarmed, were quite at a loss as to what course to take. And in despair, while one was suggesting this and another that measure for their common safety, they determined at last to make advances to John the Sheriff, who had been wont to be their refuge and their one and only protector. So by common consent it was arranged that certain of them who were their chief men in influence and power should go to him and deal with him so that, supported by his authority, they should hereafter have no cause for alarm. So they went and, passing within the castle walls, were admitted to the presence of the sheriff. They said that they had a great secret to divulge and wished to communicate secretly with him alone. Straightway, when all who were present had withdrawn, John bade them forthwith to say what they wanted, and they replied, "Look you, we are placed in a position of great anxiety, and, if you can help us out of it, we promise you a hundred marks." He delighted at the number of marks and promised that he would both keep close their secret and that, according to his power, he would not fail to give them his support on any occasion…

On that same Saturday, after sunrise, Henry de Sprowston, the forester, whom I mentioned before, mounting his horse went into the wood to see if he could find anyone who might be doing mischief by cutting down anything in the wood without a license. And it came to pass that either chance or, as I rather believe, the divine will inclined his mind as he went along toward the place where he had seen the beams of the bright light gleaming on the day before. While he was passing hither and thither in that part of the wood, suddenly he observed a man cutting wood who said that he had discovered there a boy who had been slain. Whereupon, going with the peasant as a guide, Henry found the boy, but who he was or how he had got there he could not understand. But when he had looked at him carefully to find out if by any chance he knew him, he perceived that he had been wounded, and he noticed the wooden torture in his mouth. Becoming aware that he had been treated with unusual cruelty, he now began to suspect, from the manner of his treatment, that it was no Christian but in very truth a Jew, who had ventured to slaughter an innocent child of this kind with such horrible barbarity. So, observing the place very carefully and taking note of the outlook, be became certain that this was the same place where on the day before he had seen the rays of light gleaming and flashing upwards. Accordingly, when he had pondered over these things with much wondering, Henry went back and told his wife and all his household all he had seen. Then, summoning a priest, he announced to him that the body of a little innocent who had been treated in the most cruel manner had been discovered exposed in the wood. He said that he very much wished to take it away from there and, if the priest approved, to bury it in the churchyard of Sprowston. After very earnestly deliberating about the carrying out of this intention, they came to the conclusion that, inasmuch as the festival of Easter was coming next day *[March 26, 1144]*, they should defer their arrangement till the third day and so carry into effect their devout intention more fittingly.

So the business of burying him was put off. But in the meantime, as one man after another told others their several versions of the story, the rumor was spread in all directions. When it reached the city, it struck the heart of all who heard it with exceeding horror. The city was stirred with a strange excitement; the streets were crowded with people making disturbance. Already it was asserted by the greater part of them that it could only have been the Jews who would have wrought such a deed, especially at such a time. And so some were standing about as if amazed by the new and extraordinary affair; many were running hither and thither, but especially the boys and the young men; and, a divine impulse drawing them on, they rushed in crowds to the wood to see the sight. What they sought they found. On detecting the marks of the torture on the body and carefully looking into the method of the act, some suspected that the Jews were guilty of the deed; also some, led on by what was really a divine discernment, asserted that it was so. When these returned, they who had stayed at home got together in groups, and, when they heard how the case stood, they too hurried to the sight. On their return they bore their testimony to the same effect. And thus all through Saturday and all through Easter day, all the city everywhere was occupied in going backward and forward time after time, and everybody was in excitement and astonishment at the extraordinary event.

And so the earnestness of their devout fervor was urging all to destroy the Jews. They would there and then have laid hands upon them, but, restrained by fear of the Sheriff John, they kept quiet for a while.

48. Emperor Frederick II

Refuting Ritual Murder Accusations

(1236)

Source: Chazan, *Church, State and Jew in the Middle Ages*, pp. 124–126.

[Any murder, especially of a child, occurring around Easter, was an occasion to accuse the Jews of committing the crime and of using the dead person's blood for ritual purposes. After the Norwich charges, Christians made such accusations in 1171 in Blois, France, in 1190 in Winchester, England, and then on a regular basis in the German States. While soldiers involved in the 6th Crusade were slaughtering Jewish communities in southern France, ritual murder charges against Jews spread like wildfire in Germany.

Following ritual murder accusations against the Jews of Fulda, a town northeast of Frankfort am Main, Holy Roman Emperor Frederick II ordered an exhaustive inquiry into Jewish religious practices, dietary laws and customs. He concluded that Jews could not possibly commit the crimes of which they had been accused. His logical arguments in no way convinced the populace who refused to believe in the Jews' innocence. The following, also known as the emperor's "Golden Bull," is a detailed account of Frederick II's inquiry into, and definite refutation of, Jewish guilt concerning ritual murder.]

In the name of the Holy and Undivided Trinity, Frederick II, through the favor of divine mercy august emperor of the Romans and king of Jerusalem and Sicily:

Although the preeminence of this august dignity is obligated to extend the arm of its protection to all subjects of the Roman Empire and although it is fitting, for the protection of the faith which stems from celestial dispensation, to treat the faithful of Christ with special favor, nonetheless, for the proper management of justice, it is required that we rule the non-believers properly and protect them justly, as a special group committed to our care. Thus, living with the faithful under the protection of our majesty, they shall not be violently oppressed by those stronger than themselves. Therefore, it is by the contents of the present letter that present and future generations shall know that all the serfs of our court in Germany have beseeched our majesty that we deign by our grace to confirm for all the Jews of Germany the privilege of our divine grandfather Frederick, granted to the Jews of Worms and their associates. These are the contents of that privilege...

Providing then for the security and peaceful status of the Jews of Germany, we cause this special grace to be extended to all Jews who belong directly to our court. That is to say, copying and adhering to the edicts of our aforesaid grandfather, we confirm for the Jews by our natural mercy the above privilege and those stipulations contained in it, in the same manner as our divine and august grandfather granted to the Jews of Worms and their associates.

Moreover, we wish that all present and future know the following. When a serious crime was imputed to the Jews of Fulda concerning the death of certain boys of the town, because of that terrible incident the harsh opinion of the neighboring populace, spawned by recent misfortune, was projected against the rest of the Jews of Germany, although covert attacks were not yet in evidence. In order to clarify the truth concerning the aforesaid crime, we had many of the princes and magnates and nobles of the empire, along with abbots and clerics, convened to provide counsel. When diverse views on the matter had been expressed, not adequate to produce clear counsel, as is fitting, we concluded that one could not proceed more properly against the Jews accused of the aforesaid crime than through those who had been Jews and had converted to the cult of the Christian faith. They, since opposed to Judaism, would not withhold whatever they might know against the Jews, whether through the Mosaic books or through the contents of the Old Testament. Although through the authority of many books, which our majesty distributed, our conscience had the innocence of the aforesaid Jews reasonably proven, in order to provide satisfaction for both the populace and the law, by our counsel and that of our princes, magnates, nobles, abbots, and clerics, with unanimous agreement, we sent special messengers to all the kings of the West, through whom we had many experienced experts in Jewish law sent from their kingdoms to our presence. When they had tarried in our court for some time, we commanded, in order to ascertain the truth of this matter, that they diligently conduct a study and instruct our conscience whether there survives any belief leading to the perpetrating of any act regarding human blood, which might impel the Jews to commit the aforesaid crime. When their findings were published on this matter, then it was clear that it was not indicated in the Old Testament or in the New that Jews lust for the drinking of human blood. Rather, precisely the opposite, they guard against the intake of all blood, as we find expressly in the biblical book which is called in Hebrew, "Bereshit," in the laws given by Moses and in the Jewish decrees which are called in Hebrew, "Talmud." We can surely assume that for those to whom even the blood of permitted animals is forbidden, the desire for human blood cannot exist, as a result of the horror of the matter, the prohibition of nature, and the common bond of the human species in which they also join Christians. Moreover, they would not expose to danger their substance and persons for that which they might have freely when taken from animals. By this sentence of the princes, we pronounce the Jews of the aforesaid place and the rest of the Jews of Germany completely absolved of this imputed crime. Therefore, we decree by the authority of the present privilege that no one, whether cleric or layman, proud or humble, whether under the pretext of preaching or otherwise, judges, lawyers, citizens, or others, shall attack the aforesaid Jews individually or as a group as a result of the aforesaid charge. Nor shall anyone cause them notoriety or harm in this regard. Let all know that, since a lord is honored through his servants, whoever shows himself favorable and helpful to our serfs the Jews will surely please us. However, whoever presumes to contravene the edict of this present confirmation and of our absolution bears the offense of our majesty.

In order that the present confirmation and absolution remain in unimpaired and perpetual validity, we have ordered that the present privilege be drawn up and be sealed with the golden seal bearing the symbol of our majesty.

49.   Pope Gregory X

Papal Bull Refuting Ritual Murder Charge

(October 7, 1272)

Source: Marcus, pp. 153.

[This bull was Pope Gregory X's version of the traditional Edict in Favor of the Jews issued during the beginning of many popes' reigns. After extending the usual protections, Gregory spoke sharply against Christians who charged Jews with murdering children for the purpose "...of making sacrifices of the heart and blood..." His strong statement in no way ended the continual repetition of such charges.]

Since it happens occasionally that some Christians lose their Christian children, the Jews are accused by their enemies of secretly carrying off and killing these same Christian children and of making sacrifices of the heart and blood of these very children. It happens, too, that the parents of these children, or some other Christian enemies of these Jews, secretly hide these very children in order that they may be able to injure these Jews, and in order that they may be able to extort from them a certain amount of money by redeeming them from their straits.

And most falsely do these Christians claim that the Jews have secretly and furtively carried away these children and killed them, and that the Jews offer sacrifice from the heart and the blood of these children, since their law in this matter precisely and expressly forbids Jews to sacrifice, eat, or drink the blood, or to eat the flesh of animals having claws. This has been demonstrated many times at our court by Jews converted to the Christian faith: nevertheless very many Jews are often seized and detained unjustly because of this.

We decree, therefore, that Christians need not be obeyed against Jews in a case or situation of this type, and we order that Jews seized under such a silly pretext be freed from imprisonment, and that they shall not be arrested henceforth on such a miserable pretext, unless—which we do not believe—they be caught in the commission of the crime. We decree that no Christian shall stir up anything new against them, but that they should be maintained in that status and position in which they were in the time of our predecessors, from antiquity till now...

50.   Pope Clement VI

Jews Not Responsible for the Plague

(September 26, 1348)

Source: Synan, p. 133.

[When the bubonic plague ravaged Europe in the mid 14th century, the deadly infestation felled both Jews and Christians. Jews, however, were doubly terrorized, first by the flea-born bacillus and then by mindless, frightened, and often greedy mobs of Christians who blamed them for the pestilence. Ships arriving in Genoa and Venice from Constantinople unwittingly brought the Black Death to Europe in 1346. No one knows exactly how many died, but as much as a third of Europe's population may have perished in the forty-year pandemic.

Men with medical knowledge believed people caught the plague from someone already infected. They prescribed isolation to prevent its spread. Some, believing the Black Death was God's punishment for the people's sins, said prayer and severe penance would soften the divine wrath. Other, less scrupulous men told the ignorant that Jews poisoned the wells and thus caused the plague. They urged the crowds to kill all the Jews in their communities and confiscate their property. The superstitious and terrified masses were easy prey for this accusation and call to action. For a thousand years the Church had taught that Jews were the enemies of the human race. It could not have been difficult, therefore, to accept that the "perfidious" Jews were capable of poisoning the water supplies. After all, everyone believed the myth that they murdered little children for their strange Passover rituals.

Responsible men like Pope Clement VI tried to convince the faithful that the Jews were not responsible. This rational appeal fell on deaf ears as mobs vented their fury on one Jewish community after another.]

Lately there has come to Our hearing the fame, or more precisely the infamy, that certain Christians, seduced by that liar the devil, are imputing to poisonings by Jews the pestilence with which God is afflicting the Christian people. For He is outraged by the sins of this people who, acting on their own temerity, and taking no account of age or sex, have impiously annihilated some from among the Jews. These same Jews are prepared to submit to judgment before a competent judge on the false allegation of this sort of crime, but the violence of those Christians has not grown cool on this account; rather, their fury rages all the more against them; where they offer no resistance, their aberration is taken to be proved!

Now, if the Jews were guilty, their conscience burdened by a crime so great, We would wish them struck by a penalty of suitable severity—although a sufficient one could hardly be conceived. Still, since this pestilence, all but universal everywhere, by a mysterious judgment of God has afflicted, and does now afflict, throughout the divers regions of the earth, both Jews and many other nations to whom life in common with Jews is unknown, that the Jews have provided the occasion or the cause for such a crime has no plausibility.

51. Jacob von Königshofen

The Cremation of Strasbourg Jewry: Accusations of Well Poisoning Causing the Plague in 1349

Source: Marcus, pp. 45-47.

[This stark and insightful account of the immolation of Strasbourg's Jews was written at least 20 years after the event. The author acknowledged that greed "was indeed the thing that killed the Jews." While the Black Death cut its swath through Europe, many Jewish communities disappeared in the flames. The bubonic plague finally spent itself in 1388. Not until the 1890s did scientists discover that rodent fleas acted as intermediaries carrying the deadly bacterium from infected rats to human beings. Millions in 14th-century Europe died from flea bites they probably didn't even notice. Many thousands of Jews died because of ignorance, greed, superstition, and the belief that the Jewish people were the Christians' mortal enemies.]

In the year 1349 there occurred the greatest epidemic that ever happened. Death went from one end of the earth to the other... This epidemic also came to Strasbourg in the summer of the above mentioned year, and it is estimated that about sixteen thousand people died.

In the matter of this plague the Jews throughout the world were reviled and accused in all lands of having caused it through the poison which they are said to have put into the water and the wells—that is what they were accused of—and for this reason the Jews were burnt all the way from the Mediterranean into Germany, but not in Avignon, for the pope *[Clement VI]* protected them there.

Nevertheless they tortured a number of Jews in Berne and Zofingen *[Switzerland]* who then admitted that they had put poison into many wells, and they also found the poison in the wells. Thereupon they burnt the Jews in many towns... The deputies of the city of Strasbourg were asked what they were going to do with their Jews. They answered and said that they knew of no evil of them...finally the Bishop and the lords and the Imperial Cities agreed to do away with the Jews. The result was that they were burnt in many cities, and wherever they were expelled they were caught by the peasants and stabbed to death or drowned...

[Note: The town council of Strasbourg, which wanted to save the Jews, was deposed on the 9th/10th of February, and the new council gave in to the mob, who then arrested the Jews on Friday, the 13th.]

The Jews Are Burnt

On Saturday—that was St. Valentine's Day—they burnt the Jews on a wooden platform in their cemetery. There were about two thousand people of them. Those who wanted to baptize themselves were spared. *[Note: Some say about a thousand accepted baptism.]* Many small children were taken out of the fire and baptized against the will of their fathers and mothers. And everything that was owed to the Jews was canceled, and the Jews had to surrender all pledges and notes that they had taken for debts. The council, however, took the cash that the Jews possessed and divided it among the working-men proportionately. The money was indeed the thing that killed the Jews. If they had been poor and if the feudal lords had not been in debt to them, they would not have been burnt. After this wealth was divided among the artisans some gave their share to the Cathedral or the Church on the advice of their confessors...

The Jews Return to Strasbourg

It was decided in Strasbourg that no Jew should enter the city for a hundred years, but before twenty years had passed, the council and magistrates agreed that they ought to admit the Jews again into the city for twenty years. And so the Jews came back again to Strasbourg in the year 1368 after the birth of our Lord.

52. Publishing House of Hieronymous Höltzel, Nuremberg

Host Desecration and Ritual Murder Charges Reported

(1510)

Source: Heiko A. Oberman, *The Roots of Anti-Semitism in the Age of Renaissance and Reformation* (Philadelphia: Fortress Press, 1984), pp. 97–99.

[Part of the Roman Catholic religious service called the "Mass" includes a rite called the Holy Eucharist or Holy Communion. During this ceremony, the priest consecrates or sanctifies a thin piece of bread (wafer) and wine. With this consecration, Catholics believe that the wafer—now called the "Host"—and the wine, notwithstanding their outward appearance, actually become the body, blood, soul, and divinity of Jesus Christ. This conversion is called "Transubstantiation." The congregants then drink the liquid and the priest puts the wafer in their mouths where its thinness allows it to "melt" quickly. The Eucharist or Communion is meant to wash away sin and redeem the human race. The priest's consecration permanently changes the wafer and wine; Jesus' presence is believed to remain in them even after the Communion ceremony is completed. In religious processions and festivals, the faithful worship Jesus in the miraculously altered bread and wine.

The Church first urged the belief in Transubstantiation in 1079 and one of the major purposes of the Fourth Lateran Council (see Section Two, Chapter Four) in 1215 was to give the doctrine its final form. The belief in Transubstantiation and the "miraculous" Host spread quickly throughout Christian Europe. Along with ritual murder accusations, Christians then began charging Jews with stealing and torturing the Host. Their tales of Host desecration included accounts of the wafer's bleeding Jesus' blood and of performing other miscellaneous miracles. The Jews, of course, were fiercely punished for supposedly committing these sacrilegious crimes.

Church leaders and popes failed to denounce these false charges strongly, in stark contrast to their denunciations of ritual murder accusations. They may have felt reluctant to undermine belief in the miraculous powers of the consecrated wafer. Host desecration charges occurred sporadically between 1220 and 1514 almost exclusively in the German States and Austria. They finally ended with the spread of the Protestant Reformation since Protestants tended to view the Eucharist in symbolic rather than in literal terms.

The account given below, entitled "An Incredible Event," shows the absurdity of the Host desecration charge. It assumed that the Jews themselves believed the wafer actually became Jesus' body and, therefore, out of malice, they had to try to torture and destroy it.

Note: *In the text, a "wicked Christian" is one who violates the Christian religion on a criminal impulse. A "pyx" is a lidded case for safe-guarding the holy sacrament. The "monstrance" is a container for the display and adoration of the consecrated host during prayer or in a procession. The "sacrament" is the consecrated bread and wine, or sometimes the bread alone, which Roman Catholics believe is changed during the holy rite of the Eucharist into the blood and body of Christ. The "host" is the Eucharist bread or wafer.]*

An Incredible Event

Jews from the Brandenburg Province purchase and torture the body of Christ in the year of our Lord 1510. Herewith is published what formerly has been common knowledge. The following occurred at 11:00 P.M. on the Wednesday after the Feast of the Purification of Mary. Paul Fromm, a "wicked Christian" and a native Pomeranian and resident of Bernau, a tinker and a reputed murderer, let himself be tempted by the devil. In the church of Knoblauch, Brandenburg, he broke into the tabernacle at the altar, from which he stole a gilded pyx containing two consecrated wafers, one large and one small, and one gilded monstrance of copper. When, on the following day around eight o'clock in the morning, he sat down on a stone in the vicinity of Staaken to inspect his plunder, he abused the larger wafer in an unworthy manner. Instantly he was plunged into pitch darkness, and he could neither get up nor move for over half an hour. Shortly afterwards, he headed to Spandau (two miles from Berlin, in the direction of Brandenburg, where the Havel and the Spree meet) and there offered to sell the monstrance to a Jew with the name Salomon. Salomon replied: "Where this is from, there are more." The wicked Christian then drew the sacrament from his breast pocket and demanded sixteen groschen. Salomon offered him five, and the deal was closed at nine district groschen, or six silver groschen.

Next, the man who had sold God headed toward the Wendische, but as he did not wish to stay there, he returned home, heedless of the warning that his unconscionable theft was already notorious. Once home, he threw the monstrance from his house over the city wall, but with God's providence it hung in a tree. The burgomaster of Bernau found it there and had the already-suspect man taken into custody. The man confessed immediately, without torture.

Salomon had meanwhile laid the sacrament on the edge of a table and, out of congenital Jewish hatred, battered it several times over and pierced it; even then he was unable to wound the Lord's body. Finally, beside himself with rage, he yelled out, among other curses; "If you are the Christian God, then in the name of a thousand devils, show yourself!" At that moment, in reaction to the taunt, the holy body of Christ miraculously parted itself into three, just as the priest breaks it,—but with the result that the cracks took on the color of blood. The Jew carried the three parts of the wafer on his person for four weeks.

One year earlier, Salomon had agreed with the Brandenburg Jews, Jacob and Marcus (from Stendal), that if one of them should manage to get hold of a sacramental wafer he would give each of the other two a share. And so Salomon now gave the two portions of the wafer, well packed in small boxes covered with Samian leather, to his son to take to Jacob in Brandenburg and to Marcus in Stendal.

The remaining piece, which was his own, he once again struck and pierced until blood flowed from it. He did everything he could to offend this last portion of the host—drowning it, burning it, and attempting in several other ways to destroy it—all to no avail. Finally it dawned on him to knead the sacrament into a scrap of matzo dough and to throw it into the oven at the Jewish Easter celebration. And even though it was pitch black in this oven, all of a sudden he saw (as he himself confessed)—a bright luminescence, and twice he saw floating above the bread a beautiful little child of a thumb's length. Deeply shocked at this miraculous event, and however much he wanted to fly from the spectre of the Christian prison before his eyes, it proved utterly impossible for him to move his legs and flee Spandau.

Marcus, the Jew from Stendal, likewise subjected the second portion of the wafer to all the tortures he could devise, and then sent it on to Braunschweig or, according to other reports, to Frankfurt am Main.

Similarly, Jacob of Brandenburg placed the third wafer portion on his table and gave it such a battering and piercing that one could see the grace-filled drops of blood on the table. As he could neither wash nor scratch away the blood, he knocked the blood-spattered chip from the table and took it and the wafer to Osterburg. There an affluent Jew named Mayer gave the wafer to his son Isaac, who in turn brought the holy sacrament to his wife at the marriage bed with words to the effect that she should be truly thrilled and highly honored to know that he was bringing her the God of the Christians.

During the marriage feast, the enemies of Christ subjected the sacrament once again to torture. As bridegroom, Isaac had the honor of the first blow. The wafer is also said to have ended up in Braunschweig, where now all the Jews of that town are sitting in prison. The wafer and the blood-spattered chip together with the table were brought to Berlin. There the wafer miraculously turned into bread again, and then crumbled and slowly vanished.

While they were in jail, the obstinate, blind dogs confessed that in the past few years they had purchased seven Christian children, one from his own peasant mother for twenty-four groschen, another for three guilder, and a third for ten. These children they pierced with needles and knives, tortured, and finally killed them. Then they prepared the blood with pomegranate and served it for dinner.

On this account, his majesty, the noble Landgrave Joachim of Brandenburg, sentenced the criminals to death on Friday after the fifteenth of July in Berlin, and declared their personal belongings and holdings confiscate. The Christian, Paul Fromm, was to be shredded with tongs and burned on a separate stake. Next, the thirty-eight Jews, chained by the neck, were to be burned to ashes.

And—one has to have seen it to believe it—these obstinate and impenitent Jews received their sentences with smug looks and were led away singing loud hosannas. Once on the stakes, they not only sang and laughed but some also danced and sent up shouts of jubilation, their chained hands raised high, crushing straw and stuffing it in their mouths. Without any regard for the manifest portents, they suffered their death unflinchingly, to the great horror of inconstant Christians.

Of the aforementioned Jews, Jacob and two others had themselves baptized. Jacob, whose Christian name is now Joerg, and one of the other two, were beheaded the next day and died Christians. The third, an occultist, was allowed at his own request to enter the Graue monastery in Berlin, since his guilt was limited to crimes against children only.

Nearly sixty Jews live to this day in Berlin without any knowledge of these events. It is said they will be turned out of this territory again, as is only fitting and proper.

53. *Damascus Ritual Murder Charge*

(1840)

Source: U.S. Department of State, General Records, Consular Dispatches.

[In February of 1840, a Catholic monk named Thomas and his Moslem servant disappeared in Damascus, Syria. Other members of Thomas's Capuchin order claimed Jews must have murdered the two, saving their blood to make Passover matzoh. The Damascus Affair, as this ritual murder charge became known, soon received international publicity and developed into a diplomatic confrontation between France and several other European powers all intent on expanding their influence in the Middle East.

France considered itself the protector of the Christians who lived in Moslem nations and, in this guise, the French consul in Damascus, Ratti-Menton, supported the monks in their accusation against the Jews. He reported the alleged crime to the Moslem Governor General of Syria and continued to supervise the investigation which led to the Damascus police arresting and torturing a number of Jews. They also held sixty-four Jewish children hostage in order to extract confessions from the adults. Under torture, several of the men broke down and agreed to confess to whatever tale their tormentors demanded of them. Two of the men died as a result of the torture and one, in order to avoid further pain, converted to Islam. The Damascus authorities sentenced the remaining seventy-two prisoners to death.

When the American consul in Beirut (Beyrout) heard the story, he immediately informed John Forsyth, the U.S. Secretary of State. The consul's letter, given below, shows that he completely believed the charge against the Jews, as did many other European consuls assigned to the Near East.

Note: *Reports of the Damascus Affair appeared in several European newspapers eliciting great sympathy for the accused Jews. Two prominent Jewish men, Moses Montefiore of England and Adolphe Cremieux of France, led a delegation to Egypt. There they met with Mehemet Ali, the Governor (Pasha) of Egypt who exercised control over Syria. Finally, he agreed to release the Jewish prisoners in Damascus. Later, Montefiore and Cremieux successfully persuaded the Turkish sultan to issue a Firman [edict] which denounced ritual murder accusations as completely untrue.]*

United States Consulate
Beyrout 24th March 1840

Sir,

I have the Honor to relate briefly for Your Honours consideration some details of a most Barbarous secret, for a long time suspected in the Jewish Nation, which at last came to light in the City of Damascus, that of serving themselves of Christian Blood in their unleavened Bread at Easter, a Secret which in these 1840 Years must have made many unfortunate victims.

On the 5th of February last the Rev[d] Capouchin Thomas president of the Catholic Church of Damascus together with his Servant having, all of a sudden disappeared from that City H. E. Sherif pashaw Governor General of Syria and the French Consul of Damascus employed actively the pollice for making all strict inquiries after them, and some people having declared to have seen that priest and his servant enter on that evening in the Jews quarter, the suspitions of Government fall on the Jews, that they might have assassinated them.

On that day Rev[d] Thomas had put up against the wall of a Jew Barbers shop, a written advertisement for some Articles to be sold by Auction, and was observed that the said advertisement had been removed from its place and put up again with different Wafers than those used by the priest. The Jew Barber was questioned and taken into prison, and after the application of some torments on his person he confessed that the Rev[d] Thomas had been beheaded in the house of David Arari a rich Jew, by Seven of his coreligioners of Damascus, and that, in order to take his Blood, it being ordered by their religion to make use of Christian Blood in their Unleavened Bread at Easter.

The Seven Jews thus accused, as well as all their high Priests; 64 Children, belonging to those families, and all their Butchers were immediately taken to prison, and after severe Tortures and threats several of them confessed also the fact of the murder, adding that they had since cut the body in small pieces and threw it in a Canal, after collecting all the Blood in a large Bottle for religious purposes, which Bottle they had given to their high Priest. The Pashaw and the french Consul accompanied by Massons and a multitude of People went immediately to the spot, and having searched, they found in reality the Revd Thomas's body cut in small bits, which were put in a Pinn Box and burried with a grand Prossession in the Church.

The torments on the prisoners having continued, some of them confessed that the Servant also had been beheaded in the house of another jew, his Blood taken to the last drop, and his body cut in the same way like that of the Priest was thrown in another Canal. The Pashaw and the french Consul repared to the place and found that body also in pieces together with three sharp knives. The Murderers of this last are not yet arrested they having made their escape from Damascus, but the Pollice is after them actively employ'd. The Bottle of Blood neither has been found as yet.

The inquisition against the jews in that City (in which there may be 30000. Souls of the Nation) continues with much vigour and no jew can show his face out in the streets.

The french Consul is seizing all their religious Books with a hope of clearing that abominable secret. He found a Book printed in Latin, by "Lucio Ferrajo" in which the passages are found taken from the Talmoud, which I have the honor to accompany in french.

Several of the prisoners in prison have died of the torments of the inquisition, and others turned Turks and the rest in number Seventy two are sentenced to be hanged, but the french Consul has requested to postpone their death in hope of finding out through more torments the Bottle of Blood, which they pretend to have already distributed to their coreligioners in the different other City's.

In the place where the Servants remains were found a quantity of other human Bons of old date in small bits have been discovered, which proves that they were accustomed in that house to such like umane sacrifices. A Doctor bribed by the Jews declared the Servants Bons to be those of some Beast but the Pashaw having since called a Commission of several Doctors they pronounced them to be umane.

I have the Honor to be with great respect, Sir,

　　　　　　　　　　Your Most Obedient Humble Servant
　　　　　　　　　　　　　　J. Chasseaud

54.   La Civiltà Cattolica

Ritual Murder Accusations

(1881–1882)

Source: Malcolm Hay, *Europe and the Jews* (New York: Beacon Press, 1961), pp. 310–312.

[Ritual murder accusations against Jews first surfaced in 1144. This calumnious charge continued to fire popular Christian imagination well into the 20th century. A number of popes, including Innocent IV, Gregory X, and Paul III tried to convince Christendom that there was absolutely nothing in Jewish religious ritual or tradition that mandated or even condoned the use of human blood. These popes repeated that the charge had absolutely no basis in truth and was, indeed, a slander invented by some Christians who coveted the Jews' money and possessions. In 1758, Cardinal Ganganelli, who later became Pope Clement XIV, headed a Church investigation which again completely disproved the charge. Still the belief that Jews performed ritual murder continued unabated.

In 1881–82, an Italian Catholic publication, La civiltà cattolica, *ran a series of articles that contained material claiming Jews did torture and kill Christians as part of their Passover rites. The journal had been founded by a member of the Jesuit order in 1850 and the pope at that time, Pius IX, gave it his blessing, declaring that it would serve as a mirror for the attitudes and beliefs of the Church and the Holy See.* La civilta cattolica *is still edited by Jesuits and has a solid reputation for reflecting Church views. That such slander against Jewry could appear in late 19th- century Catholic journal is evidence of the strong influence exerted by the anti-Semitic movements still reigning in Europe.*

The selections given below, although not then attributed to a particular author, were written by a Jesuit named Guiseppe Oreglia de San Stefano who was inspired by the claims of a German churchman. These defamations continued to be printed for eight months. This indicated that at least some churchmen believed the charges and may have wished to use them to reverse the economic and social freedoms the Jews had won in 19th-century Europe.]

[August 20, 1881, p. 478.]

The practice of killing children for the Paschal Feast is now very rare in the more cultivated parts of Europe, more frequent in Eastern Europe, and common, all too common, in the East properly so called. *[In the West, the Jews]* have now other things to think of than to make their unleavened bread with Christian blood, occupied as they are in ruling almost like kings in finance and journalism.

[December 3, 1881, p. 606.]

It remains therefore generally proved...that the sanguinary Paschal rite...is a general law binding on the consciences of all Hebrews to make use of the blood of a Christian child, primarily for the sanctification of their souls, and also, although secondarily, to bring shame and disgrace to Christ and to Christianity.

[January 21, 1882. p. 226.]

Opinions of the Hebrew casuists in the Middle Ages differed, as they do now, not about the substance but about the accidents of the sanguinary Paschal rites...Some hold that the blood of a child is essential, others, as we shall see, think that the blood of an adult is sufficient.

[February 4, 1882, p. 362.]

In the century which invented printing, discovered America, revived literature and science, half of Europe was full of ...Masters in Israel who bought and sold and made use of Christian blood for their piety and devotion. But now the light has been thrown on these deeds which we know even more about than our ancestors did.

[February 18, 1882, p. 472.]

In Hebrew Jubilee years, the fresh blood of a child is essential; in ordinary years the dried blood will do.

[March 4, 1882, p. 613.]

Every practicing Hebrew worthy of that name is obliged even now, in conscience, to use in food, in drink, in circumcision, and in various other rites of his religious and civil life the fresh or dried blood of a Christian child, under pain of infringing his laws and passing among his acquaintances for a bad Hebrew. How all this is still true and faithfully observed in the present century, we shall see, God willing, with all the evidence, in the next installment of our correspondence.

55.   The New York Times

The Mendel Beilis Trial

(1913)

Source: Editorial, "The Czar on Trial," *New York Times*, October 9, 1913, p. 12:2.

[Ritual murder charges also appeared on an almost regular basis in czarist Russia. Following the murder of a little girl in 1690, Russian Orthodox monks promptly declared the child a martyr. They worked to deepen the peasants' faith by displaying what they claimed were the child's bones for public veneration. Many

czars subsequently combined the unifying force of the state religion with virulent anti-Semitism in order to maintain an autocratic grip over the Russian people.

Nicholas II, the last Russian monarch, and his government, used popular anti-Jewish hatred as a tool to keep czarist government in power and to discredit the liberal and revolutionary movements springing up throughout Russia. They told the peasants that the Jews were the cause of their crushing poverty and that these same Jews controlled the revolutionary parties so opposed to their "Little Father," the czar. Government-organized, "popular" uprisings called pogroms left hundreds of Jews dead and many thousands deprived of home and livelihood. To justify its anti-Jewish actions, the Russian government deliberately supported ritual murder claims.

The most famous of these accusations involved a Jewish man named Mendel Beilis[s]. Following the death of a boy in Kiev in 1911, local police arrested Beilis on the flimsy evidence that he worked near where the child's body was found. They charged him with ritual murder. Liberals and socialists championed Beilis's cause and strongly denounced the accusation. Reactionaries used the trial to whip up anti-Semitism and undermine the movement to democratize Russia. Newspapers, including the New York Times, *sent their reporters to cover the trial and, through articles and editorials like the one presented below, kept readers informed of the testimony in Kiev [spelled Kieff in the article given below]. Finally, in 1913, with all the evidence in, the Russian court exonerated Beilis. The verdict was a humiliating political defeat for the czar.]*

In Kieff, Russia yesterday, there was placed on trial, behind closed doors, one Mendel Beiliss, charged with the murder of a Russian lad, Yuschinsky, in 1911. Beiliss is a Jew, and is accused of "ritual murder," that is to say of having killed a boy to get his blood for alleged use in the rites of the Jewish religion. There are two elements in this case which make it of great importance and interest to right-thinking persons in all parts of the world.

One is the clear presumption, on all available official Russian testimony, of the entire innocence of the accused. Immediately after the murder of the boy, M. Minschuk, Chief of the Detective Service in Kieff, with several assistants, investigated the case and reported, first, that there was no evidence against Beiliss, the accused, and second, that the boy was murdered by a gang of criminals whom he was suspected of betraying. For this report M. Minschuk was accused of manufacturing evidence to hinder the prosecution and to protect Jews, and though acquitted on one trial, was retried and condemned to prison for a year, with his assistants. That fact clearly discredits the whole case of the prosecution.

The second significant fact in the case is the nature of the accusation, the allegation of murder for Jewish ritual purposes. The crime does not and cannot exist.

It has been shown over and over again, and long ago, that there is nothing in the religious belief or practice of the Jews that remotely requires or sanctions or suggests the thing charged. Strict and searching inquiry by eminent men of science, theologians, historians, physicians, not Jews, in Great Britain, in Germany, in France, has resulted in the distinct and unqualified verdict that the belief in this crime has not the slightest foundation in fact, and that it is a foolish, blind superstition bred of prejudice upon ignorance.

It has so been held and denounced by the Pope, by the head of the Orthodox Church, by living Bishops of that Church, and by a Czar of Russia, Alexander I, in 1817, confirmed by Nicholas I in 1835. What renders this base and baseless accusation more revolting at this late day, and by the officials of a Government professedly Christian, is the fact that in the twentieth century there could be the revival of a device used by the pagans in the first century to justify the oppression and slaughter of Christians. The Government of Russia, and especially the Czar of Russia, the authoritative head of a great branch of the Christian Church, in the mad, stupid war on the Jews, is 2000 years behind the times.

For the Russian peasants who are the helpless victims of this superstition, and who accept it as a like superstition was accepted by the savage crowds of the Roman Arena, we can have pity, and even with the brutal action inspired by it we can have patience. But for educated men, particularly for Russian officials who deliberately appeal to the superstitious and incite to brutal action, we can have only indignant detestation. And that feeling is in no wise affected by the fact that this outrage is directed to those of one or another race, one or another religion. The outrage is upon humanity.

Every humane, every decently human instinct condemns it. It is true that the offense is one that cannot be dealt with in the ordinary way of international communication, though it is by no means wholly beyond them, as was very properly shown in the case of Rumania as conducted by the late Secretary Hay. But in the court of public opinion such an offense can and must be dealt with. Fortunately there is a large number of educated and fair-minded Russians who not only will recognize the jurisdiction of that court and respect its verdict, but will contribute to it. And this element in Russia is bound to gain in strength and influence. If the second trial at Kieff results in the conviction of the hapless Beiliss, and that is followed by the disorders it is calculated to produce, this element will be not weakened, but reinforced. In view of this fact and of the general protest that has been aroused it may be said the Czar and the autocracy are now on trial.

[Ritual murder accusations against Jews did not end with Mendel Beilis's acquittal. Two decades later, a year after Adolf Hitler assumed power in Germany,

the *Führer's chief propagandist, Julius Streicher, dedicated an entire issue of his newspaper,* Der Stürmer, *to ritual murder. A cartoon on the front page of this May, 1934, issue set the tone. It depicted two large-nosed, thick-lipped Jews, one piercing little blond children with a knife, the other carefully collecting their spurting blood in a platter. Such crude anti-Semitic charges became commonplace in Nazi Germany and spread to other countries as Hitler's troops conquered and occupied most of Europe.*

There is evidence that the Nazis' carefully orchestrated program of anti-Semitism left behind a smoldering legacy of hate, which included the continuing belief that Jewish religious rites required the use of Christian blood. During the summer of 1946, a nine-year-old boy in Kielce, Poland, tried to cover up why he hadn't returned home on time. He told a tale of seeing Jews commit ritual murder. Believing the story, incensed crowds attacked Kielce's Jews. Thirty-six of them died in the rioting. In reaction to the pogrom, the pitiful number of Polish Jews who had survived the Holocaust fled the country in panic.]

A wooden synagogue in Lithuania from the late eighteenth or early nineteenth century.

Section Four

Emancipation, Repression, and the Growth of Organized Anti-Semitism

Jews in Western Europe's ghettos and Eastern Europe's shtetls passed through the Renaissance, Reformation, and Age of Discovery with little or no alteration in their daily lives. The winds of change that were to lead to the modern era seemed, to them, but a faint whisper in the distance. Slowly, however, evolving social attitudes and new economic forces combined and reinforced one another to create momentous transformations which finally freed the Jews from their imprisonment.

With Oliver Cromwell's encouragement, Jews quietly re-entered England. Officially unnoticed in order to avoid public indignation, Jewish merchants contributed their skills to Britain's rise as a great economic and colonial power. Slowly, over the next two hundred years, English Jews gained citizenship, voting rights, and election to public offices.

On the continent, the French Revolution and Napoleon's conquest of much of Europe spread the idea of the liberty, equality, and fraternity of all humanity. Logically, Jews, as human beings, could not be excluded from this social movement. Even in revolutionary France, however, deeply ingrained prejudices made it difficult for most Frenchmen to see Jews as free and equal. While Napoleon's armies tore down ghetto walls, true equality and fraternity remained elusive.

Bonaparte's defeat in 1815 and the reactionary backlash which followed sent Jews back to the ghettos and stripped away their newly won rights. The Jews gradually re-won these civil rights following the 1848 revolutions in Central Europe only to face rapidly growing resentment of their new economic and social success. Unscrupulous men, pursuing their own narrow goals, fashioned this discontent into a new and popular political movement called anti-Semitism.

In Russia, the czars and their governments, whether seemingly liberal or rabidly reactionary, had only one aim with regard to the Jews: conversion to Christianity. Every manner of coercive legislation had that one goal in mind. In addition, when western revolutionary ideas seeped into the country, the czarist regimes worked to discredit those liberal ideas by linking them with the Jews, the most despised segment of the Russian community.

From Great Britain to Russia the political, economic, and social movements of the seventeenth through nineteenth centuries laid the foundation for our modern world. They also set the stage for the Jewish people's tragedies and triumphs in the turbulent 20th century.

Jews and other Russians in an open marketplace.

NAPOLÉON LE GRAND,
rétablit le culte des Israélites, le 30 Mai 1806.

Napoleon depicted extending full rights to the Jews of France.

Chapter VIII

Emancipation, Citizenship, and Equal Rights

T he basic reasons behind extending citizenship and civil rights to the Jews in the various European nations greatly influenced how the populace later reacted to growing Jewish participation in business and political affairs. Some nations attempted to turn the Jews into some common image of "useful citizens" or worked to "mainstream" them to eliminate their "strangeness" and hopefully foster their conversion. Here, disappointment sprang up as the hoped for change did not come quickly enough. The Jews then encountered increasing resistance and outright hatred which led to the phenomenon of organized anti-Semitism. In countries which extended these rights, because, in the final analysis, all citizens deserved them, Jews experienced much less opposition.

England

56.   The Houses of Parliament

An Act to Naturalize Protestants, Quakers and Jews in His Majesty's American Colonies

(1740)

Source: Morris U. Schappes, *A Documentary History of the Jews in the United States* (New York: Schocken Books, 1971), pp. 26–29. Taken from Rosendale, American Jewish Historical Society Publications, I, 1893, pp. 94–98.

[By the 1700s, Great Britain was deeply involved in mercantilism, the policy which stressed the importance of national economic interests over all individual and sectional concerns. Mercantilism called for the constant accumulation of gold by expanding exports and reducing the necessity for imports. Parliament advocated colonial development as a means toward achieving its mercantilist ends and, accordingly, supported social and political innovations meant to strengthen the colonies which would not have been acceptable at home.

To attract and keep settlers, Parliament offered British citizenship to foreigners who had lived in some colony in the Americas for at least seven years. To further qualify for naturalized citizenship, the settler had to swear allegiance to the crown, participate in the communion sacrament of some Protestant rite and take an oath "upon the true faith of a Christian." Since Quakers did not celebrate communion nor take oaths, and Jews could not take an oath upon the true faith of a Christian, they were prevented from becoming citizens. Parliament in 1740 amended citizenship laws relating strictly to colonial settlers by omitting—for Quakers and Jews—the particular oath and the requirement to take communion. This was a tremendous step forward for the Jews who had always been considered aliens even in their own homelands. Taking advantage of this freedom, increasing numbers of Jews settled in the British colonies, especially Jamaica and the Barbados. Note, however, that Catholics still could not become British citizens, even in the Americas.]

Be it therefore enacted... That from and after the first Day of June, in the Year of our Lord One thousand seven hundred and forty, all persons born out of the Ligeance of His Majesty, His Heirs or Successors, who have inhabited and resided, or shall inhabit or reside for the Space of seven Years or more, in any of his Majesty's Colonies in America, and shall not have been absent out of some of the said Colonies for a longer Space than two Months at any one time during the said seven Years, and shall take and subscribe the Oaths, and make, repeat and subscribe the Declaration appointed by an Act made in the first Year of the Reign of his late Majesty King George the First...before the Chief Judge, or other Judge of the Colony wherein such

Persons respectively have so inhabited and resided, or shall so inhabit and reside, shall be deemed, adjudged and taken to be His Majesty's natural born Subjects of this Kingdom, to all Intents, Constructions, and Purposes, as if they, and every of them had been or were born within this Kingdom...

II. Provided always and be it enacted by the Authority aforesaid, That no Person, of what Quality, Condition or Place soever, other than and except such of the People called Quakers as shall qualify themselves and be naturalized by the ways and means hereinbefore mentioned, or such who profess the Jewish Religion, shall be naturalized by virtue of the Act, unless such persons shall have received the Sacrament of the Lord's Supper in some Protestant and Reformed Congregation within this Kingdom of Great Britain, or within some of the said Colonies in America, within three Months before his taking and subscribing the said Oaths, and making, repeating and subscribing the said Declaration...

III. And whereas the following Words are contained in the latter Part of the Oath of Abjuration, *videlicet* (upon the true Faith of a Christian), And whereas the

The Great Synagogue of London, built 1722, enlarged 1790.

People professing the Jewish Religion may thereby be prevented from receiving the Benefit of this Act; be it further enacted by the Authority aforesaid, That whenever any Person professing the Jewish Religion shall present himself to take the said Oath of Abjuration in pursuance of this Act, the said Words (upon the true Faith of a Christian) shall be omitted out of the said Oath…

57.   The Houses of Parliament

The Jewish Relief Act

(July 23, 1858)

Source: A Collection of the Public General Statutes (London, 1858), pp. 258–259.

[The oath, "upon the true Faith of a Christian," had long been a stumbling block for English Jews pursuing civil and political rights. In most cases, by 1846, Jews could omit those words in order to become citizens, vote, and hold local office. They could not do so, however, to take a seat in Parliament.

In 1847, voters in the City of London elected Lionel de Rothschild to the House of Commons, but as a Jew, Rothschild could not pronounce the oath of office in its required form. Commons then voted to remove the words from the oath when taken by Jews, but when the House of Lords refused to agree, Rothschild was unable to take his seat. This charade continued, with London re-electing him and the House of Lords refusing to change the oath, until 1858. In that year Commons and Lords reached a compromise where each house would decide on its own to remove the words "upon the true Faith of a Christian" and allow a Jew to take his seat as a Member of Parliament

The final sections of the Jewish Relief Act, however, contained interesting restrictions. Part three excluded Jews from holding certain high offices in Her Majesty's (Queen Victoria's) government. Part four made sure no Jewish person could effect or gain control of any church function which might, incidentally, be included in a particular office to which a Jew had been elected or appointed.]

Be it enacted by the Queen's Most Excellent Majesty, by and with the Advice and Consent of the Lords Spiritual and Temporal, and Commons, in this present Parliament assembled, and by the Authority of the same, as follows:

1. Where it shall appear to either House of Parliament that a Person professing the Jewish Religion, otherwise entitled to sit and vote in such House, is prevented from so sitting and voting by his conscientious objection to take the Oath which by an Act passed or [is] to be passed in the present Session of Parliament has been or may be substituted for the Oaths of Allegiance,

Baron Lionel Nathan de Rothschild,
the first Jew to sit as a member of
the British House of Commons.

Supremacy, and Abjuration in the Form therein required, such House if it think fit, may resolve that thenceforth any Person professing the Jewish Religion, in taking said oath to entitle him to sit and vote as aforesaid, may omit the words "and I make this Declaration upon the true Faith of a Christian," and so long as such Resolution shall continue in force the said Oath, when taken and subscribed by any Person professing the Jewish Religion of the Oath so modified shall, so far as respects the Title to sit and vote in such House, have the same Force and Effect as the taking and subscribing by other Persons of the said Oath in the Form required by the said Act.

2. In all other Cases, except for sitting in Parliament as aforesaid, or in qualifying to exercise the Right of Presentation to any Ecclesiastical Benefice in Scotland, whenever any of Her Majesty's Subjects professing the Jewish Religion shall be required to take the said Oath, the words "and I make this Declaration upon the true Faith of a Christian" shall be omitted.

3. Nothing herein contained shall extend or be construed to extend to enable any Person or Persons professing the Jewish Religion to hold or exercise the Office of Guardians and Justices of the United Kingdom, or of Regent of the United Kingdom, under whatever Name, Style, or Title such office may be constituted, or of Lord High Chancellor, Lord Keeper or Lord Commissioner of the Great Seal of Great Britain, or Ireland, or the office of Lord Lieutenant or Deputy or other Chief Governor or Governors of Ireland, or Her Majesty's High Commissioner to the General Assembly of the Church of Scotland.

4. Where any Right of Presentation to any Ecclesiastical Benefice shall belong to any office in the Gift or Appointment of Her Majesty, Her Heirs or Successors, and such office shall be held by a Person professing the Jewish Religion, the Right of Presentation shall devolve upon and be exercised by the Archbishop of Canterbury for the time being and it shall not be lawful for any Person professing the Jewish Religion, directly or indirectly, to advise Her Majesty, Her Heirs or Successors, or any Person or Persons holding or exercising the Office of Guardians of the United Kingdom, or of Regent of the United Kingdom, under whatever Name, Style, or Title such office may by constituted or the Lord Lieutenant or Lord Deputy, or any other Chief Governor or Governors of Ireland, touching or concerning the Appointment to or Disposal of any Office or Preferment in the United Church of England and Ireland, or in the Church of Scotland, and if such Person shall offend in the Premises, he shall, being thereof convicted by due course of Law, be deemed guilty of a high Misdemeanor, and disabled for ever from holding any Office, Civil or Military under the Crown.

France

King Charles VI ended a long series of settlement invitations, restrictions, and expulsions by permanently ordering all Jews out of France in 1394. Yet by the French Revolution in 1789, approximately 40,000 Jews resided legally in four areas of France: Avignon which had been ruled by the popes; Alsace and Lorraine (including Strasbourg) which France won from the German-controlled Holy Roman Empire at the end of the Thirty Years' War; the Bordeaux region where Marranos escaping the Spanish Inquisition had settled; and Paris. They suffered, for the most part, a separate existence characterized by social isolation and repression.

---

58. The French National Assembly

Decree Recognizing the Jews of Avignon and the Sephardim as Citizens

(January 28, 1790)

Source: M. Diogene Tama, Transactions of the Paris Sanhedrin, trans. F.D. Kirwan (London, 1807), pp. 3–4.

[Following the French Revolution's overthrow of the ancien régime, *the French National Assembly met to remake France in the republican image. The Assembly's representatives confirmed the concepts of human freedom, civil rights, and equality in the 1789 Declaration of the Rights of Man and of the Citizen. The Declaration boldly stated that different religious opinions were not valid reasons for limiting rights and freedoms. Yet the Assembly could not muster a majority vote to extend full citizenship to France's Jews.*

Disappointed with the National Assembly's failure to grant citizenship to the country's Jewish population, Bordeaux's Sephardic Jewry asked for a separate hearing on the issue. They claimed their lineage was superior to that of the Ashkenazic Jews and stressed they were much better candidates for social and political equality. The Assembly, eager to find a quick way out of the thorny problem, granted their petition.]

All of the Jews known in France, under the name of Portuguese, Spanish, and Avignonese Jews, shall continue to enjoy the same rights they have hitherto enjoyed, and which have been granted to them by letters of patent.

In consequence thereof, they shall enjoy the rights of active citizens, if they possess the other requisite qualifications, as enumerated in the decrees of that national assembly.

59. *Resolution of the National Assembly*

(September 28, 1791)

Source: Tama, pp. 6–7.

[This Assembly resolution recognized the inherent requirement, according to the 1791 constitution, to fully emancipate France's Ashkenazic Jews along with the Sephardim. An important part of this resolution included that fact that in order to acquire the long sought citizenship, Jews had to take a civil oath. In doing so, the individual Jew would be giving up "all privileges granted in their favour." This referred to the separate religious, social, and judicial status enjoyed by each Jewish community as regulated by their rabbis and elders. France's Jews heartily welcomed the resolution and eagerly took the citizenship oath.]

The National Assembly, considering that the condition requisite to be a French citizen, and to become an active citizen, are fixed by the constitution, and that every man who, being duly qualified, takes the civic oath, and engages to fulfill all duties prescribed by the constitution, has a right to all the advantages it insures;—

Annuls all adjournments, restrictions, and exceptions, contained in the preceding decrees, affecting individuals of the Jewish persuasion, who shall take the civic oath, which shall be considered as a renunciation of all privileges granted in their favour.

60. Napoleon

Imperial Decree

(1806)

Source: Simeon Maslin, *Selected Documents of Napoleonic Jewry* (Cincinnati: Hebrew Union College—Jewish Institute of Religion, 1957), pp. 1–3.

[The French Revolution deeply frightened Austria and Prussia, in part because of its threat to traditional monarchy and its leaders' actions to nationalize the Catholic Church. In 1792, they invaded France to put an end to the French experiment. The French army with the aid of the citizenry, including many newly emancipated Jews, stopped the foreign advance in September of that year. At that point, Great Britain and several other nations joined Austria and Prussia to crush the revolution and restore the French monarchy. This foreign threat led to two main developments: the French government, under the Directory, became ever more radical, brutally exterminating the opposition, and the French army under the military genius Napoleon Bonaparte beat back the opposition and soon conquered much of Europe. In the wake of Napoleon's victories, the French toppled foreign

kings and imposed new constitutions which included equality for all, religious toleration, and civil rights for the Jewish people.

Returning to France as a popular hero, Napoleon helped overthrow the violently out-of-control Directory and, as First Consul, made himself virtual dictator. In 1804, he triumphantly placed the crown on his own head and became Emperor of France.

Napoleon's concern with French Jews came as a result of problems in Alsace and Lorraine. Peasants there had borrowed money from Jews to finance the purchase of land, including confiscated Church properties, and to buy seed, livestock, and other necessities for farming. When they could not repay the loans or even the accrued interest, the Jewish moneylenders foreclosed on the peasants' properties. Terrified and angry, the peasants appealed to Napoleon. The Emperor, believing that full civil rights should have ended the Jews' need to lend money at interest, reacted with outrage. He summarily canceled the peasants' debts to the Jews and set into motion a plan which he hoped would completely reform the Jewish people. He began by calling for an Assembly of Notables of the Jewish religion.]

…containing a moratorium relative to judgments rendered in favor of Jews against farmers who are engaged in commerce in several departments of the Empire.

At the Palace of Saint-Cloud,
May 30, 1806

Napoleon, Emperor of the French, King of Italy;

Due to the report which was made to us that in several of the northern departments of our Empire certain Jews, not having any other profession than that of usury, have, by the exacting of the most immoderate interest, put many farmers of the country into a state of great distress;

We have decided that we must come to the aid of those of our subjects who have been reduced to these grievous extremes by unjust greed;

These circumstances have, at the same time, made us aware of how urgent it is to revive sentiments of civil morality among those who profess the Jewish religion in the countries under our jurisdiction, sentiments which have, sadly, disappeared among a very great number of them due to the state of degradation in which they have so long languished, a state which it is not at all among our intentions to maintain nor to renew;

For the accomplishment of this plan, we have resolved to convene an assembly of the foremost Jewish notables and to communicate our intention to them by means of commissioners whom we shall name for that purpose. This assembly shall arrive at a consensus of the methods which it deems to be the most expedient in order to reestablish among its brothers the exercise of the arts and of the useful professions, the object being to replace, by honest industry, the shameful expedients to which many among them have devoted themselves from father to son for several centuries;

For these reasons,

On the report of our Grand Judge and the Minister of Justice and of our Minister of the Interior;

Our Council of State in agreement,

We have decreed and do decree that which follows:

1. The enforcement of all judgments or contracts, other than simple acts of extension, against non-commercial farmers in the departments of Sarre, Roer, Mont-Tonnerre, Haut- and Bas-Rhin, Rhin-et-Moselle, and Vosges, in which titles have been endorsed by these farmers to Jews, is hereby suspended.

2. There shall be formed on July 15 next in our good city of Paris an assembly of individuals who profess the Jewish religion and who live in French territory.

3. The members of this assembly...shall come from the departments named therein, and they shall be chosen by the prefects from among the rabbis, the land owners, and other Jews who are distinguished by their integrity and their intelligence.

4. In the other departments of our Empire...where there live from one hundred to five hundred individuals of the Jewish religion, the prefect may name one deputy; from five hundred to one thousand, he may name two deputies; and so on.

5. The deputies chosen shall arrive in Paris before July 10 and shall make their arrival and their addresses known to the secretary of our Minister of the Interior who will inform them as to the place, the day, and the hour when the assembly will open.

6. Our Minister of the Interior is charged with the execution of this decree.

Signed, Napoleon
For the Emperor;
The Secretary of State, signed,
H. B. Maret

61.   Napoleon

Note Relative to the Sanhedrin

(November 29, 1806)

Source: Maslin, pp. 17, 19, 20–23.

[The Assembly of Notables met in Paris and humbly ratified Napoleon's original plans for French Jews. The emperor next contemplated reviving the ancient Jewish Sanhedrin as a permanent assembly to oversee the changes he wished to institute in Judaism and the Jewish people. In this note on the Sanhedrin, Napoleon wrote that he wanted one-third of all marriages involving Jews to be intermarriages with Christians. Also, Jewish army conscripts could only be replaced with other Jews, and Jewish rights to own land should be severely limited. Usury and other "repugnant" Jewish economic practices needed to be eliminated. Seeing no value to the continued existence of Jews as Jews, the emperor was determined to change their culture as the first step toward weakening Jewish communal bonds and assuring eventual total assimilation.]

4. From the doctrine which will be established [by the new Great Sanhedrin] that the Jews must consider the Christians as brothers, it follows not only that marriages between Christians and Jews not be anathematized but that they be recommended because they are vital to the welfare of the nation...

6. The obligation, in every department or district of the sanhedrin or consistory, to authorize only two marriages between Jews and Jewesses out of every three marriages, the third being between Jew and Christian; if this provision appears to be extremely difficult of execution, it will be necessary to take measures of exhortation, instruction, encouragement, and command which will lead to this goal;

7. The obligation of furnishing a number of conscripts proportionate to the Israelite population without it being possible for an Israelite conscript to provide a replacement except it be another Israelite...

IV. The primary objects in mind have been to protect the Jewish people, to come to the help of country districts, and to rescue several departments from the disgrace of finding themselves vassals to the Jews, for the mortgage of a great part of the lands of a department to one people who by its morals and by its laws forms a unique nation within the French nation is actual vassalage. It is for this that, in a very short time, the threatening but unalienable right of taking possession of property will have to be curbed by certain obstacles. In addition, the property ownership of Jews extends itself unceasingly by means of usury and mortgages, and it has become essential to set limits to it. The secondary objective is to weaken, if not destroy, the tendency of

Opening of the Napoleonic Sanhedrin in Paris, February 9, 1807.

the Jewish people toward such a great number of practices which are contrary to civilization and to the good order of society in all the countries of the world.

It is necessary to put an end to the evil by preventing it; it is necessary to prevent it by changing the Jews.

All the measures proposed must lead to these two results. When, among every three marriages, there will be one between a Jew and a Christian, the blood of the Jews will cease to have any unique character.

When they are prevented from devoting themselves exclusively to usury and brokerage, they will accustom themselves to engage in the crafts, and the tendency toward usury will disappear.

When a proportion of the youth are required to enter the army, they will stop having specifically Jewish interests and feelings; they will assume French interests and feelings.

When they are submitted to the authority of civil law, all that will remain to them as Jews will be dogma, and they will leave their current state of affairs where religion is the only civil law, a situation which exists among the Moslems and which has always been the situation during the infancy of nations. It is wrong to say that the Jews are only degraded in those places where they are persecuted; in Poland, where they are necessary to fill the place of the middle class of society and where they are esteemed and powerful, they are no less vile, dirty, and given to all those customs of the basest dishonesty.

Theorizers will doubtless propose to limit themselves to ameliorative measures in their legislation; but this will not be sufficient. Good is accomplished slowly, and a mass of corrupt blood can only be improved by time. However, people are suffering; they are crying; and the intention of His Majesty is to come to their help.

It is necessary to employ the two methods concurrently, one of which aims to put a stop to the conflagration and the other of which aims to extinguish it.

That is why it is necessary to employ at the same time the Great Sanhedrin, the great assembly of Jews, and regulatory procedures deliberated by the Council of State.

The Great Sanhedrin has the best wishes and the respect of all who are enlightened among the Jews of Europe. With this support, it has the power to expunge from Mosaic legislation all those laws which are atrocious and those which can only refer to the situation of the Jews in Palestine.

Napoleon

62. Napoleon

Regulation of Commercial Transactions and Residences of Jews
(March 17, 1808)

Source: Maslin, pp. 35, 36–37, 38–39.

[The Regulation of Commercial Transactions deeply shocked France's Jews and exposed Napoleon's true aims in relation to the Jewish community. It set up special, harsh, rules (directly contrary to the French Constitution and the spirit of the

Revolution) concerning any type of business and commercial transaction undertaken by a Jew. Now, Jews not only had to obtain special business licenses, but also had to have proof of good character. The licenses needed to be renewed annually and could be revoked at the slightest suggestion of fraudulent or usurious dealings. The section on residence declared that no new Jews could move to the cities, but they could buy farm property if they devoted themselves to agriculture.

The regulation also made it impossible for a Jewish conscript to avoid the army. Napoleon wanted military service to be one of his main methods, along with intermarriage, for changing the Jews, and so conscription was forced on them much more strictly than on the general population. It was common at this time for draftees to find substitutes or to pay a certain sum of money for release from the army. This ordinance forbad Jews from buying their way out or supplying any replacements. While in the army, any Jewish laws which were at odds with general practice (e.g., dietary and Sabbath observance) had to be abandoned. In this way, the Jewish soldier would become disassociated from his ancestral faith and, when the time came, would be less resistant to intermarriage and cultural assimilation. Although Napoleon's plan was more benign, it differed little in theory from the policy Czar Nicholas I used to tear young Jewish army conscripts away from their religion and culture (see Chapter X).

The Commercial Transactions and Residences regulations were to remain in effect for ten years or as long as it took Jews to be completely assimilated.]

Napoleon Emperor of the French, etc., etc.,

On the report of our Minister of the Interior;

Our Council of State in agreement,

We have decreed and do decree that which follows:

Title II

7. From the first day of the coming July and thenceforth, no Jew shall be permitted to devote himself to any business, negotiation, or any type of commerce without having received a specific license from the prefect of his department. This license will only be granted on the receipt of precise information and of certification: 1) from the municipal council stating that the said Jew does not devote himself to any illicit business; 2) from the consistory of the district in which he lives attesting to his good conduct and his integrity.

8. This license must be renewed annually.

9. The attorneys-general of our courts are specifically instructed to revoke these licenses on the decision of the court whenever it comes to their attention that

a licensed Jew is engaging in usury or devoting himself to fraudulent business...

Title III

16. No Jew not actually now living in our department of Haut- and Bas-Rhin shall be hereafter admitted to take up residence there.

    In the other departments of the Empire, no Jew not actually now living in them shall be admitted to take up residence except in a case where he acquires a rural property and devotes himself to agriculture, without entering into any commercial or business transactions. It shall be possible to make exceptions to the provisions of this article by means of a special dispensation from us.

17. The Jewish population in our departments shall never be allowed to supply replacements for conscription; consequently, every Jewish conscript shall be subject to personal service.

General Provisions

18. The provisions included in this decree shall remain in effect for ten years in the hope that, at the end of this period and as a result of these various measures made necessary because of the Jews, there will no longer be any difference between them and the other citizens of our Empire. But, nevertheless, if our hope is disappointed these provisions shall be extended until whatever time shall be judged convenient.

19. The Jews living in Bordeaux and in the departments of Gironde and Landes, not having caused any complaints and not ever having devoted themselves to illicit business, are not included under the provisions of this decree.

Signed, Napoleon
For the Emperor;
The Minister Secretary of State, signed, Hughes B. Maret

Italy

The idealistic zeal of the French Revolution spread far beyond France's borders as its armies conquered one European country after another. The soldiers and their leaders carried the new spirit of civil liberty and equality to areas previously ruled by repressive monarchs and highly conservative theologians. Nowhere was this more true than in the Italian states ruled either by the Austrian Hapsburgs or the pope. The conditions here for Jews were among the worst in Europe.

Italian Jews, especially in the papal states of Rome, Ancona, Ferrara, and Bologna were miserably poor and confined to squalid ghettos. They were forced to wear the Jewish badge whenever there was possible contact with Christians. They were required to attend humiliating conversionary sermons, and, at times, were subject to forced baptism. Approximately 30,000 Jews lived under these conditions in Italy just prior to the French occupation. Half eked out a bare subsistence in Rome while the rest resided mainly in Florence, Venice, Verona, and Ancona.

Everywhere the French occupation forces ruled, they followed the same general plan. They ousted the former leaders, set up a liberal constitution, and formed a constituent assembly. When they encountered them, the soldiers literally beat down ghetto gates and destroyed the prison-like walls. The order of the Paduan Districts' Central Government, reproduced below, illustrates this liberation process.

---

63.   The Central Government of the Paduan Districts

Abolition of the Ghetto in Padua

(August 28, 1797)

Source: Raphael Mahler, ed. and trans., *Jewish Emancipation, A Selection of Documents, Pamphlet Series, Jews and the Post War World*, No. 1 (New York: American Jewish Committee, 1942) pp. 28–29.

The Central Government of the Paduan Delta Districts of Rovigo and Adria, having heard the reports of the Department of Justice and the chief of police,

Decrees:

First,—That the Hebrews are at liberty to live in any street they please;

Secondly, —That the barbarous and meaningless name of Ghetto, which designates the street which they have been inhabiting hitherto, shall be substituted by that of Via Libera.

A copy of these present decisions shall be sent to all the district municipalities so that they may be executed by the respective police departments in the most convenient manner. Padua, Fruttidor 11, year V of the French Republic and year I of Italian liberty.

64. The Roman Republic

First Emancipation in Rome

(February 1798)

Source: Mahler, p. 28.

[French forces, setting up and controlling the new Roman Republic, announced full emancipation and civil equality for the city's Jews in February, 1798.]

Whereas in accordance with the principles sanctified by the Constitutional Act of the Roman Republic all laws must be common and equal for all Roman citizens, the following Law is hereby decreed: Jews who meet all conditions prescribed for the acquisition of Roman citizenship shall be subject solely to the laws common to all citizens of the Roman Republic. Accordingly, all laws and particular regulations concerning Jews shall be null and void forthwith;...

[A year later, Napoleon's armies were driven out of Italy; the old rulers reclaimed their territories. They immediately abolished the French inspired liberties and returned the Jews to the ghettoes. For the next decade the fate of the Italian states seesawed between Bonaparte's forces and the allies led by Austria and Prussia. From 1809 to 1814, Rome's Jews again enjoyed equality and full citizenship under renewed French control. This happy situation, however, did not last. The French emperor's final defeat at Waterloo heralded the reestablishment of the old regime with all its restrictions. Conditions for the Jews depended greatly on the locality. For instance, Tuscany allowed its Jews to maintain some of their new rights, but the duchy of Parma forbad Jews to enter there at all. In Austrian-controlled Padua, the Jews lived under some renewed restrictions, but these were not severely debilitating.

In Rome, the pope returned to the Vatican and immediately ordered the Jews reincarcerated in the ghetto. When Leo XII ascended the Throne of Saint Peter in 1823, he insisted on legislation which, in effect, returned Rome's Jews to the Middle Ages. Conversionist sermons and forced baptisms hounded the Jewish population and almost all contact with Christians and the outside world were forbidden. The next two popes continued Leo's policies. In 1846, Pope Pius IX finally removed the ghetto gates and walls.]

65.   Victor Emmanuel II

Final Emancipation

(October 13, 1870)

Source: Mahler, p. 59.

[Slowly, with the spreading Italian Risorgimento, Jews reclaimed the rights they had lost upon Napoleon's defeat. Often the old regime's leaders, including Pius IX, granted concessions to the Jews to keep them from joining and supporting the liberation movement. This was the pope's reason for finally ending ghetto separation.

With final unification, King Victor Emmanuel II issued a royal decree in October, 1870. It made all Italians, of whatever religion, free and equal citizens with rights to vote and hold all public offices. Italy's Jews finally achieved full emancipation.]

ROYAL DECREE BY VIRTUE OF WHICH IN ROME AND IN THE ROMAN PROVINCES ALL INEQUALITIES SHALL CEASE AMONGST CITIZENS REGARDLESS OF THE RELIGION WHICH THEY PROFESS, CONCERNING THE ENJOYMENT AND EXERCISE OF CIVIL AND POLITICAL RIGHTS AND COMPETENCE TO HOLD PUBLIC OFFICES.

Vittorio Emanuele II

By the Grace of God and the Will of the Nation King of Italy

Having considered Article 24 of the Statute, and having heard the Council of Ministers, and on the proposal by the Keeper of Our Seals, Minister Secretary of State for the Affairs of Charity and Justice of Religions,

We have decreed and hereby decree:

Art.1 In Rome and in the Roman provinces all inequality between citizens whatever religion they may profess shall cease with regard to the enjoyment and the exercise of civil and political rights and to the competence for public offices.

Art.2 Every law and disposition contrary to the present Decree which becomes effectual immediately upon its publication, is abrogated.

We order that the present Decree, provided with the Seal of the State, shall be inserted in the Official Digest of Laws and Decrees of the Kingdom of Italy, instructing all concerned to observe same and to enforce the observation thereof.

Done at Firenze, on the day of October 13, 1870

Vittorio Emanuele

Germany and Austria

66.   Frederick II

The Charter Decreed for the Jews of Prussia

(April 17, 1750)

Source: Marcus, pp. 85–97.

[Frederick II, king of Prussia, was a typical example of an 18th-century "en-lightened despot." Truly considering himself a servant of the state, he manipulated his subjects and the economy to achieve his concept of a modern, functional nation. While he personally abhorred Jews, calling them "avaricious, superstitious, back-ward," Frederick the Great willingly used them to enrich his country and his coffers. In 1750, this Prussian king, facing growing complaints about Berlin's Jews, drew up a document, not to expel them, but to correct their "faults and abuses." He needed Jewish businessmen to help develop Prussia's economy and produce income for the crown, but he also needed to propitiate the burgers of Berlin who bitterly complained of Jewish competition.

This document attempted to satisfy both needs. It offered a complete, detailed regulation of Jewish economic, and, to a lesser extent, social life. It carefully listed exactly which Jewish officials could live in Berlin and serve the city's "tolerated" Jewish families. Marriage and setting up children in business were closely controlled. Prussian Jews could enter only the permissible trades, and usury and the Aleynu prayer were forbidden. Frederick was also determined not to allow any additional non-Prussian Jews into his country, except, of course, very rich ones whose skills and money he could exploit for the state's benefit.

This document is a fascinating look at how the Prussian-Jewish community was supposed to be organized and controlled. As was true for the Jews' entire past sojourn in Christian Europe, how closely this restrictive legislation actually followed the authorized plan depended greatly on the zealousness of the local officials.]

...We have noticed in our kingdom of Prussia...and particularly also in this capital *[Berlin]* various faults and abuses among the licensed and tolerated Jews, and have particularly observed that the rampant increase of these abuses has caused enormous damage and hardship, not only to the public, particularly to the Christian inhabitants and merchants, but also to Jewry itself...

For this reason we have found it necessary to make such provision...that a proportion may be maintained between Christian and Jewish business opportunities and trades, and especially that neither *[Jew or Christian]* be injured through a prohibited expansion of Jewish business activity...Therefore we establish, regulate, and order *[the following]*...

III. LIST OF THE TOLERATED COMMUNAL JEWISH OFFICIALS IN BERLIN: THE FOLLOWING LIST OF COMMUNAL OFFICIALS FOR THE CAPITAL HERE IN BERLIN HAS BEEN FIXED:

1. One rabbi or a vice-rabbi.

2. Four assistant-judges.

3. A chief and assistant cantor with his basses and his sopranos. These latter must not be married.

4. Four criers, one of whom must report daily to the police office the arrival of foreign Jews. *[These criers, or "knockers" used to call people to services at dawn by "knocking" on their doors.]*

5. Two employees in the synagogal-school.

6. Six grave diggers who also do other work for the Jewish community.

7. One cemetery guard.

8. Three slaughterers.

9. Three butchers.

10. One secretary of the meat-market and his supervisor.

11. Three bakers and one restaurant-keeper.

12. A communal scribe.

13. Two doorkeepers and one assistant. *[The doorkeepers at the city gates examined the papers of immigrant Jews.]*

14. Two hospital attendants.

15. One physician.

16. One male and one female bath attendant.

17. A fattener of fowl and cattle.

18. Eight attendants for the sick.

19. Two Hebrew printers.

20. Two teachers for girls. Both must be married...

V. PRINCIPLES THAT ARE TO BE OBSERVED IN THE SETTLEMENT OF JEWS...

The above mentioned Special Protected-Jews...are not authorized to settle a child *[in business]* nor are they to marry off a child by virtue of their privilege...

The Regular Protected-Jews, however, are allowed by virtue of their Letter of Protection to settle one child, a son or daughter...

Foreign *[non-Prussian]* Jews are not allowed to settle in our lands at all. However, if one should really have a fortune of ten thousand Reichsthalers and bring the same into the country and furnish authentic evidence of the fact, then we are to be asked about this and concerning the fee he is to pay...

XVIII. PRECISELY THE KIND OF GOODS WITH WHICH THE PROTECTED-JEWS ARE ALLOWED TO DO BUSINESS.

...they are allowed to trade and to do business with the following, namely:

With gold-cloth, fine fabrics and ribbons...domestic silk goods...

Furthermore they are permitted to deal in horses, in undressed calf and sheep hides, feathers, wigs, hair...chocolate, and foreign and domestic manufactured snuff and smoking tobacco. They are also free to trade, exchange, and do business in all sorts of old clothes, old or used furniture, house and kitchen utensils...

XXII. WHAT IS TO BE DONE WITH JEWISH BEGGARS.

It has already been decreed many times Jewish beggars are nowhere to be allowed to cross our borders...

XXIV. THE JEWS ARE ALLOWED TO LEND OUT MONEY ON PROPER PLEDGES.

Inasmuch as the money-business is a particular source of Jewish support, Jews are therefore allowed to lend money on pledges now as in the past...the Jews must be very sure in all pawning and selling that the pledges were not stolen or secretly removed and then pledged...

XXVII. INTEREST WHICH THE JEWS ARE AUTHORIZED TO TAKE.

When a Jew lends money on bills of exchange he is...authorized to take twelve percent interest if the bill of exchange is to run for twelve months or less...*[For large sums]* he must not take more than eight per cent interest, under threat of loss of the capital and all interest...

XXX. THE JEWS ARE TO BE PROTECTED IN THEIR RELIGION, CEREMONIES, AND SYNAGOGUE, AND THAT WHICH IS RELATED TO IT.

We have everywhere most graciously and firmly protected all these Jewish families in their religion and in their Jewish customs and ceremonies which they have practiced till now...This, however, on the condition that they must always refrain, under penalty of death and complete expulsion of the entire Jewry from Berlin and our other cities, from such abuses as the Jewish prayer which begins Alenu etc...

67. Emperor Joseph II of Austria

Edict of Toleration

(January 2, 1782)

Source: Mahler, pp. 18–20.

[Austrian Jewry and their brethren in the rest of the Hapsburg empire savored a short breath of freedom during Joseph II's reign. The son of strong-willed Maria Theresa, Joseph served as a co-regent for many years, but had little effective power. Upon his mother's death in 1780, he instituted a series of sweeping reforms and modernization meant to change the social, economic, and religious fabric of the diverse nations he ruled. He ordered legislation to put the Catholic Church under state control and severely curbed ecclesiastical authority. Protestants could practice their faith openly, and Jews saw many of their disabilities abolished. As an archetypical example of the "enlightened despot," Joseph II also extended ever greater imperial control over every facet of national life.

The emperor's 1782 Edict of Toleration was intended to turn the Jews, like all his subjects, into people who would be "useful and serviceable to the state." To do this, he radically changed state laws relating to the Jews. Thus he encouraged his Jewish subjects to join with Christians to develop the empire and, hopefully, modernize it. The Edict gave Jews greater freedom of movement and residence. It also repealed many of the special taxes levied solely on them. While they still could not become citizens, nor masters of the trades they were encouraged to enter, the emperor wanted Jews to take up all types of employment—manual, skilled, commercial, and professional. Only government service remained forbidden.

Joseph died six years after he issued this Edict. His brother Leopold undid much of Joseph's reform work. Significantly, Leopold reinstituted all the traditional Jewish restrictions, wiping out whatever the Jews had gained. There would be no Jewish emancipation in Austria or her territories until the Constitution of 1867 gave Jews complete citizenship.]

We, Joseph the Second, by the Grace of God, elected Roman Emperor, at all times the Enlarger of the Empire, King in Germany, Hungary and Bohemia, etc., Archduke in Austria, Duke in Burgundy and Lorraine, send Our Grace to all and graciously make known the following:

From the ascension to Our reign We have directed Our most pre-eminent attention to the end that all Our subjects without distinction of nationality and religion, once they have been admitted and tolerated in Our States, shall participate in common in public welfare, the increase of which is Our care, shall enjoy legal freedom and not find any obstacles in any honest ways of gaining their livelihood and of increasing general industriousness.

Since however the laws and the so-called Jewish Regulations pertaining to the Jewish nation prevailing in Our hereditary countries in general and particularly in Vienna and Lower Austria are not always compatible with these Our most gracious intentions, We hereby will amend them by the virtue of this present edict insofar as the difference in times and conditions necessitates it.

The favors granted to the Jewish nation by this present amendment, whereby the latest Jewish Regulation of May 5, 1764, is fully repealed consist of the following:

As it is Our goal to make the Jewish nation useful and serviceable to the State, mainly through better education and enlightenment of its youth as well as by directing them to the sciences, the arts and the crafts, We hereby grant and order...

8. Graciously, that the tolerated Jews may send their children in such places where they have no German schools of their own, to the Christian primary and secondary schools so that they have at least the opportunity to learn reading, writing and counting. And although they do not have a proper synagogue in Our residence, still We hereby permit them to establish for their children at their own expense their own school organized in the standard way with teachers appointed from amongst their co-religionists...

9. With regard to schools of higher degrees which were never forbidden to Jewish co-religionists, We hereby merely renew and confirm this permission.

10. In order to facilitate their future means of support and to prepare the necessary ways of gaining a livelihood, We hereby most graciously permit them from now to learn all kinds of crafts and trades here as well as elsewhere from Christian masters, certainly also amongst themselves, and to this end to apprentice themselves to Christian masters or to work as their journeymen, and the latter (the Christian craftsmen) may accept them without hesitation. This, however, should not be interpreted as if We wish to exercise any compulsion on Jews and Christians, We merely grant both sides full freedom to come to an understanding about this amongst themselves to their satisfaction.

11. We hereby further grant to the Jewish nation the general license to carry on all kinds of trade, without however the right of citizenship and mastership from which they remain excluded, to be carried on by them freely, only consequently as it is usual here and even then not before having obtained permission, same as Christians do, from the MAGISTRAT in this city and from the government of Lower Austria in the country...Painting, sculpture and the exercise of other liberal arts are equally permitted to them as they are to Christians,—and We further

12. Grant to the Jewish co-religionists the completely free choice of all non-civic branches of commerce and authorize them to apply for the right of wholesale trade under the same conditions and with the same liberties as are obtained and carried on by Our Christian subjects…

15. Considering the numerous openings in trades and the manifold contacts with Christians resulting therefrom, the care for maintaining common confidence requires that the Hebrew and the so-called Jewish language and writing of Hebrew intermixed with German, as well as these shall be abolished.

16. In order to facilitate the tolerated Jews in their trades also with regard to the question of servants, it shall be permitted to them from now on to employ as many Jewish as well as Christian servants as their business requires…

18. By this present Decree We hereby permit the existing restrictions with regard to definite Jewish houses to lapse and allow tolerated Jews to lease at their choice their own residences in the city as well as in the suburbs.

19. No less do We hereby completely abolish the head-toll hitherto levied on foreign Jews and permit them to enter Our residence from time to time in order to carry on their business…

23. Besides, We hereby completely remove the double court and chancellery fees hitherto in force only for Jews, and *[We remove]*

24. In general all hitherto customary distinctive marks and distinctions, such as the wearing of beards, the prohibition against leaving their homes before twelve o'clock on Sundays and holidays, the frequenting of places of public amusement and the like; on the contrary, it shall be permitted to wholesale merchants and their sons as well as to people of rank to carry swords.

25. Since by these favors We almost place the Jewish nation on an equal level with adherents of other religious associations in respect to trade and enjoyment of civil and domestic facilities, We hereby earnestly advise them to observe scrupulously all political, civil and judicial laws of the country to which they are bound same as all other inhabitants, just as they remain subject with respect to all political and legal matters to the provincial and municipal authorities within their jurisdiction and pertinent activities.

Done in Our City of Residence Vienna, the second day of January, 1782, in the eighteenth year of Our reign in the Roman Empire and in the second year of reign in Our hereditary lands.

68. Frederick William III

Emancipation in Prussia

(March 11, 1812)

Source: Mahler, pp. 32–35.

[French soldiers under Napoleon never managed to sweep through Prussia to tear down ghetto walls and emancipate the Jews. Still Prussian leaders anticipated that the Jews might agitate for freedom and citizenship. The country's first response to this fear was to increase controls and greatly limit Jewish freedom of action. This policy remained in force until Napoleon's men inflicted serious defeats on the Prussian army and Prussia lost half its territory to the French emperor. Humiliated, but not beaten, the Prussian government finally issued general reforms meant to strengthen the people's loyalty to the monarchy and to help build a strong military state.

Frederick William III needed not only to forestall any possibility of Jewish loyalty to Napoleon, but also required Jewish support to help Prussia through the current crisis. On March 11, 1812, the king ordered partial Jewish emancipation, giving Jews almost all the same rights, privileges, and responsibilities as Christians. The exceptions included a continued prohibition of government service above the municipal level, and restrictions on testimony given in, and guardianship enacted by, Berlin courts.]

We, Frederich Wilhelm, by the Grace of God, King of Prussia, etc., have resolved to grant the adherents of the Jewish faith in Our monarchy a new constitution suitable to the general welfare, and declare all laws and regulations concerning Jews *[issued]* hitherto, which are not confirmed by the present Edict as abolished, and decree as follows:

1. Jews and their families domiciled at present in Our States, provided with general privileges, patent letters of naturalization, letters of protection and concessions, are to be considered as natives and as Prussian state citizens.

2. The continuance of this qualification as natives and state citizens conferred upon them shall however be permitted only under the following obligation: that they bear strictly fixed family names, and that they use German or another living language not only in keeping their commercial books but also upon drawing their contracts and declaratory acts, and that they should use no other than German or Latin characters for their signatures...

4. After having declared and determined his family name, everyone shall receive a certificate from the Provincial Government of his domicile that he is a native

and a citizen of the state, which certificate shall be used in the future for himself and his descendants in place of the letter of protection...

7. Jews considered as natives...shall enjoy equal civil rights and liberties with Christians, in so far as this Order does not contain anything to the contrary.

8. They may therefore administer academic school teaching and municipal offices for which they qualified themselves.

As far as the admission of Jews to other public services and government offices is concerned, We leave to Ourselves its regulation by law in the course of time...

10. They are at liberty to settle in the towns as well as in the open country.

11. They may acquire real estate of any kind same as the Christian inhabitants and they may carry on any permitted trade, with the provision that they observe the general legal regulations.

12. Freedom of trade ensuing from the right of state citizenship also includes commerce...

14. Native Jews as such must not be burdened with special taxes.

15. They are, however, bound to fulfill all civic duties towards the State and the community of their domicile which Christians are obliged [to carry out] and to bear imposts equal to those of other citizens, with the exception of surplice fees.

16. Native Jews are also subject to military conscription or to the duty of serving in their cantons as well as to all other special legal regulations in connection therewith. The way and manner in which this obligation shall be applied to them, shall be determined in a more detailed manner by the regulation military conscription.

17. Native Jews may contract marriages among themselves without a special permit for it, or without having to take out a marriage license in so far as no previous consent or permission to contract a marriage depending on others is at all required under the general rules...

20. The civil legal relations of Jews shall be judged by the same laws which serve as the rule for other Prussian state citizens...

29. With regard to competence of a court and to administration by guardianship connected therewith, likewise no difference between Christians and Jews shall take place. Only in Berlin shall the special competence of a court assigned to Jews remain in force for the time being.

30. Under no conditions are Rabbis or Jewish Elders permitted to assume any court jurisdiction nor to institute or direct guardianship proceedings.

31. Foreign Jews are not permitted to take up residence in these States as long as they have not acquired Prussian state citizenship...

36. Foreign Jews may enter the country in transit or for the purpose of carrying on permissible commerce and other business. The Police authorities will be provided with a special instruction concerning the procedure to be observed by them and against them.

37. Concerning the prohibition of peddling in general, Police laws shall remain the same also with respect to Jews.

38. In Königsberg, in Prussia, Breslau and Frankfurt on the Oder, foreign Jews may stay for the duration of the fairs with the permission of the authorities.

39. The necessary regulations concerning the church conditions and the improvement in the education of Jews shall be reserved [for later issue], and when these will be considered, men of the Jewish persuasion who enjoy public confidence because of their knowledge and righteousness shall be called in and their judgment consulted.

All Our Government authorities and subjects shall be guided accordingly.

69. The Congress of Vienna

Article 16

(June 8, 1815)

Source: Mahler, p. 38.

[The Congress of Vienna was made up of the representatives of the countries that defeated Napoleon, most notably Austria, Russia, Prussia, and Great Britain. Reactionary in spirit, these people and the nations behind them intended to restore the old regime as it existed before the French Revolution. During its deliberations on the formation of post-Napoleonic Europe, the Congress appointed a committee to draw up recommendations concerning Jews and the emancipation issue. This committee turned in a resolution that substantially retained the rights Jews had won. The Congress, however, changed the phrase "<u>in</u> *the individual confederated states,"* to read *"*<u>by</u> *the individual confederated states." This one word substitution altered the whole concept of the document. "By" meant rights granted by the actual governments whose delegates were at the Congress. Since these reactionary governments, with the exception of Prussia, had not been the ones who had granted Jewish*

emancipation, they were now free to act as they saw fit. They chose to abolish most Jewish rights.

Jews were not the only groups unable to better their situation. Other peoples also reacted to the general repressive regimes set up by the Congress of Vienna. They formed revolutionary movements to fight for better conditions. Many Jews eagerly joined these groups and fought in the Revolutions of 1848.]

In the Name of the Most Holy and Indivisible Trinity

Article 16

The difference among Christian religious parties shall not form the basis of any distinction in the enjoyment of civil and political rights in the lands and areas of the German Confederation.

The Diet of the Confederation shall take into consideration the means of effecting, in the most uniform manner, an amelioration in the civil states of the confessor of the Jewish faith in Germany, as well as the means for providing and guaranteeing for the same the enjoyment of civil rights in the Confederated States in return for their assumption of all the obligations of citizens. Until then, however, the rights of the adherents of this creed already granted to them *by the individual confederated states* shall be maintained. *[Italics mine-APR.]*

70. Wilhelm I

North German Confederation and Jewish Emancipation

(July 3, 1869)

Source: Mahler, pp. 57–58.

[The 1848 revolts in Germany and the liberal constitutions that flowed from them were defeated by the combined thrusts of conservatism and the individual princes' desires to retain power and thwart the move for a united German nation. In the end, however, it was the essentially conservative forces, spearheaded by Otto von Bismarck, that forged the united German state and instituted just enough reforms to hold the new state together. Bismarck made Prussia the leading nation in German unification. The Prussian king, Wilhelm, became monarch of the North German Confederation and then Kaiser Wilhelm I of the German Empire.

The North German Confederation's constitution, promulgated by Wilhelm I and soon adapted for the German Empire, extended civil and political rights to all male citizens regardless of religion. Although this was not the complete emancipation the Jews had hoped for—they still could not serve as judges nor could they become higher government officials—they rejoiced nevertheless. As "Germans of the Jewish Persuasion," they felt their future was finally secure. They hoped to join their Christian fellow-citizens in building a powerful, modern Germany. In their enthusiasm, they hardly took seriously an ominous and growing movement which sought their political, economic, and social downfall.]

We, Wilhelm, by the Grace of God, King of Prussia, etc. with the approval of the *Bundesrath* and of the *Reichstag* decree in the name of the North German Confederation as follows:

All still existent restrictions on civil and political rights derived from the difference in religious confession are hereby repealed. In particular, the qualification for participation in communal and provincial representative bodies and for holding public offices shall be independent of religious confession.

Authentically under Our Most high Signature and with the Seal of the Confederation affixed.

Done at the Castle of Babelsberg, July 3, 1869.

Wilhelm
Count of Bismarck-Schönhausen

The guard of dishonor, drumming out Captain Alfred Dreyfus.

Chapter IX

Organized Anti-Semitism in Germany and France

A millennium and a half of anti-Jewish teachings by the Christian churches created continuing, deeply held, often folkloristic hatred and fear of the Jewish people. Jews became convenient targets, ready-made scapegoats for the innumerable social, economic, religious, and political problems of the Middle Ages. Finally, in the mid 19th century, Western European governments freed Jews from debilitating medieval restrictions and granted almost complete civil rights. The German-speaking peoples in particular were uneasy about the entrance and participation of this "foreign" element in their society. Many of those who did support Jewish emancipation clung to the belief that it would be followed, on the social level, by rapid assimilation and conversion, and, on the economic level, by the disappearance of the stereotypical money lender and petty peddler.

For their part, German Jews worked almost feverishly to become "Germans of the Jewish Persuasion." Their love of and loyalty to the new Germany was beyond question. They entered the professions in large numbers becoming doctors, lawyers, teachers, journalists. They applied their considerable commercial skills to big business which was then burgeoning as a result of the Industrial Revolution. They also invested in the stock markets and worked on the exchanges. The Jews, however, did not convert wholesale to Christianity. Instead, they "reformed" traditional Judaism making it both more relevant to their new, emancipated lives, and more like Protestantism in form and prayer service. Some Jews did become Protestants and Catholics and even more intermarried, but, on the whole, they retained their loyalty to Judaism and their ties with their co-religionists.

All of this happened at the same time growing nationalism, colonialism, and the Industrial Revolution brought about gut-wrenching changes in Western society. Unable to comprehend and deal rationally with these difficult transformations, many Germans, and to a lesser extent, Frenchmen, once again turned against the Jewish people for supposedly causing the difficulties. Some loudly claimed the Jews were attempting to destroy Christian civilization. A new term—anti-Semitism—described this movement which swept through Germany, Austria, and France in the late 19th century. Rabid anti-Semites spread spores of hatred which lay malignantly below the surface to later explode into the Nazis' murderous Final Solution.

There were two distinct varieties of organized anti-Jewish prejudice in 19th-century Germany, Austria, and France: religious (also known as political) anti-Semitism and racial anti-Semitism. Religious anti-Semitism focused on Judaism—specifically Talmud Judaism—as the basis for the existence of the "alien" Jew. Baptism and complete assimilation would quickly rectify this "Jewish problem."

Racial anti-Semitism was not as "forgiving." It developed as an adjunct to the Aryan master race myth, which claimed Teutonic Germans were superhumans. As such, they had contributed more to western civilization than any other group and were, not incidentally, destined to rule the world. Aryan racism meshed neatly with Prussian-directed nationalism and, to many, gave a *raison d'être* for the militaristic, Junker-controlled Germany. In addition, if there were a superior race of people, there had to be an inferior race also. Opportunistic demagogues quickly made use of this twisted logic to name the Jews as that inferior race. This made the very existence of the Jews an imminent threat to pure-bred Aryans: sexual relations and intermarriage with Jews polluted German blood and produced inferior, debased offspring. Racial anti-Semites believed conversion provided no solution to this problem. Only Jewish extirpation and extinction could prevent the total destruction of the German people.

Germany was particularly susceptible to these types of anti-Semitism for a number of reasons. The middle class and intellectuals, who, in other countries, supported liberal causes, were strongly drawn in by Germany's strident nationalism, which was staunchly conservative. Also, these groups were demoralized by the failure of capitalism and industrialization to bring speedy improvements in their lives. It was relatively easy for rabble rousers and unscrupulous political aspirants to claim the Jews were both traitors to the new, united Germany and blood-sucking capitalists responsible for the serious economic woes which had so adversely effected the blue- and white-collar workers.

While, for the most part, racial anti-Semitism remained the province of the lower middle classes, religious anti-Semitism was cynically manipulated by the ruling political parties. It was also tacitly accepted by Chancellor Otto von Bismarck as a method to win political support and to divert discontent. Thus religious anti-Semitism became acceptable even in polite society.

In France, on the other hand, the middle class and intellectuals tended toward liberalism and the important political parties did not make it a policy to use anti-Semitism as a method to win votes. Here it was the Catholic Church, the military, and those who supported the return of the monarchy who manufactured and used anti-Semitism, especially during the Dreyfus Affair, to achieve their political ends.

Organized anti-Semitism in Germany, Austria, and France had three major lasting effects. The movement reinvigorated and reinforced traditional anti-Jewish prejudices. It put fear and hatred of the Jews on a racial basis which even assimilation and conversion could not overcome. Finally, and most disastrously, organized 19th-century anti-Semitism laid the groundwork for National Socialist (Nazi) racism and the horrors of the Holocaust.

German Anti-Semitic Writers

71. Wilhelm Marr

The Victory of Judaism over Germandom

(1879)

Source: Mendes-Flohr and Reinharz, pp. 271–272. Wilhelm Marr, Der Sieg des Judenthums über das Germanenthum vom nicht confessionellen Standpunkt ausbetrachtet (Bern: Rudolph Costenoble, 1879), pp. 30–35, Trans. here by P. Mendes-Flohr and J. Reinharz.

[In 1855, a French diplomat, Count Joseph Arthur de Gobineau, wrote An Essay Concerning the Inequality of the Human Races. *He expounded the thesis that history was governed by racial law. He claimed a race of people he called Aryans was totally responsible for western civilization. (*Note: *"Aryan" originally referred to a family of languages also known as Indo-European.) The descendants of these ancient people, Gobineau asserted, had been found only in Central Europe. He had meant these Aryans to be the ancestors of the English, Belgians, and Northern French, but*

some Germans, as Central Europeans, soon claimed sole kinship to the chimerical Aryans. Conservative, nationalistic German writers, including historians and anthropologists, eagerly co-opted these racial fantasies, never questioning the truth of the matter. In identifying the Aryans' descendants with the German people, these writers declared the Germans to be superior to all other groups, especially the Jews.

The Aryan myth stimulated and received stimulus from German unification. Newly united, with Junker-controlled Prussia at its helm, Germany was the new kid on the block, an infant among the older nations. In modern terms, many Germans suffered from "low self-esteem." In choosing to believe their ancestors had been responsible for civilization's climb from barbarity, they eased their insecurities and in their hearts stood tall amongst the established countries of the world.

By the 1870s, Germany's Jews, although a small minority of the country's population, were well represented in banking, journalism, law, and medicine. They were professors and school teachers, artists, musicians, actors, novelists. Talented, liberal, innovative, quite a few became very successful. Many Germans, especially from the lower middle class, deeply resented what they believed—or more correctly, what they were told to believe—was the "Judaification" of their country. These people accepted the new racial theories which said Jews were inferior. Yet somehow Jews had risen to the pinnacles of success in German art, science, and business. How could this be so? The anti-Semites had a ready answer: Jews, by blood, were conspiratorial, grasping, greedy, and their ultimate aim was world domination. Against such a foe even the Aryan master race faced defeat.

Wilhelm Marr, the man who made the word "Semite" interchangeable with "Jew" and introduced the racially based term "anti-Semitism," postulated just such a theory. "The Victory of Judaism over Germandom" was so popular it went through twelve printings in six years. In it, Marr claimed the existence of a continual war between Jews and Germans, with Jews, using liberalism as a cover, coming ever closer to winning world mastery. In Marr's twisted thinking, the state, Christianity, and even the Iron Chancellor Bismarck himself were somehow the pawns of Jewish conspiracies. Thus discontent with the government's inability to deal with Germany's problems was cleverly side-tracked into racial hatred of the Jew.

In 1879, Marr moved race prejudice into the political arena when he founded the Anti-Semitic League. Although short-lived, the League served as the prototype for political movements which attracted the frustrated lower middle class with the use of racial anti-Semitic rhetoric.]

There is no stopping them...

Are there no clear signs that the twilight of the Jews is setting in?

No.

Jewry's control of society and politics, as well as its practical domination of religious and ecclesiastical thought, is still in the prime of its development, heading toward the realization of Jehovah's promise: "I will hand all peoples over to thee."

By now, a sudden reversal of this process is fundamentally impossible, for if it were, the entire social structure, which has been so thoroughly Judaized, would collapse. And there is no viable alternative to this social structure which could take its place.

Further, we cannot count on the help of the "Christian" state. The Jews are the "best citizens" of this modern, Christian state, as it is in perfect harmony with their interests...

It is not a pretentious prophecy but the deepest inner conviction which I here utter. Your generation will not pass before there will be absolutely no public office, even the highest one, which the Jews will not have usurped.

Yes, through the Jewish nation, Germany will become a world power, a western New Palestine. And this will happen, not through violent revolutions, but through the compliance of the people...

We should not reproach the Jewish nation. It fought against the western world for 1800 years, and finally conquered and subjugated it. We were vanquished and it is entirely proper that the victor shouts "*Vae Victis!*" *[Woe to the conquered!]*

German culture has proved itself ineffective and powerless against this foreign power. This is a fact; a brute inexorable fact. State, Church, Catholicism, Protestantism, Creed and Dogma, all are brought low before the Jewish tribunal, that is, the *[irreverent]* daily press *[which the Jews control]*.

The Jews were late in their assault on Germany, but once they started there was no stopping them.

Gambetta *[Note: He was not a Jew]*, Simon *[Note: He was not a Jew]*, and Cremieux were the dictators of France in 1870–1871. During the war, they drove thousands upon thousands of Frenchmen to their senseless deaths. After Sedan, the whole world believed in peace. But, no! Bismarck was lured by the rhetoric of a Jules Favre. "Blood and Iron" had to continue because of the frivolous, worthless, fanatical action of the Semites in Tours.

Poor, Judaized France!

In England, the Semite Disraeli, a German-hater (*comme il faut*), holds in his vest pocket the key to war and peace in the Orient.

Who derived the real benefit at the Congress of Berlin from the spilled blood of the Orient? Jewry. The Alliance Israelite Universelle was the first in line. Rumania was forced to open officially its doors and gates to destructive Semitism. Jewry did not yet dare to make the same demand of Russia. But, this demand, too will soon come.

Dear reader, while you are allowing the German to be skinned alive I bow my head in admiration and amazement before this Semitic people, which has us under heel. Resigned to subjugation to Jewry, I am marshalling my last remaining strength in order to die peacefully, as one who will not surrender and who will not ask forgiveness.

Can we deny the historical fact?

No!

The historical fact, that Israel became the leading social-political superpower in the nineteenth century, lies before us. It is already notorious to what extent we lack the physical and intellectual strength to de-Judaize ourselves. The raw, brutal, but completely unconscious protest against the real Judaization of society was Social Democracy. It sided, however, with the Jews, because Jewry has also infiltrated its ranks. After all, the founder of German Social Democracy, Lassalle, was a Semite.

Why are we so surprised? We have among us a flexible, tenacious, intelligent, foreign tribe that knows how to bring abstract reality into play in many different ways. Not individual Jews, but the Jewish spirit and Jewish consciousness have overpowered the world...

All this is the consequence of a cultural history—so unique in its way, so grand that everyday polemics can achieve nothing against it. With the entire force of its armies, the proud Roman Empire did not achieve that which Semitism has achieved in the West and particularly in Germany.

72.   Adolf Stöcker

What We Demand of Modern Jewry

(September 19, 1879)

Source: Paul W. Massing, *Rehearsal for Destruction: A Study of Political Anti-Semitism in Imperial Germany* (New York: Harper Brothers, 1949), pp. 278–287.

[While Wilhelm Marr popularized the term "anti-Semite" and created a tentative synthesis between anti-Semitism and German politics, Adolf Stöcker was the first person to make anti-Semitism a national issue. From a lower middle class family, Stöcker was an ordained Protestant minister who rose to become the Kaiser's Court Chaplain from 1874 to 1891. He championed social reform led by conservative Protestants. In 1878, he founded the Christian Social Workers' Party to attack both

ends of the economic spectrum, capitalism and socialism. Stöcker claimed these were controlled by Jews trying to destroy Germany's middle class. In reality, it was dislocation due to the expanding Industrial Revolution and the Economic Depression of 1873 that caused such severe hardships. Stöcker, however, cleverly diverted criticism and discontent, and, in doing so, worked to prevent a possible socialist revolution by blaming all the troubles of the middle class on the Jews.

"What We Demand of Modern Jewry" was a mixture of religious and racial anti-Semitism. In it, Stöcker reiterated many of the traditional medieval charges against Jewry and touted the superiority of Teutonic Christianity. He urged Germans to pay heed to the "rumbling of a far-off thunderstorm" by demanding legislation aimed at rooting out Jewish influence and control of Germanic life. Stöcker's position as Court Chaplain seemed to legitimize his stand and lent credence to the belief that the highest reaches of government supported his views.

In the end, however, the Reichstag enacted no anti-Semitic laws in Imperial Germany. Marr's Anti-Semitic League and Stöcker's Christian Social Workers' Party failed to obtain the legislation they demanded. This was partly due to public outcry by the Jews themselves. More important, however, was the slow improvement in the economy as the country recovered from the 1873 Depression. Better salaries and working conditions led to a decline in anti-Semitic agitation. The Jewish community, however, felt its own protests and educational efforts had brought about the decline in anti-Jewish prejudice. Some historians believe this gave them a false sense of security and led them to seriously underestimate the threat later posed by National Socialism.]

For a long time the Jewish problem has been a burning question, but in the last few months it has burst out into an open conflagration. It is not fed by religious fanaticism nor by political passion. The orthodox and the freethinkers, conservatives and liberals, all talk and write about it with the same vehemence. All alike consider the Jewish problem not a question of contending religious beliefs, but a disturbing social problem. "The social problem is the Jewish problem," writes Glagau. "Don't vote for a Jew!" exclaims W. Marr, in his third pamphlet. "The end of Germany has come," he concludes his passionate appeal to our people.

Well, we do not believe the end of the German spirit to be so near. Peoples as well as individuals can be reborn. Germany, and Berlin too, will recover and rid themselves of the foreign spirit. But there are symptoms of the presence of a disease: our national body is plagued by social abuses, and social hostility never exists without reason. Christians as well as Jews should be seriously concerned lest this enmity turn into hatred. For the rumbling of a far-off thunderstorm can already be heard. It is strange indeed that the Jewish liberal press does not have the courage to answer the charges of its attackers. Usually it invents a scandal, even if there is none… It pretends to despise its enemies and to consider them unworthy of an answer. It would be better to learn from the enemy, to recognize one's own defects, and work together toward the social reconciliation which we need so badly. It is in this light that I intend to deal with the Jewish question, in the spirit of Christian love, but also with complete social truthfulness…

I do indeed consider modern Jewry a great danger to German national life. By this I mean neither the religion of the orthodox nor the enlightenment of the reformed. Orthodox Judaism, this ossification of the Law, the Old Testament without a temple, without priests, without sacrifice, without a Messiah, is neither attractive nor dangerous to the children of the nineteenth century. It is a form of religion which is dead at its very core, a low form of revelation, an outlived spirit, still venerable but set at nought by Christ and no longer holding any truth for the present. Reformed Judaism is of even less religious significance. It is neither Judaism nor Christianity, but a pitiful remnant of the Age of Enlightenment. Its ideas did not originate on Jewish soil but in a wretched period of the Christian church, a period long since overcome by the church itself. Both factions boast, of course, that the Jews are the bearers of the loftiest religious and moral ideals…

Here we wish to make our request. We ask: *Please, be a little more modest!* We do not deny that Israel carried the knowledge of the one and only God through ancient times like a sacred flame until Christ came and bought the more perfect faith, the richer conception of God, and the higher truth. But it is a historic fact that the people of Israel time and again relapsed into the grossest idolatry, that God was able to suppress apostasy for short periods only by sending outstanding personalities. It is God's grace rather than Israel's merit that the doctrine of the one God has been preserved for mankind…

…[Jews] are quite aware of the fact that they had a caste of priests—certainly the opposite of equality; that they had slavery—certainly the opposite of freedom; that they indulged in polygamy—certainly the opposite of ideal family life. Only Teutonic-Christian life put an end to these abuses. It is true, Israel had an enlightened economic legislation, social forms of property ownership, the prohibition of usury, and the greatest charity toward the poor. But we have only to mention these things to realize the fearful chasm between the Old Testament and modern Jewry. It was German law alone that protected the concept of common property, the Christian church alone that decreed the prohibition of usury; it is precisely here that the faults and sins of modern Jewry are plainly revealed…

…The truth is that modern Jewry is most certainly a power against religion; a power which bitterly fights Christianity everywhere, uproots Christian faith as well as national feeling in the people, in their stead offering them nothing but the idolatrous admiration of Jewry such as it is, with no other content but its self-admiration…

All this may have contributed to make the Jews, especially the Jewish newspaper boys, intolerant to such a degree as to become quite intolerable. We really mean it if we address our second request to the Jewish press: *please, be a little more tolerant!* Unlike many others who have dealt with this topic, we shall not quote the Talmud with its contempt for foreign peoples and its hatred for human rights… We do not feel that present-day Jewry in its totality can be made responsible for books which were written thousands of years ago… The strict Jews still accept the Talmud as infallible, like the law. Some of them quite unreasonably declare that the whole Talmud, including all the vengeful and savage passages, is sacred to them. But it appears, nevertheless, that many years of living together with Christians and maintaining business relations with them, and the kinder spirit of modern times have caused the hatred of Christians to decline greatly in the synagogue…

The Jews are and remain a people within a people, a state within a state, a separate tribe within a foreign race. All immigrants are eventually absorbed by the people among whom they live—all save the Jews…

…They control the arteries of money, banking, and trade; they dominate the press and they are flooding the institutions of higher learning… The process of disintegration is under way; nothing will stop it, unless we turn about and make the Jews turn about too. And this is where we make our third request. Modern Jewry must take part in productive work: *a little more equality, please!*

It used to be said that emancipation would push the Jews into other occupations. Now they are emancipated, but the opposite has happened. More than ever, they cultivate those trades where they can get rich quickly and easily… They take almost no part at all in handicraft and little in industrial labor. That means that they do not enjoy work and that they do not believe in the German concept of the dignity of labor… For me the Jewish problem centers in the question as to whether the Jews who live in our midst will learn to participate in all aspects of German labor, including the hard toil of artisans, factory workers, and peasants. We should ask nothing more of them…

The question is: What shall be done? We believe that Jews and Christians must try to establish a proper relationship with each other. There is no other way. Hatred of the Jews is already flaring up here and there, and this is repugnant to the Gospels. If modern Jewry continues to use the power of capital and the power of the press to bring misfortune to the nation, a final catastrophe is unavoidable. Israel must renounce its ambition to become the master of Germany. It should renounce its arrogant claim that Judaism is the religion of the future, when it is so clearly that of the past. Let not foolish Christians continue to strengthen the self-conceit of this people. Jewish orthodoxy with its circumcision is decrepit, while reformed Judaism is not a Jewish religion at all. Once Israel has realized this, it will quietly forget its alleged mission and stop trying to rob of their Christianity people who offer it hospitality and civil rights. The Jewish press must become more tolerant—that is the first prerequisite for improving the situation. The social abuses which are caused by Jewry must be eradicated by wise legislation. It will not be easy to curb Jewish capital. Only thoroughgoing legislation can bring it about. The mortgage system in real estate should be abolished and property should be inalienable and unmortgageable; the credit system should be reorganized to protect the businessman against the arbitrary power of big capital. There must be new stock and stock exchange regulations; reintroduction of the denominational census so as to find out the disproportion between Jewish capital and Christian labor; limitation of appointments of Jewish judges in proportion to the size of the population; removal of Jewish teachers from our grammar schools, and in addition the strengthening of the Christian-Germanic spirit are the means to put a stop to the encroachment of Jewry on Germanic life, this worst kind of usury.

Either we succeed in this and Germany will rise again, or the cancer from which we suffer will spread further. In that event our whole future is threatened and the German spirit will become Judaized. The German economy will become impoverished. These are our slogans: A return to a Germanic rule in law and business, a return to the Christian faith. May every man do his duty, and God will help us.

73. Karl Eugen Dühring

The Question of the Jew is a Question of Race

(1881)

Source: Mendes-Flohr and Reinharz, pp. 273–274. From Karl Eugen Dühring, Die Judenfrage als Racen-Sitten-und Culturfrage (Karlsruhe and Leipzig: H. Reuther, 1881), pp. 3–4. Trans. here by M. Gelber.

[Some German anti-Semitic writers believed assimilation and conversion would end Germany's "Jewish problem." Many respectable intellectuals, politicians, and ordinary citizens supported their views. Others, however, held a much more militant and dangerous belief: Jews, by blood, were evil, depraved, and corrupt. Neither baptism nor assimilation would result in the betterment of the Jewish people. Indeed, social admixture and intermarriage would ultimately destroy Christian-Teutonic civilization.

Karl Eugen Dühring, a Berlin-born economist and philosopher, was one of the earliest proponents of this racial anti-Semitism. "Jews," Professor Dühring de-

clared, "are to be defined solely on the basis of race." Along with men like Fritsch and Houston Stewart Chamberlain, Dühring developed a virulent theory of fear and hatred which led directly to Adolf Hitler's "Final Solution."]

A Jewish question would still exist, even if every Jew were to turn his back on his religion and join one of our major churches. Yes, I maintain that in that case, the struggle between us and the Jews would make itself felt as evermore urgent—although the struggle certainly is felt now even when the Jews have yet to convert *[in large numbers]*. It is precisely the baptized Jews who infiltrate furthest, unhindered in all sectors of society and political life. It is as though they have provided themselves with an unrestricted passport, advancing their stock to those places where members of the Jewish religion are unable to follow. Furthermore, several doors are closed to members of the Jewish religion by our legislation, and more particularly, by the principles of our administration. Through these portals the racial Jew, who has forsaken his religion, can enter unhindered. A situation similar to the one involving the baptized Jews results as soon as all civic rights and opportunities become available to members of the Jewish religion. Thereupon, they force themselves into all aspects of social and political life, just like those who have converted to Christianity. And, in this way, their contact with the nation in which they live becomes more pronounced. This takes place despite the fact that in society *[as opposed to the state]* there is never an instance in which the members of the Jewish religion are made completely equal... I return therefore to the hypothesis that the Jews are to be defined solely on the basis of race, and not on the basis of religion. I dismiss all conclusions hitherto upheld... The Mosaic attempt to locate within the base of our people a Jewish component only makes the Jewish question a more burning issue. The diverse admixture of our modern cultures, or in other words, the sprinkling of racial-Jewry in the cracks and crevices of our national bode, must inevitably lead to a reaction. It is impossible that close contact *[between Germans and Jews]* will take effect without the concomitant realization that this infusion of Jewish qualities is incompatible with our best impulses.

74. Theodor Fritsch

The Racists' Decalogue

(1883)

Source: Massing, pp. 306–307. Theodor Fritsch, Antisemiten-Katechismus (Leipzig, 1883).

[The Racists' Decalogue, a Ten Commandments for German racial anti-Semites, first appeared in Theodor Fritsch's Anti-Semitic Catechism. *It later turned up under the title* Handbuch der Judenfrage *(The Jewish Question Handbook). Both the Handbook and Racists' Decalogue, circulated by Fritsch's own anti-Semitic pub-*

lishing house, had a strong influence on future Nazi legislation. Many sections of the Nuremberg Laws were based on these writings.

Fritsch was an ardent propagandist. He wanted all German political parties to adopt anti-Semitic platforms which would repeal Jewish emancipation and make the mixture of Aryan and Jewish blood a crime. Decades later, Fritsch proudly became a member of the Nazi party. He died in 1933 before he could see his hateful legacy reach its "logical" conclusion.]

1. Be proud of being a German and strive earnestly and steadily to practice the inherited virtues of our people, courage, faithfulness and veracity, and to inspire and develop these in thy children.

2. Thou shall know that thou, together with thy fellow Germans, regardless of faith or creed, hast a common implacable foe. His name is Jew.

3. Thou shalt keep thy blood pure. Consider it a crime to soil the noble Aryan breed of thy people by mingling it with the Jewish breed. For thou must know that Jewish blood is everlasting, putting the Jewish stamp on body and soul unto the farthest generations.

4. Thou shalt be helpful to thy fellow German and further him in all matters not counter to the German conscience, the more so if he be pressed by the Jew. Thou shalt at once take into court any offense or crime committed by the Jew in deed, word or letter, that comes to thy knowledge, lest the Jew abuse the laws of our country with impunity.

5. Thou shalt have no social intercourse with the Jew. Avoid all contact and community with the Jew and keep him away from thyself and thy family, especially thy daughters, lest they suffer injury of body and soul.

6. Thou shalt have no business relations with the Jews. Never choose a Jew as a business partner, nor borrow nor buy from him, and keep your wife, too, from doing so. Thou shalt sell nothing to him, nor use him as an agent in thy transactions, that thou mayest remain free and not become slave unto the Jew nor help to increase his money, which is the power by which he enslaves our people.

7. Thou shalt drive the Jew from thy own breast and take no example from Jewish tricks and Jewish wiles, for thou shalt never match the Jew in trickery but forfeit thy honor and earn the contempt of thy fellow Germans and the punishment of the courts.

8. Thou shalt not entrust thy rights to a Jewish lawyer, nor thy body to a Jewish physician, nor thy children to a Jewish teacher lest thy honor, body and soul suffer harm.

9. Thou shalt not lend an ear nor give credence to the Jew. Keep away all Jewish writings from thy German home and hearth lest their lingering poison may unnerve and corrupt thyself and thy family.

10. Thou shalt use no violence against the Jews because it is unworthy of thee and against the law. But if a Jew attack thee, ward off his Semitic insolence with German wrath.

75.   Houston Stewart Chamberlain

Foundations of the Nineteenth Century

(1898)

Source: Houston Stewart Chamberlain, *Foundations of the Nineteenth Century*, vol. 1, trans. by John Lees (New York: John Lane Co., 1913), pp. 253, 254, 255, 269, 271, 272, 273, 330, 331.

[Houston Stewart Chamberlain was the most influential spokesman for 19th-century German racism. Born in England to a British admiral and his German wife, Chamberlain chose to spend his adult life in Germany. Richard Wagner became his mentor, and Chamberlain enthusiastically adopted Wagner's pseudo-scientific Aryan beliefs. He later married the composer's daughter, Eva.

Chamberlain's publications, including Foundations of the Nineteenth Century *and* Race and Nation, *rewrote the story of human civilization by claiming every creation, every advance in history, had been made by a member of the Aryan race. Germans, he trumpeted, were the modern day representatives of the ancient Aryans, and, as such, they were destined to be masters of the world. The Jews, always bearing deep hatred for the human race, were the antithesis of the heroic Aryans. Jewish claims notwithstanding, the Hebrews and their descendants never contributed anything of value to humanity. He even claimed David and Jesus were really blond, blue-eyed Aryans. A main point of Chamberlain's racist theory was the claim that Jews, through sexual intercourse with Germans, contaminated pure Aryan blood.*

While most of Europe condemned Foundations of the Nineteenth Century *for its strident racism, Germans acclaimed Chamberlain's work as a scholarly description of Teutonic superiority. Kaiser Wilhelm II openly admired the book, and this encouraged greater acceptance of racism and anti-Semitism among Germany's intellectual and social elite. Chamberlain's most lasting mark, however, was on the leaders of National Socialism, a movement that began attracting adherents in the 1920's. Many of those men, including Alfred Rosenberg and Heinrich Himmler, had read Chamberlain's books and been guided by his anti-Semitic theories.]*

...Out of the midst of the chaos towers, like a sharply defined rock amid the formless ocean, one single people, a numerically insignificant people—the Jews.

This one race has established as its guiding principle the purity of the blood; it alone possesses, therefore, physiognomy and character… In comparison with Rome and still more so with Hellas their intellectual horizon appears so narrow, their mental capacities so limited, that we seem to have before us an entirely new type of being; but the narrowness and want of originality in thought are fully counterbalanced by the power of faith, a faith which might be very simply defined as "faith in self."… However, we must distinguish between Judaism and the Jews and admit that Judaism as an idea is one the most conservative ideas in the world. The idea of physical race-purity, which is the very essence of Judaism, signified the recognition of a fundamental physiological fact of life; wherever we observe life from the hyphomycetes to the noble horse we see the importance of "race"; Judaism made this law of nature sacred. And this is the reason why it triumphantly prevailed at that critical moment in the history of the world, when a rich legacy was waiting in vain for worthy heirs. It did not further, but rather put a stop to, universal disintegration. The Jewish dogma was like a sharp acid which is poured into a liquid which is being decomposed in order to clear it and keep it from further decomposition. Though this acid may not be to the taste of every one, yet it has played so decisive a part in the history of the epoch of culture to which we belong that we ought to be grateful to the giver; instead of being indignant about it, we shall do better to inform ourselves thoroughly concerning the significance of this "entrance of the Jews into the history of the West," an event which in any case exercised inestimable influence upon our whole culture, and which has not yet reached its full growth.

Nothing is so convincing as the consciousness of the possession of race. The man who belongs to a distinct, pure race, never loses the sense of it. The guardian angel of his lineage is ever at his side, supporting him where he loses his foothold, warning him like the Socratic demon where he is in danger of going astray, compelling obedience, and forcing him to undertakings which, deeming them impossible, he would never have dared to attempt… Race lifts a man above himself: it endows him with extraordinary—I might almost say supernatural—powers, so entirely does it distinguish him from the individual who springs from the chaotic jumble of peoples drawn from all parts of the world. And should this man of pure origin be perchance gifted above his fellows, then the fact of race strengthens and elevates him on every hand, and he becomes a genius towering over the rest of mankind, not because he has been thrown upon the earth like a flaming meteor by a freak of nature, but because he soars heavenward like some strong and stately tree, nourished by thousands and thousands of roots—no solitary individual, but the living sum of untold souls striving for the same goal… Would one small tribe from among all the Semites have become a world-embracing power had it not made "purity of race," its inflexible fundamental law? In days when so much nonsense is talked concerning this question, let Disraeli teach us that the whole significance of

Judaism lies in its purity of race, that this alone gives it power and duration, and just as it has outlived the people of antiquity, so, thanks to its knowledge of the law of nature, will it outlive the constantly mingling races of today.

...In contrast to the new, growing, Anglo-Saxon race, look, for instance, at the Sephardim, the so-called "Spanish Jews"; here we find how a genuine race can by purity keep itself noble for centuries and tens of centuries, but at the same time how very necessary it is to distinguish between the noble reared portions of a nation and the rest. In England, Holland and Italy there are still genuine Sephardim... This is nobility in the fullest sense of the word, genuine nobility of race! Beautiful figures, noble heads, dignity in speech and bearing. The type is Semitic in the same sense as that of certain noble Syrians and Arabs. That out of the midst of such people prophets and psalmists could arise—that I understand at the first glance, which I honestly confess that I had never succeeded in doing when I gazed, however carefully, on the many hundred young Jews—"Bochers"—of the Friedrichstrasse in Berlin...

...But this alien people, everlastingly alien, because—as Herder well remarks—it is indissolubly bound to an alien law that is hostile to all other peoples—this alien people has become precisely in the course of the nineteenth century a disproportionately important and in many spheres actually dominant constituent of our life. Even a hundred years ago that same witness had sadly to confess that the "ruder nations of Europe" were "willing slaves of Jewish usury"; today he could say the same of by far the greater part of the civilized world. The possession of money in itself is, however, of least account; our governments, our law, our science, our commerce, our literature, our art...practically all branches of our life have become more or less willing slaves of the Jews... The Indo-European *[Aryan]*, moved by ideal motives, opened the gates in friendship: the Jew rushed in like an enemy, stormed all positions and planted the flag of his, to us, alien nature—I will not say on the ruins, but on the breaches of our genuine individuality.

Are we for that reason to revile the Jews? That would be as ignoble as it is unworthy and senseless. The Jews deserve admiration, for they have acted with absolute consistency according to the logic and truth of their own individuality, and never for a moment have they allowed themselves to forget the sacredness of physical laws because of foolish humanitarian day-dreams which they shared only when such a policy was to their advantage. Consider with what mastery they use the law of blood to extend their power: the principal stem remains spotless, not a drop of strange blood comes in: as it stands in the Torah, "A bastard shall not enter into the congregation of the Lord; even to his tenth generation shall he not enter into the congregation of the Lord," in the meantime, however, thousands of side branches are cut off and employed to infect the Indo-Europeans with Jewish blood. If that were to go on for a few centuries, there would be in Europe only one single people of pure race, that of the Jews, all the rest would be a herd of pseudo-Hebraic mestizos, a people beyond all doubt degenerate physically, mentally and morally.

Anti-Semitism in France

Late 19th-century French anti-Semites were very strong Church supporters. They tended to see France, the monarchy, and the Catholic Church as extensions of related historical institutions. The Restoration following Napoleon's defeat at Waterloo put the last Bourbon, Louis Philippe, on the French throne. He ruled until the forces of the Revolution of 1848 overthrew him and declared the Second Republic. Louis Napoleon, Bonaparte's nephew, won election as president of the new republic. Almost immediately upon taking office, Louis Napoleon worked to betray the liberal republicanism which had brought him to power. His ultimate aim, like his uncle's before him, was to make himself the Emperor of France. In December, 1851, he staged a successful *coup d'état* and a year later crowned himself Napoleon III. [*Note:* Napoleon Bonaparte's son, although he died without gaining the crown, had the honorary title of Napoleon II.] The new emperor promised to restore many of the Church's privileges, and, as a result, the Catholic Church become Napoleon III's strongest ally.

Exceedingly popular for the first half of his 22-year reign, Bonaparte III worked to restore France's primacy among the nations of the world. Then, at the peak of his popularity, he suffered a long series of economic, military, and colonial defeats, the Franco-Prussian War being the most disastrous of all. His capture by the Germans encouraged French liberals to overthrow the monarchy and to declare the Third French Republic. France was now a nation utterly beaten and disillusioned as Germany became Europe's dominant continental power, rivalled only by Great Britain.

Loss of French pride only exacerbated the difficulties the nation faced as a result of growing industrialization and emerging capitalism in the 1870s. While the Third Republic received support from the generally liberal middle class, the disadvantaged lower classes were drawn to groups on the right and the left which opposed liberal republicanism. Conservative groups, including the Church, the military, and those wishing to see a return of the monarchy, further complicated the situation. They often used anti-Semitism as an expression of their discontent and as a tool to win the populace away from the Republic.

76. Edouard-Adolphe Drumont

Jewish France

(1885)

Source: Mendes-Flohr and Reinharz, pp. 276–277. Edouard-Adolphe Drumont, *La France juive*, 14th ed. (Paris: C. Marpon and E. Flammarion, 1885), vol.1, pp. 520–526. Trans. here by J. Green.

[Journalist Edouard-Adolphe Drumont became an anti-Semite following his association with extreme rightist Catholic groups. His book, La France juive, *claimed most of France's political, economic, and social problems were caused by the country's 8,000 Jews. Their clever manipulation of the nation's money, he insisted, would soon bring France to her knees. Confiscate their wealth, make them paupers, Drumont demanded, and all Christians would benefit. In 1889, Drumont founded an Anti-Semitic League in France and a right-wing newspaper,* La Libre Parole, *which echoed French Catholic opinion and often contained bitter anti-Jewish rhetoric.]*

...Actually, the transfer of property which we propose is more legitimate than that which occurred during the revolution. In effect, no one could seriously deny that Jewish wealth has, as we have said, a special character. It is not the carefully husbanded fruit of the labor of innumerable generations. Rather, it is the result of speculation and fraud. It is not created by labor, but extracted with marvelous cleverness from the pocket of real workers by financial institutions, which have enriched their founders by ruining their stockholders.

...The obstacles [placed before the workers by the Jews] are indeed considerable. Still they are not insurmountable. A man of French origin may yet arise from among the people, harboring the magnificent ambition of attaching his name to the peaceful solution [I have proposed] of the problem of the proletariat, which has already cost them still more if they follow the old path.

Likewise, a brave officer might appear, who would be acutely struck by the degradation of his county and who would risk his life to raise it up. Given the actual situation with a government scorned by all and falling apart at the seams, five hundred determined men in the suburbs of Paris and a regiment surrounding the Jewish banks would suffice to carry out the most fruitful revolution of modern times. Everything would be over by the end of the day. After seeing posters announcing that the operations of the Office of Confiscated Jewish Wealth were going to begin in two days, people would embrace in the streets.

Thus, the beautiful saying of Pierre the Venerable, Abbot of Cluny, would be realized: SERVIANT POPULIS CHRISTIANIS, ETIAM INVITIS IPIS, DIVITIAE JUDEORUM. "Let the wealth of the Jews even against their will, serve the Christian peoples."

[By the 1890s, French anti-Semitism seemed to be dying out for lack of public interest and failure of anti-Semites to win government backing. Then, in 1895, the entire situation changed. The French military accused a Jewish army captain, Alfred Dreyfus, of selling secrets to the Germans. His court martial turned into a kangaroo court. When the army could produce no real evidence against the Jewish captain, the prosecution submitted obvious forgeries created by a member of the French Intelligence Service. The military tribunal, anxious to preserve the army's reputation, accepted these brazen falsifications and dutifully convicted Dreyfus of treason. Military, Catholic and pro-monarchist groups blatantly fanned the sudden anti-Semitic frenzy which followed Dreyfus's court marital and conviction. Drumont's La Libre Parole *took the lead in inciting the populace against France's Jews in order to embarrass the liberal Third Republic.*

Before he left for Devil's Island in chains, Dreyfus stood at attention on an army parade ground while his insignia were stripped from his uniform. The jeering crowd shouted for his death and the deaths of all Jews in France. (Note: Theodor Herzl, covering the event for a Viennese newspaper, watched in silence as supposedly civilized Frenchmen spewed out their deep hatred for the Jewish people. Incredibly shaken by the experience, Herzl developed his idea of a Jewish state where Jewry would no longer have to live with Christian hatred and prejudice.)

Dreyfus's family, convinced of his innocence, appealed to anyone of influence to reopen the case in order to reverse the guilty verdict. The new head of the Intelligence Service, Colonel Picquart, reinvestigated and discovered the true spy to be a Hungarian-born military adventurer, womanizer, and heavy gambler named Esterhazy. Clearly, treasonous documents originally claimed to be written by Dreyfus actually had come from Esterhazy's hand. When Picquart presented the incontrovertible evidence of perjury and forgery, he was summarily dismissed from his post and sent abroad. Picquart managed to pass his evidence on to friends who made the materials public. The army now had to deal with a major scandal. For show, a court martial tried Esterhazy for the crime and quickly acquitted him.

In January, 1898, the highly respected writer, Emile Zola, published an open letter to the president of the Republic concerning the case and asserting Dreyfus's innocence. The banner headline, "J'accuse" ("I accuse"), appeared in huge black letters across the front page of L'Aurore. Zola's article dared to name the men who had framed Dreyfus. Soon Zola found himself convicted of libel. Following anti-Semitic riots and death threats, Zola fled for his life to England. That summer the army reopened Dreyfus's case with every intention of protecting its honor and no intention of giving the former captain a fair trial. The French Catholic Church supported the army's stance. Both the army and the Church hoped the embarrassment to the Republic would bring a return of the monarchy. The same testimony and the same lies resulted in yet another conviction in September, 1899. In hopes of calming the growing scandal, the president of the Republic pardoned Dreyfus. Not satisfied with the remaining stain on his military record, Dreyfus asked for a third trial. A court martial board, in 1906, finally declared him not guilty.

With the Dreyfus Affair at an end, the government enacted a law which forced the Church out of state affairs. Open anti-Semitism became much less common, but did continue in the guise of a French royalist movement called Action Française. Headed by Charles Maurras and kept in the public view by the newspaper L'Action française, *this ultra-nationalist group attacked Jews, Protestants, Freemasons and all foreigners. Active until 1944, Action Française directly inspired Vichy France's anti-Semitic legislation during the Second World War.]*

Émile Zola's open letter to the President of the French Republic, accusing the French military of having framed Alfred Dreyfus, January 13, 1898.

The Pale of Settlement.

Chapter X

Czarist Russia and the Jews

By the middle of the 18th century, Poland, the home of almost half the world's Jewish population, was racked by social and religious antagonisms, economic stagnation, and what amounted to political disarray verging on anarchy. Sensing Poland's weakness, surrounding nations looked greedily upon its vast agricultural and natural resources. In 1772, Prussia, Russia, and Austria invaded Poland, each tearing off and annexing chunks of territory. This first Polish Partition was followed by another in 1793. The final partition in 1795 left no rer. .ants whatever of the former Polish kingdom.

Russia's share of Poland contained a large Russian-speaking population and approximately one million Jews. While Czarina Catherine the Great reveled in the almost instantaneous twenty percent increase in Russia's land mass, she was positively dismayed by the number of Jews she now ruled. Not knowing what to do with these alien people and fearing their effect on Russian orthodoxy, she ordered their confinement to the so-called Pale of Settlement, the area which had formerly been part of Poland. Here Jews made up one-fifth of the population with approximately half residing in the cities and towns and half in the rural villages. They were by no means well off. Sixty percent earned a living as artisans; the rest were small merchants, petty traders, shopkeepers, and peddlers.

Within the Pale, Catherine guaranteed the Jews their lives, communal institutions, and the freedom to worship as they pleased. In every other facet of life they faced severe restrictions, including where they could live and travel and how they could earn a living. Following the czarina's death, each czar, with the aid and blessing of his advisors, developed his own plan for dealing with the Jews. Whether the particular course of action decreed attempts to "re-educate" the Jews, re-order their economic "contribution" to the country, force them into dire poverty and starvation, or subject them to deadly pogroms, the czars' ultimate agenda was always the same: convert the Jews to Russian Orthodox Christianity.

In their plans concerning the Jews, the czars, as the formal heads of the Russian Orthodox Church, always worked hand in hand with church officials. In Western Europe, Jews often survived persecution because the medieval kings regularly asserted their independence from papal and church authority. No such separation of church and state existed in Russia. Much as in the Spain of Ferdinand and Isabella, czarist Russia always held to the dictum of one nation, one autocratic czar, and one religion. The bitter history of the Jews under Russian rule reflected both the union between Christian Orthodoxy and monarchy, and complete intolerance toward any minority which did not accept the dominant faith and culture.

---

77. Ivan IV the Terrible

No Jews Allowed in Russia

(1550)

Source: Salo Wittmayer Baron, *A Social and Religious History of the Jews,* Volume XVII (New York: Columbia University Press, 1980), p. 122.

[The Russian monarchy and religious leadership had been strongly anti-Jewish for centuries. Their basic fear was that contact with Jews would contaminate the Russian peasantry and help create "judaized" sects which would challenge the unity of Russian Orthodox Christianity. One such sect, which did develop in the latter half of the 15th century, rejected the Trinity and the divine messiahship of Jesus. Russian leaders ruthlessly destroyed this sect and claimed these heretics had been unduly influenced by Jews and the Jewish religion. Reformation leaders in the German states made similar accusations against the Jews in relation to various heretical Protestant sects.

So paranoid were the Russian czars about Jews that Ivan IV refused to allow even the smallest group temporarily into his lands. When King Sigismund II Augustus of Poland asked Ivan IV to allow a few Jewish traders to enter Russia as part of a commercial treaty between the two nations, Ivan flatly refused.]

It is not convenient to allow Jews to come with their goods to Russia, since many evils result from them. For they import poisonous herbs into Our realm, and lead astray the Russians from Christianity. Therefore, he, the [Polish] King, should no more write about these Jews.

78. Alexander I

Statutes Concerning the Organization of Jews

(December 9, 1804)

Source: Mendes-Flohr and Reinharz, pp. 303–305. P. Levanda, Polnyi khronologicheskii sbornik zakonov i polozhenii kasaiuschikhksia evreev [Complete chronological collection of laws and ordinances relating to Jews] (St. Petersburg, 1874), pp. 53–59. Trans. here by R. Weiss.

[At the beginning of his reign, Alexander I hoped to modernize his Jewish subjects by exposing them to Christianity mixed with Russian education and culture. He also intended to alter their basic economic status. Like Napoleon at about the same time, Alexander seemed to believe that changing how Jews made a living would change them culturally and, eventually, would encourage them to convert and assimilate.

The czar's 1804 Statutes opened public schooling to Jewish children. However, if Jewish parents did not send their children to the Russian schools, the government threatened to build special schools at the Jewish communities' expense. The Statutes attempted to eliminate the Jews' everyday language, Yiddish, by making as many Jews as possible literate in Russian, German or Polish. All Jewish public documents had to be written in one of those three languages. In addition, all Jewish municipal officials had to abandon their traditional costume, including beards, and dress in the German, Polish or Russian fashion.

Jews could belong to only four main economic categories; any Jew who did not fit into the pattern would not be tolerated. The czar, again like Napoleon, encouraged the Jews to take up agriculture. He tried to move them into unpopulated areas of the Pale and permitted them to establish factories and pursue their crafts there. Only when the Jews conformed to all of Alexander's wishes would the government cease forcing them to pay special Jewish taxes.

Finally, a year before his death, Alexander I realized that his Statutes had failed to reform the "alien" Jews. He then took steps to severely reduce the size of the Pale and further restrict where Jews could live within it.]

Numerous complaints have been submitted to us regarding the abuse and exploitation of native farmers and laborers in those provinces in which the Jews are permitted to reside... The following regulations are in accord both with our concern with the true happiness of the Jews and with the needs of the principal inhabitants of those provinces...

I. Education and Language

1. Jewish children may study in all the public schools, secondary schools and universities in Russia, on equal terms with other children.

2. Jewish pupils will neither be required to renounce their religion nor will they be compelled to study subjects which are contrary to their religion...

6. If the Jews refuse, despite all these encouragements, to send their children to public schools, special schools must be built at their expense. For this purpose a special tax will be levied. The study of either Polish, Russian or German MUST be included in the curriculum...

8. All the Jews residing in the Russian Empire, although free to use their native language in all their religious and domestic affairs, are obliged, as of January 1807, to use the Russian, Polish or German language in all public documents, contracts, and bills of sale. Otherwise these documents will not be registered...

In accordance with these regulations, Jews who are elected as members of the municipal councils in the former Polish province, shall, for the sake of order and uniformity, dress in the Russian or Polish fashion; whereas Jews elected to the municipal councils in those Russian provinces in which they are permitted to reside permanently, shall dress in the German fashion. As of the year 1808, a Jew who cannot read and write either Russian, German or Polish, may not be elected to the municipal councils...

10. As of the year 1812, a person who is not literate in one of the previously mentioned languages, may not be appointed to a communal position or to the rabbinate.

II. The Status, Occupations and Rights of the Jews.

11. All the Jews are divided into four classes: (a) farmers, (b) manufacturers and craftsmen, (c) merchants and (d) city dwellers...

13. Jews who are farmers, as well as those who are manufacturers, craftsmen, merchants and city dwellers, are allowed to purchase and own property in the unpopulated areas of the provinces of Lithuania, Belorussia, Little Russia, Kiev, Minsk, Volhynia, Podolia, Astrakhan, Caucasus, Ekaterinoslav, Kherson and Tsabaria. They may sell the land, lease it, bequeath it or bestow it as a gift...

18. No Jew will be compelled to engage in agriculture in the aforementioned provinces, but those who do, shall be exempt from payment of taxes for a period of ten years. This exemption, however, does not extend to debts related to the

purchase of land. They will receive loans which will be repayable after a few years, on terms under which similar loans are given to settlers from abroad…

20. Jews are permitted to establish factories of all kinds, in those provinces in which they are permitted to settle, with the same freedom and on the same basis as that granted to all subjects of Russia…

23. In the aforementioned provinces, Jewish craftsmen may engage in any craft not prohibited by law. Managers of workshops or organizations of craftsmen may not interfere in their rights. They *[i.e., Jews]* are permitted to register as members of a craftsmen's association if it is not in conflict with local regulations…

29. When all the Jews shall evince diligence and industry in agriculture, commerce and manufacturing, the government will take steps to equalize their taxes to those of other Russian citizens.

III. The Duties of the Jews According to their Aforementioned Class.

30. If he is not registered in one of these classes, a Jew will not be tolerated anywhere in Russia. Jews who will not present a written document in standard legal form, certifying their membership in a class will be regarded as vagrants and will be treated according to the full severity of the law…

34. As of January 1, 1807, in Astrakhan, the Caucasus, Little Russia and New Russia, and the other provinces mentioned, no Jew is permitted to hold rented property in any village or settlement. They may not own taverns, pubs or inns, either in their own name or in that of a monitor…

IV. The Legal Status of Jews.

44. …No persons may coerce *[the Jews]* or disturb them in matters of their religious practice, and in civilian life generally, either in word or in deed. Their complaints, whatever they may be, will be heard before the courts and will be satisfied according to the strict letter of the law as it applies to all the citizens of Russia…

79.   Nicholas I

Statutes Regarding the Military Service of Jews

(August 26, 1827)

Source: Mendes-Flohr and Reinharz, pp. 305–306. P. Levanda, Polnyi, pp. 193–200. Trans. here by R. Weiss.

[Two days after Nicholas I ascended the throne, the "Decembrist" revolt, an insurrection by a group of military conspirators, shook the nation. Although he quelled the uprising, the thwarted rebellion left a permanent mark on Nicholas's reign. Soon known as the "Iron Czar," Nicholas I ruled Russia according to his rigid principles of "Orthodoxy, Autocracy and Nationalism."

The army became the czar's primary tool for maintaining strict discipline and peace within Russia's borders. Each province in the kingdom had to provide a certain number of conscripts eighteen years or older to serve for a period of twenty-five years. In 1827, Nicholas and his advisors developed a diabolically clever plan that would not only increase the number of new army recruits and expose a large number of Jews to Christianizing Russian influence, but would also work to destroy the cohesive fabric of every Jewish community in the Pale.

The Jewish Military Service Statutes made boys as young as twelve eligible for conscription. The law required Jewish communal leaders to turn the full quota of children over to military authorities. If they failed to do so, they or their own sons could be taken by force for military duty. Jewish kidnappers known as "Khappers"— the Pale's equivalent of bounty hunters—snatched boys as young as eight off the streets to meet the communities' quotas. Wealthier families bought exemption for their boys by replacing them with the sons of the poor. The only protection from the army was being married. Consequently, lads of six or seven often stood under the "chuppah" or wedding canopy with their equally young brides before heading off to the cheder (elementary Hebrew school) or out to play.

Children who were sent to the army faced from six to ten years in "preparatory institutions" where they were indoctrinated and often beaten and starved until they accepted baptism. Many of the children died on the forced marches from home to the "institutions." Those who entered the army at eighteen and had managed to avoid conversion encountered severe discrimination in their military units. Few of these men returned to their families after a quarter century or more of service.]

I. General Rules Applying to the Jewish People.

1. Upon being called to military service, Jews shall fulfill their obligation in a manner identical to that of other citizens who are members of that class which is required to serve in the armed forces...

II. Manner of Fulfilling Military Draft Obligations.

6. If, at the time of the call to service, it is generally permitted to substitute a sum of money for a recruit, this privilege shall be extended to Jews under the following conditions: (a) The Jewish community owes no back taxes to the government; (b) The community is not in debt to other communities or individuals...

8. Jews presented by the community for the purpose of military service must be no younger than twelve and no older than twenty-five years of age...

III.

13. The Jews of each province must fill their quota of recruits independently of the Gentile population thereof...

IV.

24. The responsibility for fulfilling the military obligations falls upon the Jewish communities themselves. They shall follow the dictates of the appropriate provincial authority...

Exemptions:

58. In addition to merchants, rabbis also are exempt from military service. They must show proper documents proving their title...

62. Jewish youths who are enrolled in general schools for a minimum of three years and who perform adequately and those apprenticed to Gentile artisans are exempt from military service for the duration of their studies...

64. Jews who have settled and who work upon land designated for agricultural purposes are exempt...

X. The Assignment of Jews to Various Branches of the Military.

74. Jewish minors—those under 18—shall be sent to preparatory institutions for military training *[i.e., cantonist units]*.

75. Jews from the age of eighteen and upwards shall be assigned to active military duty according to their physical condition, as ordered by the military command.

XI. Jews Evading the Draft.

87. Whoever discloses the names of those who hide a Jew escaping the draft, shall receive a reward in the sum of one hundred rubles from the treasury…

90. For the purpose of release from the draft, only time spent in active duty after the age of eighteen shall be taken into account.

91. Jews in active military duty are permitted to observe their religious customs during their SPARE TIME. This is in accordance with the law of the land concerning accepted religions. Commanding officers shall protect the Jews from disturbances or abuses which may be caused by their religious affiliation.

80. Nicholas I

Jew Laws in Russia

(1835)

Source: Ackerman, pp. 365–366. From Shornik Levanda. Zakarov o Yevreyakh ot 1649 do 1873 (Compendium of the laws relating to Jews from 1649 to 1873).

[The 1835 laws pertaining to the Jews repeated many of the provisions of Alexander I's Statutes issued over thirty years earlier. The legislation tried to eliminate Yiddish in Jewish public documents and again encouraged placing Jewish children in government-run Christian schools.

Generations before the Polish Partitions, Jewish families had owned and run taverns and inns. Indeed, Jews often had a virtual monopoly on the liquor trade which helped them survive, especially in times of severe persecution and economic hardship. Alexander I tried to drive them out in favor of Christian control of the business. Apparently, by Nicholas's time, peasants were deeply in debt to Jewish tavern owners, because, when they were unable to pay, they inevitably bought their drinks on credit. Nicholas summarily outlawed the sale of alcohol on anything but a cash basis. In 1861, the Russian government nationalized the liquor trade and finally forced the Jews out of the business.]

Jews in the Western districts may not settle in towns which are not at least 50 miles removed from the border.

Jews may not employ Christians as domestic servants.

Jews must use Russian or the language of their district in all official documents—under no circumstances may they use the Jewish language.

Jews engaged in legal commerce may not sell wine or other intoxicating beverages for credit on pain of cancellation of the debt.

Jewish merchants of the First Guild may leave the Pale of Settlement to attend fairs, but they may remain in the city only for the duration of the fair.

Jewish manufacturers who wish to ship products to the interior districts must affix their special sign on the goods.

Jewish craftsmen may register…in the places of their residence provided such a procedure is not contrary to the privileges granted the several cities.

Within the Pale of Settlement Jews may rent land…without thereby being classified as farmers…

The Jews are accounted members of the community of the city in which they live; in all affairs pertaining to them and for the distribution of taxes and other obligations which are theirs in particular let them appoint 3–5 representatives who shall constitute the Kahal.

The members of the Kahal shall be chosen only from among those Jews who can read and write Russian or the language used in that locality for official documents. The members of the Kahal shall serve with the approval of the District Officer for a period of three years.

It is forbidden to congregate in synagogues or Houses of Study for any purpose other than prayer or the practice of religious ceremonies.

Jewish children may be admitted to government schools in those places where their parents have the right of residence.

Upon enrolling their children in a Christian school Jews must declare their religion. Children who are accepted to those schools will not be forced to convert nor will they be compelled to attend classes in the Christian religion.

Jews who earn the degree of Doctor with the approval of the Minister of Education concerning their special abilities are eligible for appointment as teachers and civil servants, but only with the assent of higher authorities.

81. Alexander III

The May Laws

(May 3, 1882)

Source: Mendes-Flohr and Reinharz, p. 309. Nedelnaya kronica voskhoda, no. 20 (May 15, 1882), pp. 534–535. Trans. here by R. Weiss.

[When Alexander II succeeded Nicholas I as czar of all the Russias, few Jews shed any tears of grief. Russian Christians, too, had suffered because of Nicholas's unrelenting policies. The country as a whole was demoralized mentally and physi-

cally, and bankrupt militarily. Alexander was determined to reverse these trends with an open and enlightened policy toward both the peasantry and the Jews.

In 1861, the czar freed Russia's 40 million serfs and for the first time set up a jury system to try legal cases. The army could no longer conscript Jewish children. Jews now entered Russian schools and universities with markedly fewer restrictions than in the past. Some Jews became lawyers and doctors with practices that included Christian clients. The government permitted a number of privileged Jews to leave the Pale and settle in Russia's major cities. Finally, it seemed as if the winds of freedom and change had reached the steppes and swept inward to Moscow and beyond.

By the mid-1860s, Russia began to experience a revolution of rising expectations. Reform, so welcome in the beginning of Alexander's reign, was not proceeding quickly enough to satisfy some who soon became secret revolutionaries. Various nationality groups voiced their discontent, and the Polish people openly, but unsuccessfully, revolted against czarist rule.

Alexander was angered and frightened. He halted his reform measures and encouraged a strong Russian nationalist movement to counter the stirrings of the minorities. He ordered all the Jews back to the Pale and reinstituted many of their former disabilities. In 1881, a group of revolutionaries assassinated the czar by tossing a bomb under his passing carriage.

If the conspirators had hoped to speed up Russian reforms by eliminating Alexander II, they were grievously mistaken. The dead czar's son, Alexander III, had often disagreed with his father's dabblings in liberalism, and the assassination only hardened the new czar's resolve to utterly destroy any opposition to Russian autocracy. In this he had the unflagging advice and aid of a man who was a lay leader of the Orthodox Church, the Procurator of the Holy Synod, and an extreme reactionary, Konstantin Pobedonostsev.

Pobedonostsev urged the czar to suppress any possible threat to national unity, including cultural differences of non-Russian nationalities and any religious movements other than Orthodox Christianity. Under the Procurator's tutelage, Orthodoxy itself would preach faithful and unquestioning obedience to the "Little Father" or czar. Jews were now triply suspect for being not only culturally foreign and non-Orthodox, but also for being a people traditionally despised by Russians as the faithless murderers of Christ. In addition, when the czar learned that a Jewish woman had been involved in the conspiracy which led to Alexander II's death, his furious hatred for the Jews knew no bounds.

In the spring of 1881, full-scale, organized, government-directed riots against the Jews began in the Ukraine and spread to the rest of the Pale. These pogroms always followed the same pattern. Drunken crowds of local men would noisily make their way to the Jewish sections of town. They then systematically looted and burned Jewish homes and businesses, raped Jewish women, and killed indiscriminately. The police were inevitably absent or "reluctant" to use sufficient force to quell the riots. The authorities allowed the wild mobs to continue for two or three days. Finally, carrying firearms, the police ended the pogrom.

In August, 1881, the czar blamed the Jews themselves for the pogroms, claiming the murderous riots were spontaneous uprisings against intolerable Jewish exploitation. Alexander III issued a Ukase or imperial order calling for a full investigation of the Jews and their economically destructive activities.

Under the leadership of the Minister of the Interior, Ignatiev, the investigation report recommended a slow strangulation of Russia's Jewish communities. On May 3, 1882, the czar's government issued a set of "temporary" measures against the Jews. Far from transitory, the May Laws remained in effect until the beginning of the First World War in 1914. The laws, at first, did not seem much worse than other anti-Jewish legislation enacted in the past. Their implementation, however, brought disaster to the Pale's Jews.

Jews could not live outside of cities and larger townships. Government edicts reclassified small towns as rural villages where the May Laws forbad Jews to live. Overnight Jewish families lost their property, goods, and the ability to make a living. They crowded into the larger cities where, desperately, they tried to eke out an existence. Within little more than a decade, 40 percent of Russia's Jewry became paupers. The May Laws proceeded as part of Pobedonostsev's plan to eliminate the Jews. His equation was terrifyingly simple: one-third would starve to death, one-third would accept Orthodox Christianity to end finally the bitter poverty and persecution, and one-third of the Jews would emigrate.]

The Council of Ministers, having heard the presentation made by the Minister of Internal Affairs, regarding the execution of the Temporary Regulations regarding the Jews has concluded as follows:

1. As a temporary measure, and until a general re-examination of the laws pertaining to the Jews takes place by set order, it is henceforth forbidden for Jews to settle outside the cities and townships. Existing Jewish settlements which are engaged in agricultural work are exempted [from this ban].

2. The registration of property and mortgages in the name of Jews is to be halted temporarily; the approval of the leasing by Jews of real estate beyond the

precincts of the cities and townships is also to be halted temporarily. Jews are also prohibited from administering such properties.

3. It is forbidden for Jews to engage in commerce on Sundays and Christian holidays...

4. The regulations contained in paragraphs one through three apply to those provinces in which the Jews permanently reside.

The Kishinev Pogrom

Alexander III's death and his son's coronation in no way ended the Jews' misery. The last Russian czar, Nicholas II, was a weak, highly superstitious man who was unable to deal effectively with his subjects' rising discontent. His advisors, especially Minister of Interior Vyacheslav Von Plevhe, counseled Nicholas to provide scapegoats for the peasants' misery. At Von Plevhe's instigation, pogroms against the Jews became more widespread and violent. One of the most infamous pogroms took place in the Bessarabian city of Kishinev (Kishineff) on April 6–8, 1903.

82. *A Description of the Kishinev Pogrom*

(April 6–8, 1903)

Source: "The Kishineff Outbreak," *New York Times*, May 11, 1903, page 3.

[Several days before Easter in 1903, rumors spread through the Kishinev area that Jews, preparing for the "Jewish Easter" (Passover) had murdered a young Christian man. The local newspaper, Bessarabetz, *headed by its rabidly anti-Semitic publisher, Kroushevan, printed crude and inflammatory articles connecting the supposed ritual murder and Kishinev's Jews. Several leaders of the Jewish community, which made up about one-third of the city's 140,000 people, urgently appealed to Governor Von Raaben for help. He refused to intervene.*

For three days, beginning on Easter Sunday, violent mobs attacked the Jews and whatever belonged to them. On April 24, several Russian newspapers published accounts of the pogrom. People all over the world read of the anti-Jewish riots, and many nations sent official protests to the czar. At that point, Nicholas's government formally denied that any massacre had taken place. On May 11, the New York Times *printed an English translation of one of the Russian articles about the pogrom published before the government denial.]*

The Central Committee for the relief of the Kishineff sufferers said in a statement issued last night:

"The following from St. Petersburg Vuedemosti is an answer to the Russian official denial of the anti-Jewish riots in Kishineff, offering a remarkable picture of the outbreak. The Vuedemosti is subjected to strict censorship and therefore the account must be read in light of what the Government permitted to be published before it decided that no riot had taken place."

The account published on April 24 said:

"Since incendiary articles against the Jews were published in the *Bessarabetz, Novoye* and *Swiet,* rumors have been current that an anti-Jewish outbreak was imminent. The Moldavians are ordinarily, however, so peaceful that no credence was given these reports.

"In Kishineff all was quiet until Easter Sunday, when at noon *[later reports proved that rioting actually began just after sunrise]* the crowd on the Chuplinsky place, where amusement and other booths had been erected, became excited. Several Jews, who came to watch the Christians enjoying themselves, were attacked. They ran away. The cry 'Kill the Jews!' was raised, and the mob, which swelled instantly, followed in hot pursuit, particularly through Alexandrowsky Street to the new bazaar, where a fearful riot took place.

"It is impossible to account the amount of goods destroyed in a few hours. The 'hurrahs' of the rioters and the pitiful cries of the victims filled the air—wherever a Jew was met he was savagely beaten into insensibility. One Jew was dragged from a street car and beaten until the mob thought he was dead. The air was filled with feathers from torn bedding. About 3 o'clock in the afternoon the rioters were signaling and whistling in the principal streets. The miscreants began there by breaking windows.

"At nightfall quiet was restored, at least in the centre of the city, and it was presumed that the disturbance was at an end. Police, troops, and mounted gendarmes patrolled the streets, but the real assault only began on Monday morning, when armed with axes and crowbars, the mob set upon its work of destruction, damaging the best houses and shops, clothing themselves in pillaged clothing and carrying away huge bundles of loot.

"The mob ignored the order of the patrols and the police to disperse, and continued to rob, destroy and kill. Every Jewish household was broken into and the unfortunate Jews in their terror endeavored to hide in cellars and under roofs. The mob entered the synagogues, desecrated the biggest house of worship, and defiled the scrolls of the law.

"The conduct of the intelligent Christians was disgraceful. They made no attempt to check the rioting. They simply walked around enjoying the frightful 'sport.'

"On Tuesday, the third day, when it became known that the troops had received orders to shoot, the rioting ceased. The Jews then came out of their houses. The streets were piled up with the debris and they presented a horrible appearance. The big Jewish Hospital is filled with dead and wounded. Some bodies are mutilated beyond identification. From a distance there could be heard heart-rending groans and pitiable wailings of widows and orphans. The misery of the Jews is indescribable. There is an actual famine. The prices of all living commodities have gone up. Relief is being organized."

The Protocols of the Elders of Zion

In addition to secretly instigating pogroms as a means of heading off revolution, the czar's government also tried to prove that the hated Jews were directly behind Russia's revolutionary movements. Nicholas's advisors claimed to have discovered a copy of "The Protocols of the Elders of Zion" which proved that Jewish leaders all over the world were directing a conspiracy to destroy Christian civilization. Since the elders supposedly knew that the best form of government was one led by a strongly autocratic czar, they were making plans to spread liberalism, economic dislocation, and socialist discontent to topple Nicholas II.

The Protocols of the Elders of Zion came to Russia by a complex and circuitous route which began in 1864. In that year a French lawyer named Maurice Joly published a political satire criticizing Napoleon III. Entitled "Dialogues in Hell," Joly's work created an imaginary conversation between Machiavelli and the French liberal, Montesquieu. The French government banned the satire and jailed Joly, who later committed suicide. Two years later, a German anti-Semite, Hermann Gödsche, wrote a novel which contained a chapter called "The Jewish Cemetery in Prague and the Council of Representatives of the Twelve Tribes of Israel." Gödsche plagiarized much of Joly's "Dialogues," using the same themes but having the main character discuss a Jewish plot to control the world. Later Gödsche rewrote "The Jewish Cemetery," not as part of a fictional work, but as a true recounting of a rabbi's speech to a clandestine meeting of Jewish elders.

Two members of the Russian secret police in Paris copied the "Rabbi's Speech," turning it into "The Protocols of the Elders of Zion." They published it in 1905 in

Russia as part of a book entitled "The Enemy of the Human Race." This spurious account of a Jewish plot to destroy Christianity and control the world was meant to reinforce Czar Nicholas II's anti-Semitic beliefs and to keep him from granting any concession to those who wanted to modernize and liberalize Russia.

In the next two decades the Protocols spread through Europe and were published in the United States by Henry Ford in his anti-Semitic *Dearborn Independent*. The Nazis, gleefully making note of Ford's actions, used the Protocols as part of their rationale for destroying European Jewry. Even today, people who wish to attack Jews and Zionism still claim the Protocols are a true account of Zionist plans to control the world.

---

83. *The Protocols of the Meetings of the Learned Elders of Zion*

(1905)

Source: Herman Bernstein, *The Truth About "The Protocols of Zion,"* (New York: Covici, Friede Publishers, 1935), pp. 295–359.

Protocol No. 1

…What I am about to set forth, then, is our system from the two points of view, that of ourselves and that of the *goyim [i.e., non-Jews]*…

Whether a State exhausts itself in its own convulsions, whether its internal discord brings it under the power of external foes—in any case it can be accounted irretrievably lost: it is in our power. The despotism of Capital, which is entirely in our hands, reaches out to it a straw that the State, willy-nilly, must take hold of: if not—it goes to the bottom…

Our power in the present tottering condition of all forms of power will be more invincible than any other, because it will remain invisible until the moment when it has gained such strength that no cunning can any longer undermine it…

…It must be understood that the might of a mob is blind… members of the mob…though they should be as a genius for wisdom, yet having no understanding of the political, cannot come forward as leaders of the mob without bringing the whole nation to ruin.

Only one trained from childhood for independent rule *[meaning, of course, the czar]* can have understanding of the words that can be made up of the political alphabet…

It is only with a despotic ruler that plans can be elaborated extensively and clearly…a satisfactory form of government for any country is one that concentrates in the hands of one responsible person. Without an absolute despotism there can be no existence for civilisation which is carried on not by the masses but by their guide, whosoever that person may be. The mob is a savage and displays its savagery at every opportunity. The moment the mob seizes freedom in its hands it quickly turns to anarchy, which in itself is the highest degree of savagery...

In all corners of the earth the words "Liberty, Equality, Fraternity" brought to our ranks...whole legions who bore our banners with enthusiasm. And all the time these words were canker-worms at work boring into the well-being of the *goyim*, putting an end everywhere to peace, quiet, solidarity and destroying all the foundations of the *goy* States. As you will see later, this helped us to our triumph; it gave us the possibility, among other things, of getting into our hands the master card—the destruction of the privileges, or in other words of the very existence of the aristocracy of the *goyim*, that class which was the only defence peoples and counties had against us...

The abstraction of freedom has enabled us to persuade the mob in all countries that their government is nothing but the steward of the people who are the owners of the country, and that the steward may be replaced like a worn-out glove.

It is this possibility of replacing the representatives of the people which has placed them at our disposal, and, as it were, given us the power of appointment.

Protocol No. 2

...war will...be brought on to the economic ground, where the nations will not fail to perceive in the assistance we give the strength of our predominance...

In the hands of the States of to-day there is a great force that creates the movement of thought in the people, and that is the Press... It is in the Press that the triumph of freedom of speech finds its incarnation. But the *goyim* States have not known how to make use of this force; and it has fallen into our hands...

Protocol No. 3

...Nowadays, with the destruction of the aristocracy, the people have fallen into the grips of merciless money-grinding scoundrels who have laid a pitiless and cruel yoke upon the necks of the workers.

We appear on the scene as alleged saviours of the worker from this oppression when we propose to him to enter the ranks of our fighting forces—Socialists, Anarchists, Communists—to whom we always give support in accordance with an alleged brotherly rule (for the solidarity of all humanity) of our social masonry. The aristocracy, which enjoyed by law the labour of the workers, was interested in seeing that the workers were well fed, healthy and strong. We are interested in just the opposite—in the diminution, the killing out of the *goyim*...

...We shall create by all the secret subterranean methods open to us and with the aid of gold, which is all in our hands, a universal economic crisis whereby we shall throw upon the streets whole mobs of workers simultaneously in all the countries of Europe...

Protocol No. 4

...With...faith...a people might be governed by a wardship of parishes, and would walk contentedly and humbly under the guiding hand of its spiritual pastor submitting to the dispositions of God upon earth. This is the reason why it is indispensable for us to undermine all faith, to tear out of the minds of the *goyim* the very principle of Godhead and the spirit, and to put in its place arithmetical calculations and material needs...

Protocol No. 5

...In order to put public opinion into our hands we must bring it into a state of bewilderment by giving expression from all sides to so many contradictory opinions and for such length of time as will suffice to make the *goyim* lose their heads in the labyrinth and come to see that the best thing is to have no opinion of any kind in matters political, which it is not given to the public to understand, because they are understood only by him who guides the public. This is the first secret.

The second secret requisite for the success of our government is comprised in the following: To multiply to such an extent national failings, habits, passions, conditions of civil life, that it will be impossible for anyone to know where he is in the resulting chaos, so that the people in consequence will fail to understand one another. This measure will also serve us in another way, namely, to sow discord in all parties, to dislocate all collective forces which are still unwilling to submit to us, and to discourage any kind of personal initiative which might in any degree hinder our affair. There is nothing more dangerous than personal initiative... By all these means we shall so wear down the *goyim* that they will be compelled to offer us international power of a nature that by its position will enable us without any violence gradually to absorb all the State forces of the world and to form a Super-Government...

Protocol No. 6

...It is essential...for us at whatever cost to deprive them *[the aristocracy]* of their land...

...What we want is that industry should drain off from the land both labour and capital and by means of speculation transfer into our hands all the money in the world, and thereby throw all the *goyim* into the ranks of the proletariat. Then the *goyim* will bow down before us, if for no other reason but to get the right to exist...

Protocol No. 7

...In a word, to sum up our system of keeping the governments of the *goyim* in Europe in check, we shall show our strength to one of them by terrorist attempts and to all, if we allow the possibility of a general rising against us, we shall respond with the guns of America or China or Japan.

Protocol No. 8

...We shall surround our government with a whole world of economists. That is the reason why economic sciences form the principal subject of the teaching given to the Jews. Around us again will be a whole constellation of bankers, industrialists, capitalists and—the main thing—millionaires, because in substance everything will be settled by the question of figures...

Protocol No. 9

...Nowadays, if any States raise a protest against us it is only *pro forma* at our discretion and by our direction, for their anti-Semitism is indispensable to us for the management of our lesser brethren...

...And the weapons in our hands are limitless ambitions, burning greediness, merciless vengeance, hatred and malice.

It is from us that the all-engulfing terror proceeds...

...We have fooled, bemused and corrupted the youth of the *goyim* by rearing them in principles and theories which are known to us to be false although it is by us that they have been inculcated...

Protocol No. 10

...we must have everybody vote without distinction of classes and qualifications, in order to establish an absolute majority... In this way, by inculcating in all a sense of self-importance, we shall destroy among the *goyim* the importance of the family and its educational value...

Liberalism produced Constitutional States, which took the place of the only safeguard of the *goyim*, namely, Despotism...

...it is indispensable...to utterly exhaust humanity with dissension, hatred, struggle, envy and even by the use of torture, by starvation, BY THE INOCULATION

OF DISEASES, by want, so that the *goyim* see no other issue than to take refuge in our complete sovereignty in money and in all else...

Protocol No. 11

...God has granted to us, His Chosen People, the gift of the dispersion, and in this which appears in all eyes to be our weakness, has come forth all our strength, which has now brought us to the threshold of sovereignty over all the world...

Protocol No. 12

...Literature and journalism are two of the most important educative forces, and therefore our government will become proprietor of the majority of the journals...

Protocol No. 14

When we come into our kingdom it will be undesirable for us that there should exist any other religion than ours of the One God... We must therefore sweep away all other forms of belief...

Protocol No. 15

...power...is attained only by such a majestic inflexibility of might as shall carry on its face the emblems of inviolability from mystical causes—from the choice of God. Such was, until recent times, the Russian autocracy, the one and only serious foe we had in the world, without counting the Papacy...

Protocol No. 16

In order to effect the destruction of all collective forces except ours we shall emasculate the first stage of collectivism—the universities...

Protocol No. 17

We have long past taken care to discredit the priesthood of the *goyim*... Day by day its influence on the peoples of the world is falling lower. Freedom of conscience has been declared everywhere, so that now only years divide us from the moment of the complete wrecking of that Christian religion: as to other religions we shall have still less difficulty in dealing with them...

Protocol No. 22

In our hands is the greatest power of our day—gold: in two days we can procure for our storehouses any quantity we may please...

German soldiers emptying the Warsaw Ghetto in 1943.

Section Five

Change, Hope, and Tragedy

The Challenges of Communism, Zionism, and Nazism

E uropean Jewry experienced more change—both disastrous and triumphant—in the first fifty years of the 20th century than at any other time in the history of the Diaspora. Beginning in 1914, the First World War spread death and destruction throughout Europe and exposed the utter bankruptcy of czarist autocracy in Russia. Finally, in March, 1917, revolutionaries overthrew Nicholas II and set up a Provisional government headed by Alexander Kerensky, a moderate socialist. The new regime immediately emancipated Russia's Jews and guaranteed them full civil rights, religious freedom, and legal protection. The Jews rejoiced that pogroms and persecution had, at last, come to an end. Eight months later, however, radical Bolsheviks led by Lenin ousted Kerensky and imposed a communist dictatorship of the proletariat.

The new Bolshevik state claimed all people, including Jews, were equal and had equal rights. Nevertheless, it forcibly destroyed Jewish religious institutions and worked to wipe out all vestiges of Yiddish culture. As a result, the Russian Revolution, which had begun with such promise for Europe's largest and most persecuted Jewish community, resulted in almost total religious and cultural disintegration.

While Soviet Jews struggled to maintain their traditions, Zionists in the west continued working to establish a Jewish homeland. Emancipation had not eliminated anti-Semitism. The need for a safe haven from persecution was as real in the 20th century as it had been in the Middle Ages. In 1917, Great Britain made the Zionist dream seem truly possible when it publicly promised to support a national home for Jews in Palestine. The League of Nations later gave the British control of that area, instructing His Majesty's government to encourage Jewish immigration. Great Britain also agreed to set up political and economic institutions to facilitate the growth and development of the Jewish homeland while also protecting the rights of Palestine's Arab citizens.

Soon the Arabs grew fearful of the expanding Jewish presence in Palestine. They attacked Jewish agricultural settlements and carried out riots and general strikes in the cities. Slowly Britain abandoned its pro-Jewish policies and began to support the Arab side of the dispute. The once bright hope of a homeland and refuge for all persecuted Jews suddenly began to fade. In 1939, the British government announced the imminent end of all Jewish immigration to Palestine. The timing could not have been worse. During the next six years, Europe's Jews would need a safe haven more than at any other time in their long history.

Gentiles as well as Jews now refer to those war years between 1939 and 1945 as the "Holocaust." Under the aegis of National Socialism, Germany and its leaders set out to murder every Jew in Europe. They very nearly succeeded.

A Berlin synagogue, set afire on *Kristallnacht.*

Alexander Kerensky.

Chapter XI

The Russian and Bolshevik Revolutions
and the Jews

Czarist autocracy, with its single-minded goal of blocking any liberal reform, set the stage for a tragic drama which led to massive social, political, economic, and religious upheaval in Russia. By the beginning of the twentieth century, the moribund monarchy and aristocracy despotically ruled a country ripe for revolution. Peasants were little better off than they had been as serfs and a new, growing class of urban workers suffered under unrelenting exploitation. Approximately forty percent of Russia's Jews eked out a living as industrial workers, mainly in textile factories in the Pale. To work toward bettering the dehumanizing conditions, thousands joined the Jewish-Socialist Bund.

The Bund was a unique combination of strike-organizing labor union, Yiddish cultural society, and self-help organization. Its main objectives were the peaceful attainment of higher wages and better working conditions, plus the strengthening of the traditional Jewish communal spirit. Few of the Bund's members were religiously devout; most considered themselves "freethinkers." All identified strongly with the Jewish people.

Many Jews who were less bound by tradition joined more radical organizations, such as the Social Democratic Party. Most of this group's Jewish members belonged to the Menshevik faction, although several proved to be very influential on the Bolshevik side. These Jews, like the founder of communism, Karl Marx, had discarded any feelings toward or connections with Judaism and the Jewish people. Among the early Bolshevik leaders were Leon Trotsky, Lev Borisovich Kamenev, and Grigori Evseyevich Zinoviev, who denied all affiliation with their Jewish backgrounds. They placed their loyalties with their party, the Russian proletariat, and all the oppressed workers of the world. For them, and for fellow revolutionaries like Lenin and Stalin, the answer to Jewish suffering was the demolition of industrial capitalism, the elimination of the Russian monarchy (by violent means, if necessary), and the abandonment of all religious beliefs.

While both factions of the Social Democratic Party plotted the czar's downfall, Nicholas II and his officials hunted down and murdered or exiled many of the revolutionaries. At the same time, they remained unresponsive to the workers' and peasants' increasingly fervent pleas for reform. On Sunday, January 21, 1905, a huge group of workers and their families gathered and marched peacefully to the Winter Palace in St. Petersburg. Carrying portraits of the czar and singing Russian Orthodox hymns, they had come to present a humble petition asking for their monarch's help. Nicholas was not there to receive them; he and his family had quietly left the palace several days before. Nervous soldiers guarding the palace inexplicably and with no warning opened fire on the crowd, massacring hundreds. "Bloody Sunday," as protesters called this tragedy, plus Russia's humiliating defeat in the Russo-Japanese War of the same year, stunned the nation and shook the common people's faith in their "Little Father." Russia's revolutionaries deepened their resolve to eliminate the monarchy and to create in its wake a socialist, egalitarian society.

Nicholas responded to the growing revolutionary fever by refusing to initiate any real changes. He did agree to a parliament or Duma, but continually frustrated any of its attempts at reform. He instead chose to misdirect his subjects' attention. Often this strategy included violence directed specifically at the Jews. The government encouraged the formation and actions of a group called the Black Hundreds. These lawless mobs terrorized the countryside with countless bloody pogroms against Jewish communities in the Pale. The Union of the Russian People, begun in 1905, was another counterrevolutionary group with semi-official links to czarist authorities. While they were quick to blame all of Russia's problems on "disloyal" minorities such as the Poles, Armenians, Latvians, and Finns, Jews soon became their favorite targets. These tactics managed to delay needed reforms until Nicholas's participation in the First World War finally sealed the monarchy's fate.

The Kaiser's war machine, vastly superior to the poorly supplied and often ineptly led czarist forces, enabled Germany to inflict massive destruction on the hapless Russian army. The Bolsheviks took full advantage of the ensuing chaos to turn soldiers against their officers and the people against government authority. The Germans themselves encouraged the situation by transporting many Bolsheviks who had been in exile back to their homeland. Lenin was one of these men and, upon his return, he repeatedly told the people that communism offered what they wanted most: peace, bread, and land.

Finally, in March 1917, a coalition of socialist groups overthrew Nicholas II and set up a Provisional Government led by the moderate Alexander Kerensky. Russian Jews, who had suffered grievously under the czars, enthusiastically welcomed and supported the new regime. One of the Provisional Government's first acts in office was the removal of all disabilities based on race and religion. For the first time in Russian history, Jews enjoyed all the rights and privileges of equal citizenship.

Kerensky chose to continue Russia's participation in the war, in large part due to secret treaty obligations and promises of war spoils, which included possible annexation of Constantinople and the Dardanelles. With the drain caused by the war, constant disagreement among the political parties and continued Bolshevik agitation, Kerensky was unable to stem the growing anarchy which gripped the country. In November 1917, the Bolsheviks seized power by ousting the Provisional Government and immediately set up a "dictatorship of the proletariat" which they called the Russian Soviet Republic.

Seeking peace in order to consolidate and secure the revolution, the communists broke with the Allies and signed the Treaty of Brest-Litovsk with the Germans. In return for an end to hostilities, the Kaiser's government levied a staggering indemnity and forced the Soviets to give up a huge section of Russia's territory in Eastern Europe. The harsh treaty, however, brought no peace to the new communist republic. The Russian aristocracy, including most of the army's officers and those who supported the monarchy, rebelled against Bolshevik rule. The "white" armies, supported by the Allies who bitterly resented Lenin's pulling out of the war, waged a bloody two-year civil war against the "red" communist regime.

The "whites," including the infamous General Anton Ivanovich Denikin and the Ukrainian guerilla leader Semion Petliura, were fanatically anti-Semitic. They hated Jews not only because Russians traditionally detested the Jewish people, but also because they identified Jews with leftist socialism and the Bolshevik cause. At least 70,000 Jews died during the hundreds of "white"-led pogroms which swept

European Russia from 1919 to 1921. The Bolshevik forces eventually defeated the White Armies, thanks to a brilliant and ruthless military campaign directed by Leon Trotsky. Lenin was now free to carry out his plans to remake Russia and its people in the communist image. Jews, who had gained religious and civil equality under Kerensky's Provisional Government, now faced communal and ethnic dissolution at the hands of the Bolsheviks.

---

84.   The Provisional Government

Emancipation by the March Revolution

(April 2, 1917)

Source: Mahler, pp. 63–65.

[Unlike Lenin and the Bolsheviks who unswervingly centered their attention on complete social revolution, the moderate socialist-led Provisional Government tried to remedy specific problems associated with generations of czarist misrule. In doing so, Alexander Kerensky and his supporters attempted to give Russia a stable basis for free, democratic government. One of their first priorities was to emancipate politically and socially all the people formerly ruled by Nicholas II. Russia's Jews enthusiastically welcomed the new laws which directly countered all the disabilities placed upon them by the oppressive czarist regimes.

Kerensky's administration, however, attempted to unite all the contentious political factions in the socialist coalition, while, at the same time, continuing to fight the First World War. This difficult task was made utterly impossible by the Bolsheviks' continued propaganda and anti-government agitation. At just the opportune moment, the Bolsheviks overthrew the government, and captured and executed most of the Provisional leaders. Somehow, Kerensky managed to escape. He carried with him into exile Russia's hopes for freedom and a truly democratic political system.]

Whereas it is our unshakable conviction that in a free country all citizens should be equal before the law, and that the conscience of the people cannot acquiesce in legal restrictions against particular citizens on account of their religion and origin,

The Provisional Government has decreed:

All restrictions on the rights of Russian citizens which had been enacted by existing laws on account of their belonging to any creed, confession or nationality, shall be abolished.

In accordance with this:

I. All laws shall be abolished which have been in force both throughout the entire territory of Russia, as well as in any of her particular localities, and which enacted restrictions depending on the adherence of Russian citizens to any creed, confession or nationality, relating to:

1) settlement, (domicile) and freedom of movement;

2) acquisition of the right of ownership and other property rights on all kinds of movable and immovable goods as well as the disposal, use and administration of those goods and the giving or receiving of them as security;

3) any engaging in crafts, commerce and industry including mining as well as participation in government contracts, deliveries and public auctions;

4) participation in stock companies and other commercial industrial companies and associations as well as the occupation of all kinds of positions in those companies and associations either by election or by hiring;

5) hiring servants, salesmen, overseers, workmen and engaging of crafts apprentices;

6) entering of government services, civil and military alike, the rules and conditions of promotion therein, participation in elections to local self-government bodies and to all kinds of communal bodies, the occupation of all kinds of posts in government and communal institutions and the fulfillment of all duties attached to such offices;

7) entering educational institutions of all kinds, private, community and government owned alike, the attendance of courses therein and benefits from stipends, as well as engaging in instruction and education;

8) fulfillment of duties of guardians, trustees and jurymen;

9) use of languages and dialects, other than Russian in the management of private associations, in teaching in educational institutions of any kind and in the keeping of commercial books...

85. Council of People's Commissars

Attacking Anti-Semitism

(July 27, 1918)

Source: Lionel Kochan, ed., *The Jews in Soviet Russia Since 1917* (London: Oxford University Press, 1970) p. 294. As taken from Bernard D. Weinryb, "Antisemitism in Soviet Russia."

[Following Lenin's coup, counterrevolutionary armies made up of the nobility and the monarchists rebelled against the new Communist regime and plunged Russia into a disastrous civil war. The "white" forces used hatred of the Jews as a means

to attract the peasants' support. Wherever the armies went, bloody pogroms oc-
curred. The Bolsheviks strongly condemned anti-Semitism, labelling it an archaic
remnant of the barbarous czarist autocracy which directly violated socialist princi-
ples. In the following order, the Council of People's Commissars—the new govern-
ment leadership headed by Lenin, denounced the spreading terrorization and murder
of Jews.]

...the antisemitic movement and anti-Jewish pogroms are fatal to the cause of
the workers' and peasants' revolution...and directs all Sovdeps *[soviets of workers',*
peasants' and soldiers' delegates] to take such steps as will effectively destroy the
antisemitic movement at its roots. It is herewith ordered that pogromists and persons
inciting to pogroms be outlawed.

86.   Joseph Stalin

On Anti-Semitism

(1931)

Source: Kochan, p. 303. As taken from Weinryb, "Antisemitism in Soviet Russia."

[Jews in the Soviet Union increasingly abandoned religious practice, attended
state schools, and distanced themselves from Jewish traditions and Yiddish culture.
Many of their fellow citizens, nevertheless, retained deeply ingrained prejudices
against them. The short excerpt of Stalin's writings given below expressed the official
communist teaching concerning such anti-Semitism.]

National and racial chauvinism is a survival of the barbarous practices of the
cannibalistic period...serves the exploiters...to protect capitalism from the attack of
the working people...antisemitism, a phenomenon profoundly hostile to the Soviet
regime, is sternly repressed in the U.S.S.R.

Joseph Stalin and Nikita Khruschev.

Theodor Herzl at the Sixth
Zionist Congress, Basle, 1903.

Chapter XII

A Jewish Homeland

Psychologically, Diaspora Jews never accepted their exile from Judea and Jerusalem. Judaism's holy days and festivals continued to revolve around Judea's agricultural calendar and a continual state of mourning for the destroyed Second Temple permeated synagogue services. Each year the story of the Israelites's Passover escape from Egyptian slavery ended with "May the Temple be rebuilt speedily in our days" and "Next Year in Jerusalem." This yearning for the Promised Land grew particularly strong during times of persecution when Jews prayed the Messiah would redeem the Jewish people and bring them safely to their ancient home. Jews expected the Messiah's imminent arrival as they died by the Crusaders' swords, perished in flames during the Bubonic plague years, wept in memory of the 1492 Spanish expulsion, and huddled sleeplessly in fear during the czarist-inspired pogroms. There was a strong sense of fatalism in the Jews' hope for the Messiah and a return to Jerusalem. For almost fifteen hundred years, they endured persecution—if they could, died—if they had to, prayed fervently, and waited.

Jewish emancipation in Western Europe, the spread of secular Jewish enlightenment in the shtetls (Jewish sections of villages and towns) of Eastern Europe, and the growth of modern nationalism greatly influenced young Jewish intellectuals. This new generation of dreamers rejected their parents' passive longing for Zion and, instead, they created an active movement for the long overdue liberation of the Jewish people. The first concrete steps toward establishing a Jewish homeland took place independently in Russia and Vienna in the last few years of the 19th century.

In Russia, the pogroms which followed Alexander II's assassination shattered any illusions Jews may have held concerning possible emancipation and equality in Russia. Soon after a frightful pogrom in Odessa, a Russian Jew named Leon Pinsker wrote that hatred of the Jews was a mental illness that could never be cured. His pamphlet, "Auto-Emancipation," urged Jews to turn away from assimilation and to immigrate to Palestine where they could safely develop their own national consciousness. He formed a group called *Hoveve Zion*, the lovers of Zion, which encouraged young Jews to leave Russia for Palestine. Once there, Pinsker believed, they could till its soil in freedom and dignity. The first of these pioneers—the First Aliyah—went to Palestine in 1882.

A few years later, Theodor Herzl, the foreign correspondent who had witnessed Dreyfus's humiliation and the French populace's hatred for Jews, came to the same conclusion as Pinsker concerning anti-Semitism's enduring nature. Returning to Vienna, Herzl wrote *Der Judenstaat* (the Jewish State), describing a sovereign area where Jews could develop a nation safe from prejudice and persecution. Enlisting the help of influential Jews, Herzl organized the First Zionist Congress. It met in Basel, Switzerland, in 1897. Representatives of world Jewry convened to hear Herzl call for a Jewish homeland secured by public law and recognized by the major powers of Europe. Russian Jews became Herzl's strongest supporters. By the Sixth Congress in 1903, however, they were dissatisfied with Herzl's failed attempts to win Ottoman, German, and British support. The Russian delegates wanted a "practical" Zionism where Jews moved to Palestine, built up an agricultural and political base, and then presented the European governments with a *fait accompli*. The "Practicals" suspected that Herzl did not truly understand the Russian Jews' longing for the Promised Land. This feeling was reinforced at the Congress when Herzl submitted the Uganda Plan for consideration.

Following the Kishinev pogrom earlier in 1903, Herzl seriously considered a British offer for Jewish settlement in the African highlands of Uganda. Despite widespread Jewish suffering in the Pale, however, the Russian delegates would accept nothing less than Palestine as the Jewish national home. They summarily walked out of the conference. The British soon withdrew their offer and, with great sadness, Herzl accepted defeat. Zionism's founder and guiding light died the following year, but his dream continued to flourish. By 1914, the Zionist movement had succeeded in tripling Palestine's Jewish population by encouraging immigration. Zionists also purchased land through the Jewish National Fund from absentee

Ottoman-Turkish landlords. Approximately 85,000 Jews lived in scattered agricultural settlements from Lake Huleh's swamps south to Jerusalem.

The Arab people of the Near East were divided into often-feuding tribal factions. Some lived a nomadic desert existence. Others worked as agricultural laborers. All were bearers of a proud heritage which had languished under 600 years of harsh Ottoman rule. On the eve of the First World War, the days of Turkish suzerainty over this area were coming to an end. When the Turkish Empire finally died, two seemingly irreconcilable movements, Zionism and Arab nationalism, arose to fulfill their long-awaited destinies.

Jewish Pioneers in Palestine before World War I.

87. *The Balfour Declaration*

(November 2, 1917)

Source: Walter Laqueur, *A History of Zionism* (New York: Schocken Books, 1972), picture section, page 312+.

[The Balfour Declaration was the first official governmental statement supporting the idea of a home in Palestine for the Jewish people. It gave Zionism increased legitimacy in the eyes of the world and encouraged Zionists to make concrete plans for the eventual establishment of an independent Jewish state. The declaration was the result of the combined efforts of Jews who saw a homeland as the realization of biblical prophecy and Christians who believed the Jewish people deserved a national home after so many years of exile and persecution.

> Foreign Office,
> November 2nd, 1917.
>
> Dear Lord Rothschild,
>
> I have much pleasure in conveying to you, on behalf of His Majesty's Government, the following declaration of sympathy with Jewish Zionist aspirations which has been submitted to, and approved by, the Cabinet
>
> "His Majesty's Government view with favour the establishment in Palestine of a national home for the Jewish people, and will use their best endeavours to facilitate the achievement of this object, it being clearly understood that nothing shall be done which may prejudice the civil and religious rights of existing non-Jewish communities in Palestine, or the rights and political status enjoyed by Jews in any other country"
>
> I should be grateful if you would bring this declaration to the knowledge of the Zionist Federation.

The Balfour Declaration.

Chaim Weizmann, a Russian-born, naturalized British citizen, was the man most responsible for keeping the homeland issue before British government officials. An influential and respected Jewish chemist, Weizmann had recently invented a high explosive that helped Great Britain sustain its war effort against Germany. His plea for a homeland made little real headway with Prime Minister Asquith's government, which was working to convince Arabs to support the British side. The situation changed, when, in December, 1916, David Lloyd George became the new prime minister. Lloyd George and two of his key cabinet members, Foreign Secretary Arthur James Balfour and the assistant foreign secretary, Lord Robert Cecil, warmly supported the Zionists' cause. They envisioned plans for a Jewish refuge in Palestine with Britain acting as its protector.

There was some opposition to a pro-Zionist move. Surprisingly, it came from a small group of important British Jews. Simply put, they were afraid anti-Semites would use the existence of a Jewish homeland to question the true loyalties of those Englishmen who professed the Jewish religion. The British public, including the majority of England's Jews, did not agree with this argument.

Lloyd George's cabinet, after receiving favorable comments from France, Italy, the United States, and the Pope in Rome, asked the Zionists to formally request a British protectorate. At that point, Lord Walter Rothschild, Britain's chief rabbi, wrote a draft proposal and submitted it. After more debate, several revisions, and the addition of words meant to protect the rights of non-Jews in Palestine and Jews who chose to remain in the Diaspora, Balfour sent Lord Rothschild an official letter of support to pass on to Zionist officials.

The Balfour Declaration was not the dream document Weizmann and the Zionist Federation had hoped for. It did not suggest the possibility of a Jewish "state." Nevertheless, Weizmann accepted it as a major step toward Zionism's goal. Soon Zionists, the British press, and the general public considered the eventual creation of a Jewish state a foregone conclusion. In reality, it took thirty-one years, two world organizations, another world war, six million Jewish deaths, and an active Jewish resistance movement in Palestine to turn the national homeland for Jews into the sovereign State of Israel.]

Foreign Office
November 2nd, 1917

Dear Lord Rothschild,

I have much pleasure in conveying to you, on behalf of His Majesty's Government, the following declaration of sympathy with Jewish Zionist aspirations which has been submitted to, and approved by, the Cabinet.

His Majesty's Government view with favour the establishment in Palestine of a national home for the Jewish people, and will use their best endeavours to facilitate the achievement of this object, it being clearly understood that nothing shall be done which may prejudice the civil and religious rights of existing non-Jewish communities in Palestine, or the rights and political status enjoyed by Jews in any other country.

I should be grateful if you would bring this declaration to the knowledge of the Zionist Federation.

Yours...,

Arthur James Balfour

88.   Malcolm MacDonald

White Paper of 1939

Source: United Kingdom. British Parliamentary Papers. Cmd. 6019, Palestine, 1939.

[The situation between Jews and Arabs in Palestine worsened with renewed Arab violence in 1938. Jewish immigration had greatly increased as a result of Germany's ever more stringent application of the anti-Semitic Nuremberg Laws. Again Palestine's Arabs feared losing their land, culture, and identity to the growing Jewish community in Palestine [Yishuv]. In February, 1939, the British brought representatives from both sides to London hoping they could reach some kind of peaceful agreement between themselves. When this failed, the leaders of the United Kingdom declared they would impose a solution unilaterally. The new policy was issued by Malcolm MacDonald, the secretary of state for the colonies and for Dominion affairs, in the White Paper of 1939.

The White Paper began by "clearing up" long-standing "misinterpretations" of previous agreements with both the Arabs and the Jews. With reference to the Jews, the government made clear that the framers of the Balfour Declaration had never intended the creation of a Jewish state nor would the United Kingdom help the Jews work toward such an entity. Furthermore, the White Paper redefined "Jewish national home" to mean an internationally guaranteed Jewish right to a self-governing body within a larger Arab territory. Since this separate Jewish communal body was now alive and well in Palestine, Great Britain felt it had fulfilled all its Balfour and Mandate obligations. The British now chose to view the Jewish homeland mainly as a place Jews could point to with pride rather than as a home and secure refuge from persecution for all Jews who wished to go there.

On the other side, the British government said the Arabs completely misunderstood British-Arab communications during the First World War: Palestine west of the Jordan River had never been promised as part of a future independent Arab state. Palestine would become independent, possibly within ten years, but as a state in which Arabs and Jews shared authority. Until that time, His Majesty's Government would carefully guide Palestine toward self-rule. This policy proved to be incredibly naive and, of course, satisfied no one.

The truly tragic impact of the White Paper of 1939 came in the sections dealing with Jewish immigration. This is where Prime Minister Neville Chamberlain and his cabinet gave into violent Arab demands the way they had previously capitulated to Hitler in Munich. As the White Paper itself indicates, the British knew there were German, Austrian, and Czech Jews who desperately needed a refuge from Nazi anti-Semitism. They knew of Kristallnacht and the Nuremberg Laws (see Chapter

XIII). They knew no country in the world would accept a large number of Jewish refugees. They knew the Zionists in the Yishuv wanted these persecuted Jews. But they also knew that the Arabs would continue to riot if more Jews came to Palestine. The British government opted to appease the Arabs. They did so because they needed Arab oil and they wanted Arab support [which, for the most part, they did not get] in the war against Germany that was sure to come. They did not have to curry Jewish favor as they had done during the First World War because they knew world Jewry would never back Hitler and the Nazis.

The British declared that the Mandate's new goal was to let Jewish numbers increase until they made up one-third of the country's population. With that policy in mind, the White Paper declared that 75,000 more Jews would be allowed to immigrate to Palestine, 10,000 maximum during each of the next five years. In addition, 25,000 Jewish refugees might enter above this quota, but only if they could be "adequately" provided for. When the five-year limit was up, the British would allow no more Jews in unless the Arabs agreed to their continued immigration.

Great Britain could not have picked a worse time to restrict immigration. Within four months Germany invaded Poland to begin the Second World War. The Nazis extended their anti-Semitic persecutions in all the countries they soon conquered and occupied. The Nuremberg Laws' legal disabilities were but the first step in Hitler's plan to totally destroy European Jewry. With no place to go, with no country to welcome them, Europe's Jews were trapped in a continent-wide slaughterhouse. The one place that wanted them, Palestine's Jewish community, was declared off-limits by Arab unrest and British policy.]

May 17, 1939

In the Statement on Palestine, issued on the ninth of November, 1938, His Majesty's Government announced their intention to invite representatives of the Arabs of Palestine, of certain neighbouring countries and of the Jewish Agency to confer with them in London regarding future policy. It was their sincere hope that, as a result of full, free and frank discussion, some understanding ought to be reached... Certain proposals were laid before the Arab and Jewish delegations as the basis of an agreed settlement. Neither the Arab nor the Jewish delegations felt able to accept these proposals, and the conferences therefore did not result in an agreement. Accordingly His Majesty's Government are free to formulate their own policy, and after careful consideration they have decided to adhere generally to the proposals which were finally submitted to, and discussed with, the Arab and Jewish delegations...

3. The Royal *[Peel]* Commission and previous Commissions of Enquiry have drawn attention to the ambiguity of certain expressions in the Mandate, such as the

expression "a national home for the Jewish people," and they have found in the ambiguity and the resulting uncertainty as to the objectives of policy a fundamental cause of unrest and hostility between Arabs and Jews. His Majesty's Government are convinced that in the interests of the peace and well-being of the whole people of Palestine a clear definition of policy and objectives is essential. The proposal of partition recommended by the Royal Commission would have afforded such clarity, but the establishment of self-supporting independent Arab and Jewish States within Palestine has been found to be impracticable. It has therefore been necessary for His Majesty's Government to devise an alternative policy which will, consistently with their obligations to Arabs and Jews, meet the needs of the situation in Palestine. Their views and proposals are set forth below under the three heads, (I) The Constitution, (II) Immigration, and (III) Land.

I. THE CONSTITUTION

4. ...His Majesty's Government therefore now declare unequivocally that it is not part of their policy that Palestine should become a Jewish State. They would indeed regard it as contrary to their obligations to the Arabs under the Mandate, as well as to the assurances which have been given to the Arab people in the past, that the Arab population of Palestine should be made the subjects of a Jewish State against their will.

5. The nature of the Jewish National Home in Palestine was further described in the Command Paper of 1922 as follows:

"...When it is asked what is meant by the development of the Jewish National Home in Palestine, it may be answered that it is not the imposition of a Jewish nationality upon the inhabitants of Palestine as a whole, but the further development of the existing Jewish community, with the assistance of Jews in other parts of the world, in order that it may become a centre in which the Jewish people as a whole may take, on grounds of religion and race, an interest and a pride. But in order that this community should have the best prospect of free development and provide a full opportunity for the Jewish people to display its capacities, it is essential that it should know that it is in Palestine as of right and not on sufferance. That is the reason why it is necessary that the existence of a Jewish National Home in Palestine should be internationally guaranteed, and that it should be formally recognised to rest upon an ancient historic connection."

6. His Majesty's Government adhere to this interpretation of the Declaration of 1917 and regard it as an authoritative and comprehensive description of the character of

the Jewish National Home in Palestine. It envisaged the further development of the existing Jewish community with the assistance of Jews in other parts of the world… The growth of the Jewish National Home and its achievements in many fields are a remarkable constructive effort which must command the admiration of the world and must be, in particular, a source of pride to the Jewish people.

7. In the recent discussions the Arab delegations have repeated the contention that Palestine was included within the area in which Sir Henry McMahon, on behalf of the British Government, in October, 1915, undertook to recognise and support Arab independence… His Majesty's Government regret the misunderstandings which have arisen as regards some of the phrases used. For their part they can only adhere, for the reasons given by their representatives in the Report, to the view that the whole of Palestine west of Jordan was excluded from Sir Henry McMahon's pledge, and they therefore cannot agree that the McMahon correspondence forms a just basis for the claim that Palestine should be converted into an Arab State…

8. …His Majesty's Government are unable at present to foresee the exact constitutional forms which the government in Palestine will eventually take, but their objective is self-government, and they desire to see established ultimately an independent Palestine State. It should be a State in which the two peoples in Palestine, Arabs and Jews, share authority in government in such a way that the essential interests of each are secured.

9. …A transitional period will be required before independence is achieved, throughout which ultimate responsibility for the Government of the country will be retained by His Majesty's Government as the Mandatory authority, while the people of the country are taking an increasing share in the Government, and understanding and co-operation amongst them are growing. It will be the constant endeavour of His Majesty's Government to promote good relations between the Arabs and the Jews.

10. In the light of these considerations His Majesty's Government make the following declaration of their intentions regarding the future government of Palestine:

(1) The objective of His Majesty's Government is the establishment within ten years of an independent Palestine State in such treaty relations with the United Kingdom as will provide satisfactorily for the commercial and strategic requirements of both countries in the future…

(2) The independent State should be one in which Arabs and Jews share in government in such a way as to ensure that the essential interests of each community are safeguarded.

(3) ...During the transitional period the people of Palestine will be given an increasing part in the government of their country...

(7) His Majesty's Government will require to be satisfied that in the treaty contemplated...adequate provision has been made for:

   (a) the security of, and freedom of access to, the Holy Places, and the protection of the interests and property of the various religious bodies.

   (b) the protection of the different communities in Palestine in accordance with the obligations of His Majesty's Government to both Arabs and Jews and for the special position in Palestine of the Jewish National Home...

(8) ...If, at the end of ten years, it appears to His Majesty's Government that contrary to their hope, circumstances require the postponement of the establishment of the independent State, they will consult with representatives of the people of Palestine, the Council of the League of Nations and the neighbouring Arab States before deciding on such a postponement...

II. Immigration

12. ...Although it is not difficult to contend that the large number of Jewish immigrants who have been admitted so far have been absorbed economically, the fear of the Arabs that this influx will continue indefinitely until the Jewish population is in position to dominate them has produced consequences which are extremely grave for Jews and Arabs alike and for the peace and prosperity of Palestine. The lamentable disturbances of the past three years are only the latest and most sustained manifestation of this intense Arab apprehension. The methods employed by Arab terrorists against fellow-Arabs and Jews alike must receive unqualified condemnation. But it cannot be denied that fear of indefinite Jewish immigration is widespread amongst the Arab population and that this fear has made possible disturbances which have given a serious setback to economic progress, depleted the Palestine exchequer, rendered life and property insecure, and produced a bitterness between the Arab and Jewish populations which is deplorable between citizens of the same country...

14. It has been urged that all further Jewish immigration into Palestine should be stopped forthwith. His Majesty's Government cannot accept such a proposal. It would damage the whole of the financial and economic system of Palestine and thus affect adversely the interests of Arabs and Jews alike. Moreover, in the view of His Majesty's Government, abruptly to stop further immigration would be unjust to the Jewish National Home. But, above all, His Majesty's Government are conscious of the present unhappy plight of large numbers of Jews who seek a refuge from certain European countries, and they believe that Palestine can and should make a further

contribution to the solution of this pressing world problem. In all these circumstances, they believe that they will be acting consistently with their Mandatory obligations to both Arabs and Jews, and in the manner best calculated to serve the interests of the whole people of Palestine, by adopting the following proposals regarding immigration:

(1) Jewish immigration during the next five years will be at a rate which, if economic absorptive capacity permits, will bring the Jewish population up to approximately one-third of the total population of the country. Taking into account the expected natural increase of the Arab and Jewish populations, and the number of illegal Jewish immigrants now in the country, this would allow of the admission, as from the beginning of April this year, of some 75,000 immigrants over the next five years. These immigrants would, subject to the criterion of economic absorptive capacity, be admitted as follows:-

   (a) For each of the next five years a quota of 10,000 Jewish immigrants will be allowed on the understanding that a shortage in any one year may be added to the quotas for subsequent years, within the five-year period, if economic absorptive capacity permits.

   (b) In addition, as a contribution towards the solution of the Jewish refugee problem, 25,000 refugees will be admitted as soon as the High Commissioner is satisfied that adequate provision for their maintenance is ensured, special consideration being given to refugee children and dependents…

(3) After the period of five years no further Jewish immigration will be permitted unless the Arabs of Palestine are prepared to acquiesce in it.

(4) His Majesty's Government are determined to check illegal immigration and further preventive measures are being adopted. The numbers of any Jewish illegal immigrants who, despite these measures, may succeed in coming into the country and cannot be deported will be deducted from the yearly quotas.

15. His Majesty's Government are satisfied that, when the immigration over five years which is now contemplated has taken place, they will not be justified in facilitating, nor will they be under any obligation to facilitate, the further development of the Jewish National Home by immigration regardless of the wishes of the Arab population.

III. LAND

16. …The Reports of several expert Commissions have indicated that, owing to the natural growth of the Arab population and the steady sale in recent years of Arab land to Jews, there is now in certain areas no room for further transfers of Arab land,

whilst in some other areas such transfers of land must be restricted if Arab cultivators are to maintain their existing standard of life and a considerable landless Arab population is not soon to be created. In these circumstances, the High Commissioner will be given general powers to prohibit and regulate transfers of land...

18. In framing these proposals His Majesty's Government have sincerely endeavoured to act in strict accordance with their obligations under the Mandate to both the Arabs and the Jews... Each community has much to contribute to the welfare of their common land, and each must earnestly desire peace in which to assist in increasing the well-being of the whole people of the country. The responsibility which falls on them, no less than upon His Majesty's Government, to co-operate together to ensure peace is all the more solemn because their country is revered by many millions of Moslems, Jews and Christians throughout the world who pray for peace in Palestine and for the happiness of her people.

Benito Mussolini and Adolf Hitler.

German soldiers enforce a boycott of Jewish shops in pre-war Germany.

Chapter XIII

Holocaust

Germany emerged from the First World War a defeated nation unsure why it had lost the war. Not one inch of German territory had been lost in battle, yet the kaiser had fled and the government had summarily collapsed. The triumphant Allies vindictively stripped Germany of its rich industrial and coal regions, forbad it to raise and maintain armed forces, and compelled it to pay a huge indemnity.

The new, democratic republic set up at Weimar immediately faced difficult economic and political problems. These became insurmountable following the worldwide depression beginning in 1929. Skyrocketing inflation made the German mark worthless. Massive unemployment spread throughout the country. Hungry, cold, discontented, Germans in the 1930s proved much more receptive to anti-Semitism than they had during the rapid industrialization era of the late 19th century.

A rabble-rouser named Adolf Hitler, representing the radical National Socialist Party, proposed militant solutions to Germany's problems. He repeatedly told Germans the Jews were to blame for all the nation's misfortunes. An ever increasing number listened and believed. They elected National Socialist (Nazi) candidates to the Reichstag (parliament).

In 1933, the Weimar Republic's aging president, Paul von Hindenburg, appointed Hitler chancellor. The moderates and conservatives hoped to use the Nazis' numerical strength as a basis for a coalition government; they were confident they could control the Nazi Party's violent excesses. They were wrong. In a little over a year, Hitler viciously eliminated all political competition and became the supreme dictator of a ruthless fascist state.

Hitler immediately began redressing what he considered Germany's grievances. He re-armed the nation by building a huge standing army, developing the Navy and creating the Luftwaffe or air force. The growing war machine created jobs and all but eliminated unemployment. His troops marched into territories such as the Rhineland, which Germany had lost in 1918. Germans were jubilant. Hitler had restored their pride. Furthermore, he sold them the myth that they were Aryan supermen. Their newfound strength was ample proof of the Führer's (leader's) claim. For the blond, blue-eyed Germans to be supermen, however, there seemed to be a need for an opposite race of inferior beings. To Hitler, the Nazis, and a growing number of Germans, the Jewish people became the dreaded sub-humans who supposedly threatened to destroy the Aryan race.

In 1935, the Nazis began the enactment of a series of laws which defined racial purity and denied citizenship to Jews based on their sub-human status. The Nuremberg Laws, over the next few years, carefully excised Jews from German political, economic and social life. To be sure, the Jews were frightened by these actions, but they considered them to be signs of a *Kinderkronkheit,* a childhood illness of the new regime. They clung to the belief that this radical anti-Jewish phase would pass as had so many others in their history. The events of November 10, 1938, destroyed that naive hope.

On that night, the Nazis orchestrated and carried out a nationwide pogrom against Germany's Jewish community. All over the country, violent mobs burnt synagogues, destroyed Jewish businesses, dragged Jews from their homes, attacked them and, in some cases, beat them to death. This night of terror—named the Night of Broken Glass (Kristallnacht) after the shattered glass windows of thousands of Jewish businesses—convinced the Jews that the Nazis posed a deadly threat. Desperately trying to get out of the country, thousands now besieged foreign embassies. But no nation, including the United States, would accept more than a mere handful of these frantic refugees.

Germany's invasion of Poland the following September began the Second World War. With Hitler's lightening attacks (blitzkrieg) against the nations of Europe, almost the entire continent's Jewish population came under Nazi domination. From the beginning, the Nazi leadership carried on three separate wars: a military conflict against the Allies, reprisals against any members of the conquered nations who dared oppose German rule, and a war to annihilate European Jewry.

At first, special command units marched local Jewish populations out of their villages and executed them by machine-gun fire. They then dumped the lifeless bodies into huge pits and covered them with soil. This soon proved too inefficient and time consuming. Eventually, Polish, French, Italian, Greek, Dutch, Belgian, Czech, Austrian, Russian, Yugoslavian, Hungarian, Finnish, Norwegian, and German Jews (*Note:* Bulgaria and Rumania, Germany's allies, chose to deal with their Jews themselves) were sent by train to concentration camps where they were poisoned by Zyklon B gas or worked and starved to death as slave laborers.

Genocide involving an entire continent and millions of victims could not have been carried out without, at the very least, the silent acquiescence of the majority of Europe's population. They remained silent not only because they feared for their own lives, but also because they carried within themselves a millennia and a half of church-taught hatred and fear of the Jewish people. Certainly Catholic and Protestant churches did not cause the Holocaust. They would never have agreed with such torture and murder. But the churches' crusade of the past 1500 years to convince Christians that Jews were evil children of the devil—as shown by many of the documents in this collection—made anti-Semitism an integral part of European culture.

The Nazis' major theoretical innovation (borrowed from 19th-century anti-Semites such as Fritsch and H.S. Chamberlain) was the belief that nothing, not even baptism, could wash away the Jews' evil nature. And so in one occupied country after another, with the major exception of Denmark, the Germans faced little opposition in collecting and transporting the Jews to their deaths. Even the Allies largely remained silent, choosing to believe that the best way to help the Jews was to win the war against Germany. Not until 1944 did any of the Allied nations officially recognize the special character of the Nazis' war against the Jewish people. In January of that year U.S. President Franklin Roosevelt created the War Refugee Board to help Jews escape the Holocaust. Tragically, it was too little, too late.

Theory

89.   Adolf Hitler

Mein Kampf

(1924)

Source: Adolf Hitler, Mein Kampf, translated by Ralph Manheim (Boston: Houghton Mifflin, London: Hutchinson, 1971), pp. 51–52, 56, 57, 58, 59–60, 61, 63, 64–65, 153, 235, 246, 286–287, 315–316, 324–325, 328, 562, 623, 679.

[Adolf Hitler grew up in Linz, Austria, the son of a minor customs official. After his father's death, he travelled to Vienna where he hoped to study painting at the Academy of Arts. The school turned down his application, telling him he did not have the aptitude to be an artist. This rejection and his consequent attempts to make a living in the lower class sections of Austria's capital permanently influenced how he viewed the world. It left him with the most extreme views on economics, politics, Aryan racial theories, and anti-Semitism

Hitler left Austria in 1914 and moved to Munich. Soon after his arrival, the First World War began, and he patriotically enlisted in the German army. In August, 1918, he was injured as a result of a poison gas attack while serving as an infantry corporal. After Germany's surrender, he returned to Munich and became deeply involved in the National Socialist German Workers Party (NSDAP), a small, paramilitary and highly nationalist group which he soon dominated. His party's attempt to seize control of the Bavarian government—the infamous Beer Hall "Putsch" of November, 1923—resulted in Hitler's nine-month confinement in Landsberg Fortress prison. While at Landsberg, Hitler wrote what eventually became known as Mein Kampf (My Struggle).*

Mein Kampf is part autobiography, part Hitler's own interpretations of history, politics, economics, and foreign relations, and part fanatical tract on the endless struggle between the superhuman Aryan-Germans and the subhuman, evil Jews. The former corporal wrote Mein Kampf *to prove to his party rivals that he possessed both a clear philosophy and a plan of action. This was meant to secure his position as the undisputed leader of National Socialism.*

A large part of the book is filled with vicious slanders against Jews: everything Hitler considered wrong in Germany—indeed, in the whole world—was the result of Jewish conspiracies to destroy civilization. He wrote that while in Vienna he was shocked and disgusted by the traditional Orthodox Jews he encountered. After reading many anti-Semitic pamphlets and newspapers, he began his journey toward racial anti-Semitism. He first rejected the idea that Jews were merely Germans of a different religious persuasion. Soon he came to the conclusion that Jews were not even human beings. In spite of Hitler's claims that Vienna was the birthplace of his racial theories, many historians believe that he first acquired his anti-Semitic beliefs as a youth in Linz. His family belonged to the lower middle class, and this section of society had been strongly influenced by the 19th-century anti-Semitic movement in Germany and Austria.

Whatever the direct origin of this fanatical anti-Jewish hatred, Hitler clearly understood the usefulness of anti-Semitism in German politics. Mein Kampf is filled with references to the Jewish "problem" not only because it made up such a large part of Hitler's psyche, but also because he knew this prejudice appealed to his intended audience. In the book's early chapters, Hitler offers a somewhat disjointed explanation for the reasons behind his anti-Semitism. He then continues throughout most of the remaining chapters to interpret history and contemporary issues with an emphasis on the endless and universal evil of the Jews. Here, Hitler especially warns against the dire threat posed by Marxist Socialism, which he declares is another Jewish conspiracy to destroy German society. Toward the end of Mein Kampf, Hitler gives broad hints concerning how the Jews should be treated.

Mein Kampf clearly highlights Hitler's obsession with racial purity, an idea which originated with the Folkish (Volkish) movement of the previous century. This movement glorified the Germanic peasant as the epitome of purity and decency. Folkish thinkers believed modern industrialization, capitalism, democracy, liberalism and city life—all manifestations of the Jews' conspiracy against the German people—threatened to destroy idyllic peasant existence. The Folkish movement had spread fear of racial defilement and preached against sexual contact and intermarriage with Jewish subhumans. Hitler accepted these ideas and firmly believed "…the question of preserving or not preserving the purity of the blood will endure as long as there are men." Because of this overwhelming preoccupation, Hitler and the Nazis literally stopped at nothing to safeguard the Aryan race from Jewish blood-pollution. From the First Racial Definition in 1933, Nazi Germany continually escalated its response to the "Jewish Problem" until the need to transport Jews to the death camps actually took priority over moving and supplying German troops in the last stages of the Second World War. Hitler's onslaught against the Jewish people, first outlined in Mein Kampf, did not end until the Allies completely defeated Germany and the Third Reich finally ceased to exist.]

[pp. 51–52]…There were few Jews in Linz. In the course of the centuries their outward appearance had become Europeanized and had taken on a human look; in fact, I even took them for Germans. The absurdity of this idea did not dawn on me because I saw no distinguishing feature but the strange religion. The fact that they had, as I believed, been persecuted on this account sometimes almost turned my distaste at unfavorable remarks about them into horror.

Thus far I did not so much as suspect the existence of an organized opposition to the Jews.

Then I came to Vienna...

[p. 56] Once, as I was strolling through the Inner City, I suddenly encountered an apparition in a black caftan and black hair locks. Is this a Jew? was my first thought.

For, to be sure, they had not looked like that in Linz. I observed the man furtively and cautiously, but the longer I stared at this foreign face, scrutinizing feature for feature, the more my first question assumed a new form:

Is this a German?...

Yet I could no longer very well doubt that the objects of my study were not Germans of a special religion, but a people in themselves; for since I had begun to concern myself with this question and to take cognizance of the Jews, Vienna appeared to me in a different light than before. Wherever I went, I began to see Jews, and the more I saw, the more sharply they became distinguished in my eyes from the rest of humanity...

[p. 57]...Was there any form of filth or profligacy, particularly in cultural life *[in Vienna]*, without at least one Jew involved in it?

If you cut even cautiously into such an abscess, you found, like a maggot in a rotting body, often dazzled by the sudden light—a kike!

What had to be reckoned heavily against the Jews in my eyes was when I became acquainted with their activity in the press, art, literature, and the theater...

[p. 58]...This was pestilence, spiritual pestilence, worse than the Black Death of olden times, and the people was *(sic.)* being infected with it!...

The fact that nine tenths of all literary filth, artistic trash, and theatrical idiocy can be set to the account of a people, constituting hardly one hundredth of all the country's inhabitants, could simply not be talked away; it was the plain truth...

[pp. 59–60]...But then a flame flared up within me. I no longer avoided discussion of the Jewish question; no, now I sought it. When I learned to look for the Jew in all branches of cultural and artistic life and its various manifestations, I suddenly encountered him in a place where I would least have expected to find him.

When I recognized the Jew as the leader of the Social Democracy, the scales dropped from my eyes. A long soul struggle had reached its conclusion...

[p. 61] I took all the Social Democratic pamphlets I could lay hands on and sought the names of their authors: Jews…I had at last come to the conclusion that the Jew was no German.

Only now did I become thoroughly acquainted with the seducer of our people…

[p. 63] I didn't know what to be more amazed at: the agility of their tongues or their virtuosity at lying.

Gradually I began to hate them…

[pp. 64–65] For me this was the time of the greatest spiritual upheaval I have ever had to go through.

I had ceased to be a weak-kneed cosmopolitan and become an anti-Semite… If, with the help of his Marxist creed, the Jew is victorious over the other peoples of the world, his crown will be the funeral wreath of humanity and this planet will, as it did thousands of years ago, move through the ether devoid of men.

Eternal Nature inexorably avenges the infringement of her commands.

Hence today I believe that I am acting in accordance with the will of the Almighty Creator: BY DEFENDING MYSELF AGAINST THE JEW, I AM FIGHTING FOR THE WORK OF THE LORD…

[p. 153] The following theorem may be established as an eternally valid truth: Never yet has a state been founded by peaceful economic means, but always and exclusively by the instincts of preservation of the species regardless whether these are found in the province of heroic virtue or of cunning craftiness; the one results in Aryan states based on work and culture, the other in Jewish colonies of parasites…

[p. 246]…In future days the Jew will certainly continue to raise a mighty uproar in his newspapers if a hand is ever laid on his favorite nest, if an end is put to the mischief of the press and this instrument of education is put to the service of the state and no longer left in the hands of aliens and enemies of the people. But I believe that this will bother us younger men less than our fathers. A thirty-centimeter shell had always hissed more loudly than a thousand Jewish newspaper vipers—so let them hiss!

[pp. 286–287]…The result of all racial crossing is therefore in brief always the following:

(a) Lowering of the level of the higher race;

(b) Physical and intellectual regression and hence the beginning of a slowly but surely progressing sickness.

To bring about such a development is, then, nothing else but to sin against the will of the eternal creator.

And as a sin this act is rewarded...

[pp. 315–316] And this nationality he [the modern Jew] guards as never before. While he seems to overflow with 'enlightenment,' 'progress,' 'freedom,' 'humanity,' etc., he himself practices the severest segregation of his race. To be sure, he sometimes palms off his women on influential Christians, but as a matter of principle he always keeps his male line pure. He poisons the blood of others, but preserves his own. The Jew almost never marries a Christian woman; it is the Christian who marries a Jewess. The bastards, however, take after the Jewish side.

[pp. 324–325] ...With satanic joy in his face, the black-haired Jewish youth lurks in wait for the unsuspecting girl whom he defiles with his blood, thus stealing her from her people. With every means he tries to destroy the racial foundations of the people he had set out to subjugate...

And so he tries systematically to lower the racial level by a continuous poisoning of individuals.

And in politics he begins to replace the idea of democracy by the dictatorship of the proletariat.

[p. 328] Only by examining and comparing all other problems of life in the light of this one question [blood purity] shall we see how absurdly petty they are by this standard. They are all limited in time—but the question of preserving or not preserving the purity of the blood will endure as long as there are men.

[p. 562]...Systematically these black parasites of the nation [Jews] defile our inexperienced young blond girls and thereby destroy something which can no longer be replaced in this world... The folkish-minded man, in particular, has the sacred duty, each in his own denomination, of making PEOPLE STOP JUST TALKING SUPERFICIALLY OF GOD'S WILL, AND ACTUALLY FULFILL GOD'S WILL, AND NOT LET GOD'S WORD BE DESECRATED.

[p. 623] AND SO THE JEW TODAY IS THE GREAT AGITATOR FOR THE COMPLETE DESTRUCTION OF GERMANY. WHEREVER IN THE WORLD WE READ OF ATTACKS AGAINST GERMANY, JEWS ARE THEIR FABRICATORS, JUST AS IN PEACETIME AND DURING THE WAR *[the First World War]* THE PRESS OF THE JEWISH STOCK EXCHANGE AND MARXISTS SYSTEMATICALLY STIRRED UP HATRED AGAINST GERMANY UNTIL STATE AFTER STATE ABANDONED NEUTRALITY AND, RENOUNCING THE TRUE INTERESTS OF THE PEOPLES, ENTERED THE SERVICE OF THE WORLD WAR COALITION.

[p. 679] ...If at the beginning of the *[First World]* War and during the War twelve or fifteen thousand of the Hebrew corrupters of the people had been held under poison gas, as happened to hundreds of thousands of our very best German workers in the field, the sacrifice of millions at the front would not have been in vain. On the contrary: twelve thousand scoundrels eliminated in time might have saved the lives of a million real Germans, valuable for the future.

Laws

90.   The Nuremberg Laws

Law for the Protection of German Blood and Honor

(September 15, 1935)

Source: Dov Weinryb, *Jewish Emancipation Under Attack* (New York: The American Jewish Committee, 1942), p. 45.

[The Law for the Protection of German Blood and Honor was enacted in Nuremberg and thus became one of the many "Nuremberg Laws." It made all sexual relations and intermarriage between Aryans and Jews illegal. Precedent for this legislation against racial "defilement" came from earlier anti-Semitic writings such as Theodor Fritsch's "The Racists' Decalogue" and, of course, Hitler's Mein Kampf. *Paragraph three of this law also banned women of reproductive age from working in Jewish homes. This type of legislation was not unique to the Nazis. The Catholic Church had tried to enforce almost identical regulations since the reign of Constantius in 339 C.E. Evidently, Church leaders for 1500 years, like Nazis in 1935, presumed Jewish men would automatically take advantage of any Christian women they employed. In the Church's case, the fear was eventual conversion of the Christian women to Judaism. For the Third Reich, the sin was racial pollution.]*

Imbued with the conviction that the purity of the German blood is the pre-requisite for the future existence of the German People, and animated with the unbending will to ensure the existence of the German nation for all the future, the Reichstag has unanimously adopted the following law, which is hereby proclaimed:

Paragraph 1

   (1) Marriages between Jews and state members of the German or cognate blood are forbidden. Marriages concluded despite this law are invalid, even if they are concluded abroad in order to circumvent this law.

   (2) Only the State Attorney may initiate the annulment suit.

Paragraph 2

   Extra-marital relations between Jews and state members of German or cognate blood are prohibited.

Paragraph 3

Jews must not engage female domestic help in their households among state members of German or cognate blood, who are under 45 years.

Paragraph 4

(1) The display of the Reich and national flag and the showing of the national colors by Jews is prohibited.

(2) However, the display of the Jewish colors is permitted to them. The exercise of this right is placed under the protection of the state.

Paragraph 5

(1) Whosoever acts in violation of the prohibition of Paragraph 1, will be punished with penal servitude.

(2) Whosoever acts in violation of Paragraph 2, will be punished with either imprisonment or penal servitude.

(3) Whosoever acts in violation of Paragraph 3 or Paragraph 4, will be punished by imprisonment up to one year, with a fine or with either of these penalties...

Paragraph 7

This law goes into effect on the day following promulgation, except for Paragraph 3 which shall go into force on January 1, 1936.

91.   *First Ordinance to the Reich Citizenship Law*

(November 14, 1935)

Source: Raul Hilberg, *Documents of Destruction; Germany and Jewry, 1933–1945* (Chicago: Quadrangle Books, 1971), pp. 19–21. *Reichsgesetzblatt* (Reich Legal Gazette) 1935, I, 1333.

[The First Ordinance, enacted two months after the Reich Citizenship Law, attempted to provide a clearer definition of who was a Jew and who could be considered a "part-Jew." A person who had one or two fully Jewish grandparents was a part-Jew or Mischling (half-breed). Part-Jews would be treated by law as full-Jews if they were married to Jews, if they were children of an Aryan-Jewish marriage which took place after September 15, 1935, or if they were born out of wedlock after July 31, 1936 (in other words, conceived after the Nazis passed the Law for the Protection of German Blood and Honor). Part-Jews who had no such affiliations, were, for the time being, exempt from the anti-Jewish laws. More detailed definitions of Mischling appeared in the 1942 Wannsee Protocols (see below) that

determined which classes of part-Jews, along with full Jews, were scheduled for liquidation in death camps.

In addition to racial definitions, the First Ordinance specifically stripped Jews of their citizenship, the right to vote, and the right to hold office. It also forcibly retired the last remaining Jews in any branch of government employment.]

On the basis of article 3 of the Reich Citizenship Law of September 15, 1935 (Reich Legal Gazette I, 1146) the following is ordered:

Article 1

1. Until the issuance of further regulations for the award of citizenship, nationals of German or related blood who possessed the right to vote in Reichstag elections at the time when the Reich Citizenship Law entered into force or who were granted provisional citizenship by the Reich Minister of Interior acting in agreement with the Deputy of the Führer, are provisionally considered Reich citizens.

2. The Reich Minister of Interior acting in agreement with the Deputy of the Führer may revoke provisional citizenship.

Article 2

1. The regulations of Article 1 apply also to nationals who were part Jews *[judische Mischlinge]*.

2. Partly Jewish is anyone who is descended from one or two grandparents who are fully Jewish *[volljudisch]* by race, insofar as he is not to be considered as Jewish under article 5, section 2. A grandparent is to be considered as fully Jewish if he belonged to the Jewish religious community.

Article 3

Only a Reich citizen as bearer of complete political rights may exercise the right to vote in political affairs or hold public office. The Reich Minister of Interior or an agency empowered by him may make exceptions with regard to an admission to public office during the transition. The affairs of religious communities will not be affected.

Article 4

1. A Jew cannot be a Reich citizen. He is not allowed the right to vote in political affairs; he cannot hold public office.

2. Jewish civil servants will retire as of December 31, 1935. If these civil servants fought for Germany or her allies in the World War *[World War I]*, they will

receive the full pension to which they are entitled by their last position in the pay scale, until they reach retirement age; they will not, however, advance in seniority. Upon reaching retirement age their pension is to be based on pay scales which will prevail at the time.

3. The affairs of religious communities will not be affected.

4. The provisions of service for teachers in Jewish public schools will remain unaltered until new regulations are issued for the Jewish school system.

Article 5

1. A Jew is he who is descended from at least three grandparents who are fully Jewish by race. Article 2, paragraph 2, sentence 2 applies.

2. Also to be considered a Jew is a partly Jewish national who is descended from two fully Jewish grandparents and

   a) who belonged to the Jewish religious community, upon adoption of the [Reich Citizenship] Law, or is received into the community thereafter, or

   b) who was married to a Jewish person upon adoption of the law, or marries one thereafter, or

   c) who is the offspring of a marriage concluded by a Jew (as defined in paragraph 1) after the entry into force of the Law for the Protection of German Blood and Honor of September 15, 1935 (Reich Gazette I, 1146) or

   d) who is the offspring of an extramarital relationship involving a Jew (as defined in paragraph 1) and who is born out of wedlock after July 31, 1936.

Article 6

1. Requirements for purity of blood exceeding those of article 5, which are made in Reich laws or regulations of the National Socialist German Workers' Party and its organizations, remain unaffected.

2. Any other requirements for purity of blood, exceeding those of article 4, may be made only with the consent of the Reich Minister of the Interior and the Deputy of the Führer. Insofar as requirements of this type exist already, they become void on January 1, 1936 unless they are accepted by the Reich Minister of the Interior acting with the agreement of the Deputy of the Führer. Acceptance is to be requested from the Reich Minister of the Interior.

Article 7

The Führer and Reich Chancellor may grant exemptions from the stipulations of the implementory ordinances.

Berlin, November 14, 1935

The Führer and Reich Chancellor
Adolf Hitler

The Reich Minister of the Interior
Frick

The Deputy of the Führer
R. Hess
(Reich Minister without Portfolio)

92. Nazi Documents

Kristallnacht

(November 10, 1938)

Source: Ingeborg Hecht, *Invisible Walls; A German Family Under the Nuremberg Laws* (San Diego: Harcourt Brace Jovanovich, Publishers, 1985), p. 49.

[In October, 1938, the Third Reich expelled Polish-born Jews and their families who had been living in Germany. The Nazis shipped these people by train to the eastern border where they forcibly marched the men, women, and children into Polish territory. The authorities permitted the Jews to keep 10 Reichsmarks and the possessions they could personally carry. Everything else, they confiscated.

Zindel Grynszpan, one of the evacuated Jews, wrote to his son Herschel in Paris. He described the deportation and the brutal treatment he and his family had endured. Enraged by the news, Herschel vowed to make the Germans pay for their cruelty. He got a gun and made his way to the German embassy. When he could not find the ambassador, he shot the first person he saw—Ernst vom Rath, the third undersecretary. Vom Rath died two days later.

When the Nazi leadership, meeting in Munich to celebrate the anniversary of the Beer Hall Putsch, learned of vom Rath's death, they exploded in fury. Joseph Goebbels, the Minister of Popular Enlightenment and Propaganda, suggested that Germany's Jews be punished for Grynszpan's crime. He insisted, however, that the forthcoming attack appear to be a spontaneous uprising of the people's indignation. Chief of Security Police and the S.S Security Service Reinhard Heydrich telegraphed orders to begin the pogroms that evening, November 10. That night, in cities and villages throughout Germany, frenzied mobs directed by Nazis in civilian clothing attacked Jews, burnt synagogues, and destroyed Jewish businesses. The shattered windows of thousands of Jewish shops gave the pogrom its name—Kristallnacht, the Night of Broken Glass.

Vom Rath's death was the casus belli *for Kristallnacht, but it was not the real reason the pogrom occurred when it did. The Nazis had long wanted to thoroughly terrorize the Jews, but they needed to do it without risking international protests and censure. By November, 1938, Hitler, Hermann Göring, and Goebbels were reasonably confident they could get away with a massive anti-Semitic action. The Germans had recently occupied the Rhineland, taken over Austria, and annexed Czechoslovakia's Sudetenland, all without effective opposition.*

The Führer was also aware that a conference on refugees held the previous July at Evian-les-Bains, France, had failed to encourage any country to open its doors to Jews fleeing Nazism. He took great delight in the knowledge that other nations were no more fond of Jews than was Germany. Indeed, Hitler may even have believed the world was handing Germany a carte blanche *to deal with the Jews in any way the Third Reich saw fit.]*

Measures to Be Taken against Jews Tonight

Immediate preparations and consultations with police chiefs in attendance. Only those measures may be taken which carry out no threat to German lives and property. (Synagogues to be burned only when there is no risk to the surrounding area.) No Jewish homes or business premises to be destroyed or looted; non-Jewish business premises to be protected; no Jews of foreign nationality to be molested. Summary confiscation by the police of documentary records belonging to Jewish religious communities. In all districts, as many Jews—well-to-do Jews in particular—are to be detained as can be accommodated in the detention centers available. Upon their *[the police]* request, the appropriate concentration camp must be contacted forthwith, so that they *[the Jews]* can be accommodated there as soon as possible. All State Police *[Gestapo]* headquarters are instructed not to intervene by taking countermeasures.

Broken windows of a Jewish typesetting firm the morning after *Kristalnacht.*

Practice

93. *Protocols of the Wannsee Conference*

(January 20, 1942)

Source: Protocols of the Wannsee Conference, International Military Tribunal, "Nuremberg Trials," Nuremberg document No. NG 2586.

[As German forces occupied the conquered nations of Europe, representatives of the Reich Security Main Office immediately began identifying and registering the Jewish citizens of these countries. They then separated the Jews and confined them

to ghettoes. In Poland and Russia, special units known as Einsatzgruppen formed firing squads to murder Jewish communities en masse.

By the summer of 1941, with Nazi leadership confident of eventual total victory in Europe, Hitler verbally informed Hermann Göring that the time had come to plan and carry out the complete annihilation of European Jewry. Such an undertaking, so vital to the Führer's vision of Aryan domination, would require the close cooperation of many Reich departments. Göring ordered Heydrich to convene a secret meeting of state and party ministers, and police and S.S. officials to discuss plans for the "Final Solution."

The conference met on January 20, 1942, in the pleasant Berlin suburb of Am Grossen Wannsee. Adolf Eichmann took minutes while Heydrich explained the scope of the "Jewish problem" and what measures had already been instituted. The fact that firing squads had already murdered three-quarters of a million Russian and Polish Jews was not mentioned directly in the protocols.

Next—and this was a the crucial part of the meeting—Heydrich listed what needed to be done to complete Hitler's plan. Jews from all over Europe had to be moved to camps where the strongest would be used as slave laborers and the rest would be murdered by poison gas. The gas, Zyklon B, had already been tested and approved. Gas chambers and cremation ovens were being constructed. Now, all state and party agencies had to cooperate closely to set up an operation that functioned smoothly and efficiently. Göring and Heydrich had expected some resistance from the secretaries of state to this plan for organized mass murder, but none materialized. In fact, the general feeling was one of impatient urgency to get the job done.

The Protocols of the Wannsee Conference are a chilling insight into Nazi thinking concerning the murder of the Jews. The session was conducted as if it were a simple business meeting, and yet, even amongst this elite group, Heydrich continued to use typical Nazi euphemisms. The word "evacuation" translated as forced removal and transportation. "Resettlement to the east" actually meant being sent to imminent death. "Practical experience being gathered" referred to mass gassing experiments on Jews, Russian soldiers and others, and the testing of various ways to dispose of the dead bodies while recovering valuables such as gold teeth.

As a result of the Wannsee Conference, the Nazis began the massive transportation of Europe's Jews to the death camps of Auschwitz, Chelmno, and Treblinka, to name but a few. Heydrich's conference at Wannsee had been successful. The operation was well organized, efficient, methodical.]

Minutes of Discussion

I. The following persons took part in the discussion about the final solution of the Jewish question which took place in Berlin, am grossen Wannsee No. 55/58 on 20 January 1942.

Gauleiter Dr. MEYER and Reichsamtsleiter Dr. LEIBBRANDT—Reich Ministry for Occupied Eastern territories

Under Secretary of State Dr. STUCKART—Reich Ministry of the Interior

Under Secretary of State NEUMANN—Plenipotentiary for the Four-Year Plan

Under Secretary of State Dr. FREISLER—Reich Ministry of Justice

Under Secretary of State Dr. BUEHLER—Office of the Government General

Unterstaatssekretaer LUTHER—Foreign Office

SS-Oberfuehrer KLOPFER—Party Chancellery

Ministerialdirektor KRITZINGER—Reich Chancellery

(handwritten note) D III. 29 Top Secret.

SS-Gruppenfuehrer HOFMANN—Race and Settlement Main Office

SS-Gruppenfuehrer MUELLER—Reich Main Security Office

SS-Obersturmbannfuehrer EICHMANN

SS-Oberfuehrer Dr. SCHOENGARTH—Security Police and SD Chief of the Security Police and the SD in the Government General

SS-Sturmbannfuehrer Dr. LANGE—Security Police and SD Commander of the Security Police and the SD for the General-District Latvia, as deputy of the Commander of the Security Police and the SD for the Reich Commissariat "Eastland."

II. At the beginning of the discussion SS-Obergruppenfuehrer HEYDRICH *[Chief of the Security Police and the SD]* gave information that the Reich Marshal *[Göring]* had appointed him delegate for the preparations for the final solution of the Jewish problem in Europe and pointed out that this discussion had been called for the purpose of clarifying fundamental questions. The wish of the Reich Marshal to have a draft sent to him concerning organisatory, factual and material interests in relation to the final solution of the Jewish problem in Europe, makes necessary an initial common action of all Central Offices immediately concerned with these questions in order to bring their general activities into line.

He said that the Reich Fuehrer-SS and the Chief of the German Police (Chief of the Security Police and the SD) *[Heinrich Himmler]* was entrusted with the official

Jewish survivors in the Warsaw ghetto rounded up for concentration camps.

handling of the final solution of the Jewish problem centrally without regard to geographic borders.

The Chief of the Security Police and the SD then gave a short report of the struggle which has been carried on against this enemy, the essential points being the following:

a) the expulsion of the Jews from every particular sphere of life of the German people,

b) the expulsion of the Jews from the Lebensraum *[living space]* of the German people.

In carrying out these efforts, an increased and planned acceleration of the emigration of Jews from the Reich territory was started, as the only possible present solution...

...537,000 Jews were sent out of the country between the day of the seizure of power and the deadline 31 October 1941. Of these as from 30 January from Germany proper approx. 360,000 from 15 March 1938 from Austria (Ostmark) appr. 147,000 from 15 March 1939 from the Protectorate, Bohemia and Moravia appr. 30,000.

The Jews themselves, or rather their Jewish political organizations financed the emigration. In order to avoid the possibility of the impoverished Jews staying behind, action was taken to make the wealthy Jews finance the evacuation of the needy Jews...

...Up to 30 October 1941, the foreign Jews donated approx. $9,500,000.

In the meantime the Reich Fuehrer-SS and Chief of the German Police had prohibited emigration of Jews for reason of the dangers of an emigration during war-time and consideration of the possibilities in the East.

III. Another possible solution of the problem has now taken the place of emigration, i.e. the evacuation of the Jews to the East, provided the Fuehrer agrees to this plan.

Such activities are, however, to be considered as provisional action, but practical experience [*Note:* no doubt this refers to mass gassing] is already being collected which is of the greatest importance in relation to the future final solution of the Jewish problem.

Approx. 11,000,000 Jews will be involved in this final solution of the European problem, they are distributed as follows among the countries:

[Note: numbers are not accurate, but will show the Nazi mode of thought on this subject]

COUNTRY		NUMBER
A.	Germany proper	131,800
	Austria	43,700

	Eastern territories	420,000
	General Government	2,284,000
	Bialystok	400,000
	Protectorate of Bohemia and Moravia	74,200
	Estonia	no Jews
	Latvia	3,500
	Lithuania	34,000
	Belgium	43,000
	Denmark	5,600
	France/Occupied France	165,000
	Unoccupied France	700,000
	Greece	69,600
	Netherlands	160,000
	Norway	1,300
B.	Bulgaria	48,000
	England	330,000
	Finland	2,300
	Ireland	4,000
	Italy, incl. Sardinia	58,000
	Albania	200
	Croatia	40,000
	Portugal	3,000
	Roumania, incl. Bessarabia	342,000
	Sweden	8,000
	Switzerland	18,000
	Serbia	10,000
	Slovakia	88,000
	Spain	6,000
	Turkey (European Turkey)	5,500
	Hungary	742,800
	USSR	5,000,000
	Ukraine 2,994,685	
	White Russia	
	with the exception	
	of Bialystok 446,484	
	Total	over 11,000,000

The number of Jews given here for foreign countries includes, however, only those Jews who still adhere to the Jewish faith as the definition of the term "Jew" according to racial principles is still partially missing there. The handling of the problem in the individual countries will meet with difficulties due to the attitude and conception of the people there, especially in Hungary and Roumania. Thus, even today a Jew can buy documents in Hungary which will officially prove his foreign citizenship.

The influence of the Jews in all walks of life in the USSR is well known. Approximately 5 million Jews are living in the European Russia, and in Asiatic Russia scarcely 1/4 million...

Under proper guidance the Jews are now to be allocated for labor to the East in the course of the final solution. Able-bodied Jews will be taken in large labor columns to these districts for work on roads, separated according to sexes, in the course of which action a great part will undoubtedly be eliminated by natural causes.

The possible final remnant will, as it must undoubtedly consist of the toughest, have to be treated accordingly, as it is the product of natural selection, and would, if liberated, act as a bud cell of a Jewish reconstruction (see historical experience).

In the course of the practical execution of this final settlement of the problem, Europe will be cleaned up from the West to the East. Germany proper, including the protectorate Bohemia and Moravia, will have to be handled first because of reasons of housing and other social-political necessities.

The evacuated Jews will first be sent, group by group, into so-called transit-ghettos from which they will be taken to the East.

SS-Obergruppenfuehrer HEYDRICH went on to say that an important provision for the evacuation as such is the exact definition of the group of persons concerned in the matter.

It is intended not to evacuate Jews of more than 65 years of age but to send them to an old-age-ghetto—Theresienstadt is being considered for this purpose.

Next to these age-groups—of the 20,000 Jews still in Germany proper and Austria on 31 October 1941, approximately 30% are over 65; Jews disabled on active duty and Jews with war-decorations (Iron Cross I) will be accepted in the Jewish old-age-ghettos. Through such expedient solution the numberous *[numerous]* inter-ventions will be eliminated with one blow...

In Slovakia and Croatia the difficulties arising from this question *[evacuation]* have been considerably reduced, as the most essential problems in this field have already been brought near to a solution. In Roumania the Government in the meantime has also appointed a commissioner for Jewish questions. In order to settle the question in Hungary it is imperative that an *adviser in Jewish questions be pressed upon the Hungarian government without too* much delay.

As regards the taking of preparatory steps to settle the question in Italy SS-Obergruppenfuehrer HEYDRICH considers it opportune to contact the chief of the police with a view to these problems.

In the occupied and unoccupied parts of France the registration of the Jews for evacuation can in all probability be expected to take place without great difficulties.

Assistant Under Secretary of State LUTHER in this connection calls attention to the fact that in some countries, such as the Scandinavian states, difficulties will arise if these problems are dealt with thoroughly and that it will be therefore advisable to defer action in these countries. Besides, considering the small numbers of Jews to be evacuated from these countries this deferment means not essential limitation.

On the other hand, the Foreign Office anticipates no great difficulties as far as the South-East and the West of Europe are concerned...

IV. The implementation of the final solution-problem is supposed to a certain extent to be based on the Nuermberg Laws, in which connection also the solution of the problems presented by the mixed-marriages and the persons of mixed blood is seen to be conditional to an absolutely final clarification of the question...

Under Secretary of State Dr. BUEHLER stated that it would be welcomed by the Government General if the implementation of the final solution of this question could *start in the Government General,* because the transportation problem there was of no predominant importance and the progress of this action would not be hampered by considerations connected with the supply of labor. The Jews had to be removed as quickly as possible from the territory of the Government General because especially there the Jews represented an immense danger as a carrier of epidemics, and on the other hand were permanently contributing to the disorganization of the economic system of the country through black market operations. Moreover, out of the two and a half million Jews to be affected, the majority of cases was *unfit for work...*

Towards the end of the conference the various types of possible solutions were discussed; in the course of this discussion Gauleiter Dr. MEYER as well as Under Secretary of State Dr. BUEHLER advocated the view that certain preparatory measures incidental to the carrying out of the final solution ought to be initiated immediately in the very territories under discussion, in which process, however, alarming the population must be avoided.

With the request to the persons from the Chief of the Security Police and the SD that they lend him appropriate assistance in the carrying out of the tasks involved in the solution, the conference was adjourned.

94. P. Joseph Goebbels

Diary Entry

(March 27, 1942)

Source: Goebbels, P. Joseph, *The Goebbels Diaries*, edited and translated by Louis P. Lochner (Garden City: Doubleday & Company, Inc., 1948), pp. 147–148.

[The immediate results of the Wannsee Conference were evident in this diary entry made by Dr. Joseph Goebbels, the Nazis' Minister of Propaganda. The third most powerful man in the Third Reich, he had received a Ph.D. degree in 1921. Goebbels recorded—with obvious satisfaction—that the trains which carried Jews to the slave labor and death camps were making their regular runs. There was no doubt in Dr. Goebbels' mind of the necessity for the "Final Solution." Without the complete elimination of the Jewish people, whom he referred to as a "bacillus," Aryan Germany had no future.]

March 27, 1942

...Beginning with Lublin, the Jews in the General Government are now being evacuated eastward. The procedure is a pretty barbaric one and not to be described here more definitely. Not much will remain of the Jews. On the whole it can be said that about 60 per cent of them will have to be liquidated whereas only about 40 per cent can be used for forced labor.

The former Gauleiter of Vienna, who is to carry this measure through, is doing it with considerable circumspection and according to a method that does not attract too much attention. A judgment is being visited upon the Jews that, while barbaric, is fully deserved by them. The prophesy which the Führer made about them for having brought on a new world war is beginning to come true in a most terrible manner. One must not be sentimental in these matters. If we did not fight the Jews, they would destroy us. It's a life-and-death struggle between the Aryan race and the Jewish bacillus. No other government and no other regime would have the strength for such a global solution of the question. Here, too, the Führer is the undismayed champion of a radical solution necessitated by conditions and therefore inexorable. Fortunately a whole series of possibilities presents itself for us in wartime that would be denied us in peace time. We shall have to profit by this.

The ghettos that will be emptied in the cities of the General Government will now be refilled with Jews thrown out of the Reich. This process is to be repeated from time to time. There is nothing funny in it for the Jews, and the fact that Jewry's representatives in England and America are today organizing and sponsoring the war against Germany must be paid for dearly by its representatives in Europe—and that's only right.

United States soldiers force German civilians to view bodies of Jewish women who starved during a forced 300-mile march, April 1945. Many Germans did not believe that these atrocities actually took place.

Chapter XIV

Holocaust Rescue: Heroes and Rhetoric

When Adolf Hitler became Germany's chancellor and the Nazi Party began putting its racial theories into practice, German Jews had two courses of action open to them. They could do nothing, assuming the worst of the anti-Semitism would soon pass, or they could leave Germany and settle elsewhere. The overwhelming desire of most German Jews was to remain in the country they loved and "weather out the storm."

As the Nazis grew bolder and more vicious, however, an increasing number of German and post-Anschluss Austrian Jews sought to emigrate. This was exactly what the Nazis wanted. In fact, much of the anti-Jewish legislation was meant to encourage Jews to leave the Reich. The real difficulty at this time lay not so much in getting out, as in finding a place to go. In addition to legalizing persecution and discrimination, the Nazis systematically robbed the Jews of all their wealth and possessions. Few countries were interested in accepting these pauperized Jews as new immigrants.

Most of the Jews who managed to emigrate before the war resettled in western Europe where anti-Semitism was a good deal less evident than in central and eastern Europe. Some families immigrated to Canada, Mexico, and several of the Latin American states. The United States, however, allowed only the merest handful to enter and these people were generally prominent scientists (e.g., Albert Einstein) or religious and social leaders. The Yishuv—the Jewish community in Palestine—desperately wanted to provide a refuge for their persecuted brothers and sisters, but the British adamantly refused to let these refugees in. His Majesty's Government, bowing meekly to Arab pressure, issued the 1939 White Paper which all but ended Jewish immigration to Palestine.

Why were the nations of the world so reluctant to accept Jewish immigration? Economic difficulty caused by the Great Depression in the 1920s and 1930s was one of the major reasons. With large segments of the population out of work, few people cared to welcome new immigrants who would compete with native residents for the few jobs available. In addition to this factor, most countries were relatively homogeneous in religion and culture. Large groups of Jews were viewed as an unassimilable, foreign element which would cause social problems in the future. Much more difficult to prove, but undoubtedly one of the major reasons behind the rejection of Jewish refugees, was the long-standing tradition of anti-Semitism in the Western, Christian world.

While they offered only token refuge, the leaders of the western nations engaged in a sham ritual of first discussing the refugee problem and then appointing committees to further investigate it. On July 6, 1938, representatives of thirty countries met at Evian-les-Bains, France, to discuss the situation created by the Third Reich. Each nation—including the United States and Great Britain—sympathized, but regretfully, could offer no help. Only the Netherlands and Denmark, small states that had already settled many refugees, said they would continue to offer a safe haven to those in need. The sole outcome of the Evian Conference was the establishment of an Intergovernmental Committee on Refugees, which, without cooperation from the free nations of the world, accomplished next to nothing.

The policies of apathy, isolationism, and appeasement which allowed Hitler to pursue his plans of conquest against the Rhineland, Austria, and Czechoslovakia also allowed him to carry out his anti-Jewish policy with impunity. The refugee "problem" turned into a full-blown crisis following Kristallnacht when tens of thousands of Jews frantically applied for immigration visas from any country which would grant them. Most applied in vain. Ten months later, on September 1, 1939, Germany attacked Poland. Great Britain and France declared war on September 3. Germany and the other nations of Europe sealed their borders. The Jews were trapped.

With terrifying swiftness, the Nazi war machine conquered most of the European continent. The Germans transformed legalized persecution against the Jews into a massive effort to murder every Jew in Europe. The scenes of possible rescue action now shifted to the occupied nations. Here, with one notable exception, the Nazis rounded up, transported, and killed millions of Jews with very little or no resistance from the Christian populations. Some individuals did risk their lives to hide endangered Jews, but, overall, the frightened civilians considered their Jewish fellow-citizens expendable. Only in Denmark did the majority of the country's population heroically save their Jewish friends and neighbors. Elsewhere, especially in Poland, parts of eastern Europe, and in European Russia, many locals silently applauded and even openly aided the Nazis in Jewish extermination.

Compounding the tragedy of this general indifference and open hostility, the Allies who might have taken some action to help the Jews, namely the United States, Great Britain, and the U.S.S.R., did next to nothing. Great Britain actively thwarted rescue plans and possible ransom deals with the Nazis because they did not want to let rescued Jews into Palestine. The British government callously closed its eyes to confirmed evidence of mass murders and continued to enforce the 1939 White Paper. The Soviet Union refused to acknowledge that Jews were the special objects of the Nazis' wrath. Stalin's government maintained a continually negative attitude toward Jewish refugees and purposely refused to publicize information about Nazi atrocities against the Jews. The U.S. government was nearly as obstructionist as the Kremlin.

By mid-1942, the American government had enough reliable information in its possession to leave no doubt that the Nazis were carrying out their plans to completely eliminate European Jewry. The Roosevelt administration, nevertheless, refused to publicly mention the specifically Jewish character of the suffering. Washington did not want anyone to assume the U.S. was fighting the war primarily to save the Jews. Apparently F.D.R. and his advisors feared such a belief, especially by Americans who harbored some degree of anti-Semitic feeling, would compromise public support for the war. Also, some influential people in the administration still did not fully comprehend the true situation in Europe. They argued that singling out the Jews for special mention would merely result in more ruthless Nazi retaliation. Even at the Bermuda Conference called to discuss pressing Jewish refugee problems, the delegates continued to use the euphemism "refugees of all races and nationalities" when everyone really meant "Jewish refugees."

After the Japanese attack on Pearl Harbor drew the United States into the war, American military leaders steadfastly vetoed all suggested plans which might have helped save some of the doomed Jews. At the same time, the State Department refused to consider any scheme to ransom the Jews in Nazi occupied countries and held up funds desperately needed to sustain refugees who had managed to escape. Someone at State also sabotaged efforts to inform the administration and the American public concerning the details of the Final Solution. When finally presented with evidence of the State Department's obstructionist tactics, President Roosevelt agreed to take refugee matters out of the department's hands. In January, 1944, he signed an executive order creating the War Refugee Board (WRB) whose specific assignment was to do everything possible to rescue Europe's Jews. Thousands of Jews survived and reached safety in 1944 and 1945 thanks to the efforts of the WRB's special attachés.

In spite of heroic efforts and presidential support, the WRB was never able to convince the U.S. military to cooperate. Nor could it elicit more than token response from the Allies, the neutral nations, the International Red Cross or the pope in the Vatican. In the final analysis, the Nazis' fanatic desire to make Europe "Judenrein" (free of Jews) would have required a rescue effort as monumental as the general war effort itself. Enthusiasm for that type of mission never existed. Military expediency, social and economic fears, latent anti-Semitism, and refusal to take any action seen as incompatible with the war effort resulted in an inability to act which doomed any chances of saving the Jews from the Nazi onslaught.

[*Note:* Sadly, time has dulled the world's senses and faded the stark pictures of genocide. Fifty years later, many world leaders again admonish Jewry not to claim exclusive rights to the memory of Holocaust suffering. Some groups have even claimed that Hitler and the Nazis never carried out the "Final Solution" at all. In a sadistic attack on all the victims and survivors, these revisionists declare that the Holocaust never happened. To them, the claim of six million deaths was all Jewish propaganda used to generate sympathy for the establishment of a Jewish state.]

95. Rescue of Jews in Denmark

German Proclamation to the Danes

(October 2, 1943)

Source: Harold Flender, *Rescue in Denmark* (New York: Simon and Schuster, 1963), pp. 67–68.

[*The Scandinavian countries provided the few bright exceptions to the general indifference toward Hitler's plan to exterminate the Jews. Neutral Sweden accepted all refugees who entered her territory and often extended Swedish citizenship and protection to otherwise helpless Jews. Finland, which became a nominal German ally only after Hitler's armies attacked their common enemy—the Soviet Union—re-*

fused to go along with the persecution and deportation of its Jewish minority. Occupied Norway's population objected to Germany's anti-Jewish policies and spirited as many Jews as possible across its borders into Sweden. The people of Denmark, however, became shining examples of moral courage and humanitarianism. They not only refused to distinguish between Jew and non-Jew, but also risked their lives to hide and, later, to move safely to Sweden, almost their entire Jewish population.

When the German army invaded Denmark on April 9, 1940, the Danes had little defense capability and, therefore, offered no resistance. The Germans set up a "model protectorate" which kept the monarchy and treated the Danes as brother Aryans. The Nazis did this, in part, because the Reich needed Danish agricultural and industrial produce. Himmler and Heydrich were anxious to institute the Nazis' racial policies, but were cautioned that the Danes might not go along with them as had the other occupied nations. When the Germans hinted they would require the Jews to wear yellow Stars of David on their clothing, King Christian spoke for his whole country when he refused to allow such an action. The Nazis dropped the plan, but then tried to round up German-born Jews who had settled in Denmark after Hitler's rise to power. The Danish government forced the Nazis to back down again stating they did not differentiate between foreign and native-born Jews.

By late summer 1943, the Danes' passive acceptance of German occupation was rapidly coming to an end. Sabotage and strikes became more common. The Nazis declared a state of emergency and arrested many Danish soldiers. Himmler and Heydrich now felt the time was right to begin arresting and deporting Denmark's Jews. The actions would commence on October 1. At this point two absolutely unique events occurred. The general in charge of the German army in Denmark refused to allow his men to participate in the roundup. Then another German, aware of the plan, passed on the information to an influential Dane. With lightning speed, the news travelled though the small country, and the Jews were warned in time to go into hiding.

The Nazis tried to convince the populace that the Jews were their enemies and were responsible for all their recent troubles. This ploy had always worked before. The Danes, however, would have none of it. On October 2, the Nazis offered to end the state of emergency and free the arrested soldiers if the Danes turned their Jews over to the Germans. Still the Danish people and government refused. Their replies, two of which appear below, left no doubt that Denmark would never participate in Hitler's plans to destroy European Jewry. In the next few weeks, thousands of Danish Christians secretly moved the country's Jews to the coast where fishermen ferried them safely to Sweden.

In the end, only 472 Danish Jews were caught. These were mostly ill and elderly people incapable of going into hiding. They were sent to Theresienstadt, the "model" concentration camp. Thanks to constant inquiries from King Christian and a massive effort to send packages and supplies—return receipt requested—on a regular basis, these people received better treatment from the Germans than did Jews from the other European countries. Almost all these Danish Jews survived to see the Allies liberate their camp.]

Since the Jews, who, with their anti-German provocation and their moral and material support to terrorism and sabotage, to a considerable extent contributed to the aggravated situation in Denmark, and since, thanks to the precautions taken by Germans, these Jews have been secluded from public life and prevented from poisoning the atmosphere, the German command will, in order to fulfill wishes cherished by most of the Danish people, begin to release within the next few days interned Danish soldiers, and this release will continue at a pace decided by the technical possibilities.

96. The Danish Reply

Christmas Møller, Danish Minister of Trade

(October 2, 1943)

Source: Flender, p. 68.

[Christmas Møller fled German-controlled Denmark in May 1942. He made this strong protest against Nazi persecution from his exile in London.]

It is as if the Nazis' latest infamy, the persecution against the Jews, had destroyed the last, weak dikes which—strangely enough—in some places still stopped the stream of indignation... The persecution of the Jews has hit the Danes in the sorest point of their conception of justice; even the much too tolerant, the passive, the lukewarm can feel this meanness and shrink from it... People say they're surprised that the Germans really had the courage to do it. We cannot take part in this astonishment...from this power we expect no better than racial persecution. We know that this kind of brutality has been the Third Reich's specialty since 1933... The Germans should not think that the sending home of soldiers or the formal annulment of the state of emergency will subdue the wave of indignation created by this infamy... We couldn't yield to the German threats when the Jews' well-being was at stake. Nor can we yield today, where hard punishment and the probability of being taken to Germany await us if we help our Jewish fellow countrymen. We have helped them, and we shall go on helping them by all the means at our disposal. The episodes of the past two nights have to us become a part of Denmark's fate, and if we desert the Jews in this hour of their misery, we desert our native country.

97. *Letter from Danish Lutheran Bishops to German Occupation Officials*

(October 3, 1943)

Source: Flender, p. 69.

We will never forget that the Lord Jesus Christ was born in Bethlehem of the Virgin Mary, according to God's promise to the Chosen People of Israel.

Persecution of the Jews conflicts with the humanitarian conception of the love of neighbors and the message which Christ's church set out to preach. Christ taught us that every man has a value in the eyes of God.

Persecution conflicts with the judicial conscience existing in the Danish people, inherited through centuries of Danish culture. All Danish citizens, according to the fundamental law, have the same right and responsibility under the law of religious freedom. We respect the right to religious freedom and to the performance of divine worship according to the dictates of conscience. Race or religion should never in themselves cause people to be deprived of their rights, freedom or property.

Notwithstanding our separate religious beliefs we will fight to preserve for our Jewish brothers and sisters the same freedom we ourselves value more than life. The leaders of the Danish Church clearly comprehend the duties of law-abiding citizens, but recognize at the same time that they are conscientiously bound to maintain the right and to protest every violation of justice. It is evident that in this case we are obeying God rather than man.

98. *Executive Order 9417, War Refugee Board*

(January 22, 1944)

Source: War Refugee Board Papers, Franklin D. Roosevelt Library.

[As tensions in Europe increased during the late 1930s, isolationist sentiment in the United States also increased. A majority of Americans had no desire to become entangled again in Europe's problems. These feelings helped fuel a nativist paranoia concerning immigration to the United States. President Roosevelt, who relied greatly on public opinion to guide his policy decisions, let the State Department know he contemplated no changes in the country's restrictive immigration laws. The State Department, for its part, went far beyond the president's desires by zealously guarding America's shores from "dangerous" foreign elements.

From 1938 on, the number of visas the State Department and its foreign consuls issued fell well below those actually available under the 1924 Johnson Immigration Act quotas. This was in spite of a steep rise in applications. The man in charge of the Visa and Special Problems Divisions, Assistant Secretary of State Breckinridge Long, harbored an almost paranoid fear of refugees—especially Jewish refugees—believing most of them to be communists and radicals. With the aid of a few men of similar views (men at State), Long came close to halting the admission of all refugees. By an ironic twist of fate, one of Long's responsibilities included control of the State Department's refugee rescue activities.

When the State Department received reliable reports in the months following the Wannsee Conference of the German plans to destroy European Jewry with Zyklon B gas, Long and his division purposely suppressed the information. The assistant Secretary carefully managed the agenda for the Bermuda Conference, guaranteeing its failure ahead of time. His division also delayed concrete plans to save many French and Rumanian Jews in 1943 until any possibility of effective aid became impossible. This unconscionable procrastination continued for five months after the Treasury Department authorized the transfer of funds to help rescue these people.

Stunned by the State Department's long delay, several Treasury Department officials began a careful investigation of State's handling of refugee affairs. On January 13, 1944, they delivered the results of their research to Henry Morgenthau, Jr., the Secretary of the Treasury. Their "Report to the Secretary on the Acquiescence of the Government in the Murder of the Jews" listed detailed accounts of the State Department's "gross procrastination and willful failure to act."

Morgenthau, one of several prominent Jews in Roosevelt's administration and an old friend of the president, redrafted the report. Three days later he presented it directly to F.D.R. His "Personal Report to the President" hinted at a nasty public scandal unless refugee aid and rescue were taken out of the State Department's jurisdiction. The Treasury Secretary then presented the president with a rough draft for the creation of an interdepartmental committee whose express purpose was to save Jewish refugees. On January 22, President Roosevelt signed Executive Order 9417, officially creating the War Refugee Board.]

WHEREAS it is the policy of this Government *[The United States]* to take all measures within its power to rescue the victims of enemy oppression who are in imminent danger of death and otherwise to afford such victims all possible relief and assistance consistent with the successful prosecution of the war:

NOW, THEREFORE, by virtue of the authority vested in me by the Constitution and the statutes of the United States, as President of the United States and as Commander in Chief of the Army and Navy, and in order to effectuate with all possible speed the rescue and relief of such victims of enemy oppression, it is hereby ordered as follows:

1. There is established in the Executive Office of the President a War Refugee Board (hereinafter referred to as the Board). The Board shall consist of the Secretary of State, the Secretary of the Treasury and the Secretary of War. The Board may request the heads of other agencies or departments to participate in its deliberations whenever matters specially affecting such agencies or departments are under consideration.

2. The Board shall be charged with the responsibility for seeing that the policy of the Government, as stated in the Preamble, is carried out. The functions of the Board shall include without limitation the development of plans and programs and the inauguration of effective measures for (a) the rescue, transportation, maintenance and relief of the victims of enemy oppression, and (b) the establishment of havens of temporary refuge for such victims. To this end the Board, through appropriate channels, shall take the necessary steps to enlist the cooperation of foreign governments and obtain their participation in the execution of such plans and programs.

3. It shall be the duty of the State, Treasury and War Departments, within their respective spheres, to execute at the request of the Board, the plans and programs so developed and the measures so inaugurated. It shall be the duty of the heads of all agencies and departments to supply or obtain for the Board such information and to extend to the Board such supplies, shipping and other specified assistance and facilities as the Board may require in carrying out the provisions of this Order. The State Department shall appoint special attachés with diplomatic status, selected by the Board, to be stationed abroad in places where it is likely that assistance can be rendered to war refugees, the duties and responsibilities of such attachés to be defined by the Board in consultation with the State Department.

4. The Board and the State, Treasury and War Departments are authorized to accept the services or contributions of any private persons, private organizations, State agencies, or agencies of foreign governments in carrying out the purposes of this Order. The Board shall cooperate with all existing and future international organizations concerned with the problems of refugee rescue, maintenance, transportation, relief, rehabilitation, and resettlement.

5. To the extent possible the Board shall utilize the personnel, supplies, facilities and services of the State, Treasury and War Departments. In addition the Board, within the limits of funds which may be made available, may employ necessary personnel without regard for the Civil Service laws and regulations and the Classification Act of 1923, as amended, and make provisions for supplies,

facilities and services necessary to discharge its responsibilities. The Board shall appoint an Executive Director who shall serve as its principal executive officer. It shall be the duty of the Executive Director to arrange for the prompt execution of the plans and programs developed and the measures inaugurated by the Board, to supervise the activities of the special attachés and to submit frequent reports to the Board on the steps taken for the rescue and relief of war refugees.

6. The Board shall be directly responsible to the President in carrying out the policy of this Government, as stated in the Preamble, and the Board shall report to him at frequent intervals concerning the steps taken for the rescue and relief of war refugees and shall make such recommendations as the Board may deem appropriate for further action to overcome any difficulties encountered in the rescue and relief of war refugees.

99. Angelo Roncalli (later Pope John XXIII)

Helping Budapest's Jews

(August 18, 1944)

Source: War Refugee Board Papers.

[The War Refugee Board (WRB) was blessed with a dedicated staff determined to cut through diplomatic red tape in order to speedily rescue as many Jews as possible. John Pehle, one of Treasury's men who had investigated and reported on the State Department's failure to aid refugees, became the Board's director. He targeted the neutral nations as the best places to arrange possible rescue. He sent special attachés to these areas with orders to bend rules, if necessary, to save lives. Ira Hirschmann was the WRB's first overseas representative. A New York business-man and vice president of Bloomingdale's Department Store, he had a long-standing interest in refugee rescue work and a reputation as a man who managed to "get the job done." He left for Turkey a week after Roosevelt issued Executive Order 9417.

Turkey, virtually next door to the Balkans, was a potential staging area for rescuing Jews from south-eastern Europe. British delaying tactics and Turkish disinterest, however, frustrated that effort. In the next few months, Hirschmann turned the Turkish bottleneck into a much more smoothly functioning apparatus which saved thousands of Jewish lives.

Hungary soon became another main focus of the WRB's rescue efforts. A German ally, Hungary, like Rumania and Bulgaria, had refused to turn its Jews over to the Nazis for "resettlement to the east." Homegrown anti-Semitic groups made Hungar-

ian-Jewish life difficult, but Hungary's government would not countenance a "Final Solution." In March 1944, literally overnight, the situation changed. Frustrated at Hungarian failure to carry out Nazi policies, Hitler overthrew the government, sent in his army, and put Germans in control. With the Third Reich now firmly in charge, Himmler ordered Colonel Adolf Eichmann's Sondereinsatzkommando to take care of Hungary's "Jewish problem" as quickly as possible. In a matter of weeks Eichmann's men arrested and transported to Polish death camps almost all of the country's Jews who lived outside of Budapest. The colonel then prepared to wipe out the last untouched segment of Jewry left in occupied Europe.

This time, however, the War Refugee Board was functioning and determined to thwart the Nazis' plan. Pehle called on all the neutrals to send more observers to Hungary's capital. Perhaps Eichmann would move more slowly knowing the world was watching. Only Raoul Wallenberg of Sweden volunteered to be one of those observers. Over the next few months his inventive and courageous efforts saved thousands of Budapest's Jews.

In Turkey, Hirschmann, too, worked to save Hungarian Jewry. He persuaded the Rumanians, through their ambassador in Turkey, to allow Hungarian Jews fleeing the Nazis to travel though Rumania to the Black Sea. There the WRB chartered boats to ferry them to safety. Hirschmann also decided to contact the Vatican's representative in Turkey to see what the Catholic Church could do to help.

The Vatican's response to Hitler's war against the Jews was almost non-existent. Pope Pius XII, perhaps wanting to prevent any retaliation against Catholics in Germany and the occupied countries, refused to condemn the Nazis publicly. He authorized no official Church efforts to intercede on behalf of the Jews. WRB entreaties to the Vatican were met with stony silence. On the other hand, individual priests and nuns had often risked their lives to save Jews from transport to the death camps.

On July 31, 1944, Hirschmann met with the Papal Nuncio (the Pope's ambassador) to Turkey, Monsignor Angelo Roncalli. He inquired what the Italian prelate could do to help save Hungary's Jews from certain death. Roncalli was sincere in his desire to help and asked Hirschmann to prepare a list of specific questions concerning rescue and relief which the Monsignor would answer in writing. That document appears below. Hirschmann's original questions are in the brackets which precede Roncalli's answers.

The Papal Nuncio to Turkey expressed confidence that the Vatican was doing everything in its power to save the Jews. Unfortunately, his faith in this matter proved to be misplaced. Of much greater import was the fact that Roncalli had already sent thousands of "Immigration Certificates" for Budapest's Jews. He made it clear to

Hirschmann that he would willingly send many more. The term "Immigration Certificates" was Roncalli's code for certificates of baptism. Priests in Budapest handed out Roncalli's baptism certificates freely; they did so to save lives, not to convert Jews. With these baptismal papers and the fact that the Nazis tended to round up converted Jews last, many thousands managed to avoid transport to Auschwitz. After the war, the Church made no claim that these people had actually become Roman Catholics.

Monsignor Angelo Roncalli, a humane man who acted in the face of his superiors' refusal to become involved, later became Pope John XXIII.]

Istanbul, August 18, 1944

Dear Mr. Hirschmann,

I hope you will not regard my delay in answering your letter and questionnaire of August 1, as an indication of my lack of interest in you[r] humanitarian work. The many requests for the charitable intervention of the Apostolic Delegation in connection with the recent political events in Turkey have prevented an earlier reply.

I trust you will find the enclosed answers satisfactory and I repeat that I am always ready to help you in your charitable work as far as in my power and as far as circumstances permit.

With sentiments of cordial regard, I am, dear Mr. Hirschmann,

Very sincerely yours,

Angelo Roncalli

Reply to the Questionnaire Presented to the Apostolic Delegation by Mr. Ira A. Hirschmann on August 1, 1944.

1. [What information does Your Excellency have regarding the present situation of Jewish people in Hungary?]

> Because of the purely religious character of its mission and of the lack of official contact with the Diplomatic Corps, the Apostolic Delegation in Istanbul has no information regarding the present situation of the Jewish people in Hungary apart from that received from the Jewish agency for Palestine and from the daily newspapers. The enclosed copy of the recent legislation of the Hungarian Government on this matter was the only communication received from the Hungarian Legation in Ankara on this subject.

2. [What are the specific steps which Your Excellency has been able to take thus far in connection with the rescue or assistance of Jewish people, or others, who are under oppression in Hungary as a result of present policies there?]

> A: At the request of the Jewish Agency for Palestine and of Chief-Rabbi Herzog, the Apostolic Delegation urged the Papal Secretariat of State to do all in its power to save the Jews in Hungary. The Secretariat of State replied that this was already being done and that the Apostolic Nuncio in Budapest was actively engaged in the same work.

> B: The Apostolic Delegation *[meaning Roncalli personally]* has forwarded by diplomatic courier several thousands of "Immigration Certificates" *[Roncalli's code words for baptism certificates]* destined for Jews in Hungary. These were delivered to the persons concerned by the good offices of the Apostolic Nunciature in Budapest and the same Apostolic Nuncio later informed that those certificates had enabled their owners to escape transportation and to obtain the necessary permissions for Emigration.

3. [I understand that strong representations were made by Your Excellency in telegrams of July 6th, both to Rumania and Hungary, regarding the release of Jewish people in those countries. Would you feel free to let us have the contents of those telegrams?]

> The telegrams of July 6th were merely further representations to the Papal Secretariat of State to intervene on behalf of the Jews in Hungary and Roumania. The actual text of these telegrams may not be revealed without the special permission of the Vatican authorities.

4. [Is it your Excellency's intention to make any further telegraphic representations to help effectuate the release of Jewish people, and others similarly oppressed, and to impress upon the Hungarian and the German authorities the attitude of the Church regarding their anti-humanitarian acts?]

5. [Does Your Excellency feel that you can do anything to extend protection to the oppressed people in Hungary now or to protect them against future deportation in the event that this procedure recommences?]

> 4&5 It is not the intention of the Apostolic Delegation to make any further representation on behalf of the Jewish people in Hungary: the only means of doing so is through the Papal Secretariat of State and it seems certain the Vatican has done and is doing its best, both directly and through the Apostolic Nuncio in Budapest, to ameliorate the conditions of the oppressed peoples. The Apostolic Delegation in Istanbul is always willing to transmit by courier to Budapest Immigration certificates or other non-political documents which may by useful. It is also willing to recommend particular cases to the special care

of the Apostolic Nuncio, as has been done, for example, in the case of Rabbi Salomon Halberstam.

6. [Can Your Excellency be helpful in protecting people in Hungary who are Jewish by definition, but who are Catholic or of other religions by faith?]

> There is no evidence that the Vatican has been instrumental in procuring special treatment for persons who are Jewish by definition but Christians by faith. The dispositions, however, promulgated by the Hungarian Government on July 8th…do distinguish between Jews in religion and converted Jews.

7. [To Your Excellency's knowledge, has the Holy See obtained visas for any country for so-called non-Aryan Christians, or are such projects in prospect?]

> In years past, the Holy See, in agreement with the respective Governments, was able to obtain Immigration visas for some of the South American countries for limited numbers of Italian and German Jews. The Apostolic Delegation is unable to state whether any such projects are now in prospect.

8. [If possible, could Your Excellency be helpful in any way in organizing or taking intervening steps in connection with the emigration of Jewish people from Hungary?]

> In the present circumstances it would seem that the only assistance which the Apostolic Delegation can render in facilitating the emigration of Jews is in forwarding by courier the Immigration Certificates.

9. [Would Your Excellency feel free to inquire of the Apostolic Delegate in Budapest whether, by his presence as an observer of events, he might ascertain that the Hungarian government abides by the representations it has made in its recent announcement through the International Red Cross of its intention to initiate certain ameliorating conditions in its treatment of Jewish people in Hungary?]

> The Apostolic Delegation has already made the desired inquiry and shall communicate immediately the reply of the Apostolic Nuncio in the matter.

10. [Would Your Excellency feel free to make use of your offices in securing protection, assistance, or release from jails of anti-Nazis or other political leaders in Hungary or Rumania who, because of their past activities or their political status, have been subject to oppression in their respective countries? In this connection, there are attached hereto lists of prominent persons in Rumania and Hungary who have been subjected to oppression, in part at least, for political reasons.]

> Owing to the political nature of the accusations brought against the persons mentioned in the lists, the Apostolic Delegation feels that it is not in a position to take any action in the matter. Such representations would be better made

directly to the Governments concerned through the medium of the American Embassy at the Vatican and the Papal Secretariat of State.

11. [Does Your Excellency have any knowledge or information regarding such steps as might have been taken to the present by the Holy See in assisting financially so-called non-Aryan Christians, or others, in Hungary who are subject to oppression? Would it be possible for you to be of assistance in the transmission of funds for such purposes, should they become available?]

The Apostolic Delegation has no information regarding financial aid given by the Vatican to oppressed peoples in Hungary, though it feels sure that such assistance has been rendered.

Owning to certain inconveniences which have arisen in the past out of the forwarding of sums of money on behalf of oppressed peoples, the Apostolic Delegation regrets that it cannot be of any assistance in the transmission of such funds to Hungary or to any other country.

[In spite of everything the War Refugee Board and the people working with it tried to do, a large percentage of Hungary's Jews perished. The Board never received the whole-hearted cooperation of Great Britain or the neutral nations. John Pehle was never able to change the U.S. War Department's mind about refusing to bomb rail lines leading to the death camps. Nor could he persuade the Department to ship Jews out of Europe in empty troop transports. The United States never altered its restrictive immigration quotas during the war. Finally, the small WRB staff in Washington, D.C., London and the neutral capitals were no match for the Third Reich's absolute and single-minded mania to kill every Jew in Europe.]

European Jews emigrating to Israel by ship in 1949 catch sight of their new home.

Section Six

The Post-Holocaust World

Jewry in the Latter Half of the 20th Century

E uropean Jewry suffered massive destruction and dislocation as a result of the Nazi assault. The six million who perished represented two-thirds of Europe's and over one-third of the world's Jewish population. Whole communities with their cultural and learning centers, plus an entire generation of scholars, scientists, and religious and secular leaders ceased to exist. The enormously rich traditions of Eastern European shtetl life—the very heart of Ashkenazi Jewry—simply disappeared. All past persecutions paled when compared to the systematic murder of so many millions for no reason other than their Jewish ancestry. The history of the Jewish people during the last half of the 20th century has been a saga of remembering and trying to overcome the Holocaust.

Whether directly touched or not, every Jew—then and since—has been deeply traumatized by the Nazi horror. Every single Jew knows that it could have been him or her in the gas chamber. Every single Jew knows that if it were to happen again, friends, neighbors, and governments could refuse to help, or, even worse, could aid and abet the killing. Because of this, Jews are now very quick to respond to and protest any perceived threat to any Jews anywhere. Critics and friends alike often accuse them of being overly sensitive, but the world is a very different place to the Jewish people as a result of the Second World War.

One of the major factors in dealing with post-Holocaust trauma has been the existence of the State of Israel. The Jews of the world possess an almost universal commitment to insure the survival and success of the Jewish state. Firmly believing that anti-Semitism will always exist and that the nations of the world would very likely refuse them asylum, world Jewry looks to Israel for survival in the event of renewed persecutions. Israel, however, has come into continual conflict with Arabs concerning the Jewish homeland's right to exist. Over forty years of tension and open strife have only made the problem worse. Moreover, Arab Palestinians—many of whom are perpetrators and supporters of worldwide terrorism—have gained international sympathy for their fight against Israeli occupation. Some Jews see the growing anti-Israeli attitude as anti-Semitism in another guise. It may well be so.

Anti-Semitism also continued to be a problem in the Soviet Union. Here, too, it existed under the guise of anti-Israeli and anti-cosmopolitan prejudice. Forced by the communist regime to give up all allegiance to Judaism and the Jewish people, the Jews of the U.S.S.R., nevertheless, remained aliens in their own country. Finally, following Israel's victorious Six-Day War, Soviet Jews recognized the futility of their position and began demanding permission to immigrate to Israel.

Religious and "racial" anti-Semitism reappeared as an unforeseen consequence of Mikhail Gorbachev's liberal reforms. Right-wing groups claimed that all of the Soviet Union's economic and political troubles had been caused by the Jews. After a long delay, Gorbachev and the Soviet press, including Pravda, publicly condemned this resurgent anti-Semitism.

A little more than a year later, a group of hard-line communist conservatives surrounded Gorbachev's vacation home and put him under house arrest. They then tried to seize control of the government in a bid to undo the new reforms. The coup failed when the people of Moscow and Leningrad rose up to oppose it. Their bravery in the face of tanks and machine guns both inspired and was inspired by Boris Yeltsin, a liberal government official and frequent critic of Gorbachev's measured reforms. Yeltsin, later elected president, oversaw the dissolution of the communist system, the break-up of the U.S.S.R., and the establishment of the loosely knit Commonwealth of Independent States (CIS).

The problems of the new CIS are many and varied, and include an attempt to create a modern, functioning free market economy. The future of Jews in this area of the world may well depend on how quickly the government can reform and build up the Russian economy and how strongly it denounces any attempts to make Jews the scapegoats for popular dissatisfaction.

In the West, overt anti-Semitism is generally out of fashion and is openly practiced only by radical fringe groups. New developments, however, have led to a rise in fascist-style bigotry. The dismantling of the Berlin Wall in November 1989 and the uniting of East and West Germany eleven months later resulted in economic hardship for many former East Germans. Roving gangs of disaffected youth expressed their dissatisfaction with the strained economy and rising unemployment by viciously attacking immigrants and desecrating Jewish cemetaries. The spectre of rising neo-Nazi racism has caused thousands of ordinary Germans to protest publicly the prejudice and persecution in their country.

Two new movements have also entered the scene in recent decades. Anti-Israeli sentiment is masquerading as a socially acceptable form of anti-Semitism, and historical revisionists in Europe, Canada, the United States, and Australia are claiming that the Holocaust never happened.

In spite of these negative signs, the area of Christian-Jewish relations seems to offer hope for the future. After centuries of anti-Jewish teachings, Catholic and Protestant churches have begun revising and reinterpreting their religious literature and worship to eliminate material which engenders hatred toward Jews. This movement came as a direct result of anti-Semitism's deadly ferocity in Nazi Europe. Liberal church leaders now recognize the part Christian prejudice played in setting the stage for the slaughter. The clergy of most denominations are trying to increase dialogue and understanding between Christians and Jews.

Tent camps in post-1948 Israel provide the first home for new immigrants.

David Ben-Gurion reads the Proclamation of the State of Israel at the first meeting of the Provisional Council in the Tel-Aviv Museum, May 14, 1948.

Chapter XV

The State of Israel

The creation of a Jewish homeland—recognized and secured by international law—began with the British Balfour Declaration. The League of Nations put that declaration into effect when it gave the 1922 Palestine Mandate to Great Britain. The League Mandate was designed to facilitate Jewish immigration and to help establish an organization, the Jewish Agency, to govern the growing Jewish community in Palestine (Yishuv). The Mandate also instructed the British to encourage the development of both Palestinian Arab and Jewish economies. Within a few years, however, events in Europe threatened to change the existing relationship between Arabs and Jews. Hitler's meteoric rise to power and the passage of the Nazi Party's all-encompassing anti-Semitic laws forced many Jews to seek safety outside Germany. Palestine was one of the places these refugees sought to enter. The Jewish Agency actively encouraged this immigration since the major purpose of a Jewish homeland was to provide a safe haven for all persecuted Jews. Zionism—the movement to create that homeland—envisioned a community in Palestine where Jews could freely express their own culture and religion without interference and/or persecution. That necessitated the existence of specifically Jewish government, laws, school systems, and businesses. With greatly increased immigration, the Jewish Agency believed Palestine could become a self-contained unit providing everything that made modern life possible.

The country's Arab population resented the Jewish refugee influx and feared that Palestine would soon be dominated by a culture which was non-Arab and non-Moslem. The Arab Palestinians saw their own existence threatened by people fleeing a problem which the Moslem world had not helped create. Throughout the

1930s, Palestinian Arabs reacted to these concerns by attacking Jewish farm settlements, rioting in the cities, and staging general strikes which disrupted the country.

As tension between Arabs and Jews escalated, the English colonial bureaucracy in Palestine grew increasingly pro-Arab and, in effect, anti-Jewish. The Foreign Office in London, influenced by Arab oil and a naive belief in Arab pro-western sentiment, chose to calm Arab fears by freezing the size of Palestine's Jewish community. They did so by outlawing land transfers to Jews and by calling a halt to future Jewish immigration. The British government hoped the 1939 White Paper which promulgated these new regulations would postpone trouble and, with luck, would give the situation time to resolve itself. His Majesty's Government could not have been more shortsighted, and the White Paper could not have come at a worse time.

It is impossible to speculate how many Jews might have been saved from the Holocaust if Great Britain had honored the terms of the Palestine Mandate. Yet even after the war ended and the world learned of the death camps, the British still saw their foreign policy in terms of Arab conciliation. They still refused to alter or cancel the White Paper's restrictions. The Foreign Office would not allow the traumatized remnant of European Jewry to rebuild their lives in the Jewish homeland.

Holocaust victims became Displaced Persons (DPs) as the United States, Great Britain, and the U.S.S.R. freed Europe from Nazi control. In Germany and Austria, which were under Anglo-American supervision, approximately 50,000 Jews languished in DP camps, many of which had formerly been concentration camps. The British allowed a mere 1,500 Jews a month to go to Palestine. Deducted from this total was the estimated number of Jews who managed to get into Palestine illegally.

The Soviets, now in control of Eastern Europe, ordered the liberated Jews back to their pre-war home towns. Once there, an awful reality faced them. Most of their loved ones were dead, and their homes and jobs had been taken over by others. The situation in Poland was particularly difficult. Nazi-fomented racism and centuries of anti-Jewish hatred nurtured by the Polish Catholic Church did not suddenly disappear when the war ended. After numerous attacks on Jewish survivors and a pogrom against the Jews of Kielce, thousands of Polish Jews fled in panic to the British and American controlled zones. The new refugees greatly complicated the already difficult DP problem.

After reading a detailed report on this situation, President Harry Truman asked the British government to let 100,000 displaced Jews into Palestine immediately. The Foreign Office resented the American leader's request and it tried to delay action and deflect criticism by suggesting another study of the Palestine problem, this time vis-à-vis the DP issue. In December 1945, the Anglo-American Committee of Inquiry began interviewing concentration camp survivors and displaced persons in Europe, as well as Arabs and Jews in Palestine. On May 1, 1946, the committee released its unanimous report: abolish the White Paper restrictions by admitting 100,000 Jews to Palestine at once, but, because of the possibility of war between Arabs and Jews, postpone any definite plans concerning Palestine's future. The British government rejected the committee's conclusions.

Meanwhile, the Palestinian Jews were determined not only to bring the Holocaust survivors to Palestine, but also to create an independent Jewish state. The Haganah (the clandestine army of Palestinian Jewry), through the secret Aliyah Bet program, moved Jews out of the DP camps and tried to land them illegally in Palestine. The British usually intercepted these refugee ships and interned the passengers in camps on Cyprus. In some cases they sent the illegals back to Germany. In Palestine, the Haganah concentrated on disrupting British communications and transportation, but made every effort not to risk English lives. Two other Jewish groups, the Irgun Zvai Leumi and the Stern Gang, however, pursued bloody terrorist methods to fight both the British and the Arabs. Two particularly brutal attacks, the bombing of the King David Hotel and the massacre of Arab villagers in Deir Yassin, outraged the overwhelming majority of Jews and resulted in even more stringent repression against the Yishuv. While Arab attacks against Jews increased, the British seemed to openly side with the Arabs by either looking the other way or by confiscating the Jews' weapons.

Finally, in early 1947, the British government announced it would quit the Mandate and turn the whole matter over to the infant United Nations. Thus the U.N., created to put an end to open conflict, assumed responsibility for its longest enduring peacekeeping problem.

100. United Nations General Assembly

Palestine Partition [Resolution 181]

(November 29, 1947)

Source: United Nations General Assembly. Official Records. Res. 181. 1947.

[After London's announcement in 1947 that it intended to turn the Palestine quagmire over to the United Nations, the newly created U.N. Special Committee on Palestine (UNSCOP) prepared a detailed study of its own concerning the DP problem and the Arab-Jewish impasse. UNSCOP's majority report recommended the partition of Palestine and the creation of independent Arab and Jewish states linked by some sort of economic union. It also recommended that Jerusalem be administered by the U.N. as an international city in order to protect and keep access open to the holy sites.

The Jews reluctantly accepted UNSCOP's suggested plan. It did not give them a great deal of territory—only the areas where Jews were in the clear majority, but it did offer them a seaport and land "adequate to provide facilities for a substantial immigration." The Arabs had no intention of sharing Palestine with the Jews, whom they considered interlopers. They rejected the plan in its entirety. On November 29, 1947, the General Assembly, in a majority decision which included both the United States and the Soviet Union, with Great Britain abstaining, voted to accept UNSCOP's Palestine Partition plan. The U.N. then authorized a commission to oversee the British withdrawal and to assume the Mandatory functions. It would delineate the territorial extent of the future Arab and Jewish states and coordinate the steps necessary to set up the new states on democratic bases.

In response to the plan, Palestinian Arabs escalated their attacks on the Yishuv. *The withdrawing British colonial administration either could not or would not control these attacks. As the time for Britain's complete pull-out neared and in the face of escalating violence, some countries, including the United States, hinted they would reverse their support for partition. On May 14, 1948, as the last British forces left and before U.N. members could change their minds on independence, David Ben-Gurion declared the creation of the State of Israel.*

Both Truman and Stalin quickly recognized Israel. Other countries soon followed. The Arab nations' response was an armed invasion meant to destroy Israel and rid the area of its Jewish inhabitants. Swedish Count Folke Bernadotte, the UN's representative, arranged a truce to halt fighting from June 11 to July 9. He hoped to work out some compromise that would allow the two belligerents to coexist peacefully.

The four-week hiatus proved to be a blessing for the Israelis. It gave time for Diaspora Jewry—particularly American Jews who were deeply committed to Israel's continued existence—to send arms and money to help build up Israeli defenses. When the Arabs renewed hostilities on July 9, the Jews were much better prepared with arms and workable strategies. Bernadotte again called for a truce. This time he announced a possible settlement plan which gave the Arabs part of the Jews' original land area. In blind anger, Jewish terrorists assassinated Bernadotte on September 17.

Fighting resumed again, but in one front after another the Israelis pushed the Arabs back well beyond the original partition borders. Finally, Dr. Ralph Bunche, an American diplomat representing the U.N., set up a truce which gave the Israelis, at least temporarily, the land which they had won from the Arabs. The Jews, satisfied they could defend these new borders, accepted the situation. The Arab nations refused the status quo and vowed to recapture the land at some future time.

The legacy of this settlement was disastrous for the Arab Palestinians (hereinafter referred to as Palestinians), who were now homeless. When the combined Arab armies invaded the newly created Jewish state, the Palestinians fled. The Israelis believed they left because Arab leaders, including the Grand Mufti of Jerusalem, told them the Jews would soon be beaten and they could return to take all the Jews' property and wealth. The Palestinians claim they were fleeing a dangerous war zone and that because of the massacre at Deir Yassin and other Israeli threats, they also feared Israeli retaliation. The Israelis denied forcing the Palestinians out, but refused to allow them to return to their homes. Jordan summarily annexed the remainder of Palestine, and the Arab nations refused to accept the Palestinian refugees for resettlement. Thus approximately one million Palestinians became permanent refugees living in camps administered by the U.N. Relief and Works Agency (UNRWA). These dispossessed people would become the focus of future conflicts and terrorism aimed not only at Israel, but the entire world.

For the time being, the Israelis, and Diaspora Jewry along with them, rejoiced that after almost two thousand years the Jews had a country of their own. Never again would the Jewish people suffer persecution or be forced to be strangers in someone else's land. To them the State of Israel was nothing less than the realization of ancient prophecy.]

THE GENERAL ASSEMBLY,

Having met in special session at the request of the mandatory Power to constitute and instruct a special committee to prepare for the consideration of the question of the future government of Palestine at the second regular session;

Having constituted a Special Committee and instructed it to investigate all questions and issues relevant to the problem of Palestine, and to prepare proposals for the solution of the problem, and

Having received and examined the report of the Special Committee (document A/364) including a number of unanimous recommendations and a plan of partition with economic union approved by the majority of the Special Committee,

Considers that the present situation in Palestine is one which is likely to impair the general welfare and friendly relations among nations;

Takes note of the declaration by the mandatory Power that it plans to complete its evacuation of Palestine by August 1, 1948;

Recommends to the United Kingdom, as the mandatory Power for Palestine, and to all other Members of the United Nations the adoption and implementation, with regard to the future government of Palestine, of the Plan of Partition with Economic Union set out below;

REQUESTS THAT

(a) The Security Council take the necessary measures as provided for in the plan for its implementation;

(b) The Security Council consider, if circumstances during the transitional period require such consideration, whether the situation in Palestine constitutes a threat to the peace. If it decides that such a threat exists, and in order to maintain international peace and security, the Security Council should supplement the authorization of the General Assembly by taking measures, under Article 39 and 41 of the Charter, to empower the United Nations Commission, as provided in this resolution, to exercise in Palestine the functions which are assigned to it by this resolution;

(c) The Security Council determine as a threat to the peace, breach of peace or act of aggression…any attempt to alter by force the settlement envisaged by this resolution;

(d) The Trusteeship Council be informed of the responsibilities envisaged for it in this plan;

Calls upon the inhabitants of Palestine to take such steps as may be necessary on their part to put this plan into effect;

Appeals to all Governments and all peoples to refrain from taking any action which might hamper or delay the carrying out of these recommendations…

Plan of Partition with Economic Union
Part I—Future Constitution and Government of Palestine

A. *Termination of Mandate: Partition and Independence*

1. The Mandate for Palestine shall terminate as soon as possible but in any case not later than August 1, 1948.

2. The armed forces of the mandatory power shall be progressively withdrawn from Palestine, the withdrawal to be completed as soon as possible but in any case not later than August 1, 1948.

   The mandatory Power shall use its best endeavours to ensure that an area situated in the territory of the Jewish State, including a seaport and hinterland adequate to provide facilities for a substantial immigration, shall be evacuated at the earliest possible date and in any event not later than February 1, 1948.

3. Independent Arab and Jewish States and the Special International Regime for the City of Jerusalem, set forth in part III of this plan, shall come into existence in Palestine two months after the evacuation of the armed forces of the mandatory Power has been completed but in any case not later than October 1, 1948. The boundaries of the Arab State, the Jewish State, and the City of Jerusalem shall be described in parts II and III below. [Editor's Note: parts II and III have not been included in this volume.]

4. The period between the adoption by the General Assembly of its recommendation on the question of Palestine and the establishment of the independence of the Arab and Jewish States shall be a transitional period.

B. *Steps Preparatory to Independence*

1. A Commission shall be set up consisting of one representative of each of five Member States. The Members represented on the Commission shall be elected by the General Assembly on as broad a basis, geographically and otherwise, as possible.

2. The administration of Palestine shall, as the mandatory Power withdraws its armed forces, be progressively turned over to the Commission...

3. On its arrival in Palestine the Commission shall proceed to carry out measures for the establishment of the frontiers of the Arab and Jewish States and the City of Jerusalem in accordance with the general lines of the recommendations of the General Assembly on the partition of Palestine...

8. The Provisional Council of Government of each State shall, within the shortest time possible, recruit an armed militia from the residents of that State, sufficient in number to maintain internal order and to prevent frontier clashes...

9. The Provisional Council of Government of each State shall, not later than two months after the withdrawal of the armed forces of the mandatory Power, hold elections to the Constituent Assembly which shall be conducted on democratic lines...

Arabs and Jews residing in the City of Jerusalem who have signed a notice of intention to become citizens, the Arabs of the Arab State and the Jews of the Jewish State, shall be entitled to vote in the Arab and Jewish States respectively.

Women may vote and be elected to the Constituent Assemblies...

10. The Constituent Assembly of each State shall draft a democratic constitution for its State and choose a provisional government to succeed the Provisional Council of Government appointed by the Commission...

C. Declaration

A declaration shall be made to the United Nations by the provisional government of each proposed State before independence. It shall contain *inter alia* the following clauses:

GENERAL PROVISION

The stipulations contained in the declaration are recognized as fundamental laws of the State and no law, regulation or official action shall conflict or interfere with these stipulations, nor shall any law, regulation or official action prevail over them.

Chapter 1.—Holy Places, Religious Building and Sites

1. Existing rights in respect of Holy Places and religious buildings or sites shall not be denied or impaired...

Chapter 2.—Religious and Minority Rights

1. Freedom of conscience and the free exercise of all forms of worship, subject only to the maintenance of public order and morals, shall be ensured to all.

2. No discrimination of any kind shall be made between the inhabitants on the ground of race, religion, language or sex...

8. No expropriation of land owned by an Arab in the Jewish State ([or] by a Jew in the Arab State) shall be allowed except for public purposes. In all cases of expropriation full compensation as fixed by the Supreme Court shall be paid previous to dispossession.

Chapter 3.—Citizenship, International Conventions and Financial Obligations

1. Citizenship. Palestinian citizens residing in Palestine outside the City of Jerusalem, as well as Arabs and Jews who, not holding Palestinian citizenship, reside in Palestine outside the City of Jerusalem shall, upon the recognition of

independence, become citizens of the State in which they are resident and enjoy full civil and political rights...

101. United Nations General Assembly

Resolution on the Internationalization of Jerusalem [Resolution 303]

(1949)

Source: United Nations General Assembly. Official Records. Resolution 303. 1949.

[No area on earth is as holy to Judaism and the Jewish people as the city of Jerusalem. For twenty centuries Diaspora Jewry mourned their eviction from Jerusalem and the destruction of the Second Temple there. As Jews trod the far-flung lands of this planet, their hearts and prayers remained fixed on the City of David and the Temple remnants called the Wailing Wall. While modern Jews celebrated and gave thanks for Israel's statehood in 1948, they grieved deeply over the loss of the old part of Jerusalem to Jordanian forces during the "War of Independence" of the same year.

Spurred by Christian denominations, especially the Roman Catholic Church, the U.N. General Assembly voted to make Old and New Jerusalem (and surrounding areas containing Christian holy sites) a permanently international city. The U.N. itself would administer the area, presumably guaranteeing the protection of, and free access to, the places holy to Christianity, Judaism, and Islam. Israeli and Diaspora Jewry, however, remembering the lessons of history, objected strenuously to this resolution. They questioned its true purpose, considering the fact that almost all the Christian sites were in the Old City under Jordanian control, not the Israeli New City.

The Israeli government replied by making Jerusalem the capital of Israel. By relocating its government offices and the Knesset (Parliament) there, Israel stressed the importance of the city to the Jewish people and made clear its resolve never to lose Jerusalem again.]

December 9, 1949

THE GENERAL ASSEMBLY,

Having regard to its resolution 181 (II) of 29 November 1947 and 194 (III) of 11 December 1948,

Having studied reports of the United Nations Conciliation Commission for Palestine set up under the latter resolution,

I. Decides

In relation to Jerusalem,

Believing that the principles underlying its previous resolutions concerning this matter, and in particular its resolution of 29 November 1947, represent a just and equitable settlement of the question,

I. To restate, therefore, its intention that Jerusalem should be placed under a permanent international regime, which should envisage appropriate guarantees for the protection of the Holy Places, both within and outside Jerusalem and to confirm specifically the following provisions of General Assembly resolution 181 (II):

(1) The City of Jerusalem shall be established as a *corpus separatum* under a special international regime and shall be administered by the United Nations...and

(3) The City of Jerusalem shall include the present municipality of Jerusalem plus the surrounding villages and towns, the most eastern of which shall be Abu Dis; the most southern, Bethlehem; the most western Ein Karim...

II. Calls upon the States concerned, to make formal undertakings, at an early date and in the light of their obligations as Members of the United Nations, that they will approach these matters with good will, and be guided by the terms of the present resolution.

[The creation of the State of Israel was one of the most momentous events in Jewish history. Along with the fulfilled dream, however, came massive problems. Israel's Arab neighbors continued to reject a Jewish presence in their midst. They made no secret that their ultimate goal was the complete destruction of the Zionist state. No site in Israel was safe from terrorist incursions. Many agricultural settlements lived with frequent bombardment from Arab artillery across the border. Security and defense became permanent and costly concerns.

At the same time Israel resettled, educated, and trained the impoverished, traumatized, displaced Jews of Europe. The Israelis also welcomed the overwhelmingly poor, unskilled, and uneducated Jews from the now-hostile Arab nations. In the first three years of its statehood, Israel's population nearly doubled. The nation which had been created to provide refuge for persecuted Diaspora Jewry survived because of steadfast support from Jews all over the world. In effect, Israeli and Diaspora Jewry formed a partnership which benefitted both groups.

Diaspora Jews—mainly American Jewry which emerged from the Second World War as the largest and most secure Jewish community in the world—gladly provided

Israel with strong financial support. They purchased Israel Bonds, donated money to a plethora of charities, and, in the United States, urged the President and Congress to support and provide foreign aid to the new, democratic nation.

In return, Israel gave the world's Jews a new sense of unity and consciousness. There was a renewed pride in being Jewish and a reason to look with hope to the future, which the Holocaust had almost completely destroyed. In addition, and perhaps of ultimate psychological importance, Israel gave the Diaspora a sense of security: in times of trouble, Jews could now find a safe haven from prejudice and persecution.]

102. United Nations Security Council

Resolution on the Middle East [Resolution 242]

(November 22, 1967)

Source: United Nations Security Council. Official Records. Resolution 242. 1967.

[From 1948 to 1956, Israel and the Arab nations maintained an uneasy peace based on the Jewish state's overall superior military capabilities. As the years passed, however, the Soviet Union upset the balance by supporting, arming and training Arab forces, particularly those in Egypt. The U.S.S.R's main aim was to bring the Arabs to its side during the Cold War. In 1956, Egypt's Gamal Nasser felt strong enough to challenge the British and the French. He nationalized the Suez Canal, the all-important waterway which linked the Mediterranean area to India and the Far East. British and French troops attacked Egypt by air. Israel, whose economic link to the outside world was also threatened, invaded the Egyptian-controlled Sinai peninsula. The U.N. called for a cease-fire which Great Britain and France reluctantly obeyed.

Israeli forces halted fighting only after Nasser agreed to stop terrorist raids from Egyptian soil and to grant Israel the right to use the Gulf of Aquaba and the Suez Canal. The U.N. then stationed peacekeeping forces on the Egyptian side of the border to prevent incursions into Israel. Nothing was really settled; Arab raids did not stop—now they came from Syria and Jordan— but another decade passed before open warfare broke out again.

In May, 1967, as in 1956, Nasser, buoyed by Soviet aid, once more tried to cut off Israel economically. He closed the Straits of Tiran to block the Gulf of Aquaba to Israeli shipping and, after demanding the withdrawal of U.N. forces, moved his troops into the Sinai. Syria, Iraq, Jordan, Saudi Arabia, and Kuwait joined Egypt in calling for Israel's annihilation. In spite of Israel's protests, the U.N. took no action. In June, the war of nerves exploded into a war of bullets.

In six days Israeli forces won a sweeping victory. They pushed the Egyptians out of the Sinai, captured the Old City of Jerusalem and evicted Jordan from the West Bank. Israel's army also forced Syria off the Golan Heights. The U.N. Security Council ordered a cease-fire beginning on June 11. While the Israelis agreed to lay down their arms, they adamantly refused to hand back the newly won territory unless the Arab nations committed themselves to direct negotiations. Still denying the Jewish state's existence, the Arabs refused.

The Security Council attempted to settle the problem itself by requiring each side to satisfy the demands of the other. Israel was to pull out of the captured territories, and all Middle Eastern nations were to respect the right of all other nations to "...live in peace within secure and recognized boundaries..." This did not, however, answer Israel's need for face-to-face negotiations. They therefore refused to return the captured lands and, to end calls to internationalize Jerusalem, officially united the Old and New City under Israeli administration.

The Six-Day War gave the Jewish people free access to Jerusalem and the Wailing Wall. It left Israel with occupied territories which not only provided a buffer from Arab border raids, but also provided potential bargaining chips for face-to-face talks. The same territories, however, were filled with hostile Palestinians who detested the Israeli occupation. The Palestinians' attempts to win independence and statehood changed how the West viewed Israel and soon held the whole world hostage to terrorist threats and actions.]

THE SECURITY COUNCIL,

Expressing its continuing concern with the grave situation in the Middle East. Emphasizing the inadmissibility of the acquisition of territory by war and the need to work for a just and lasting peace in which every state in the area can live in security.

Emphasizing further that all member states in their acceptance of the Charter of the United Nations have undertaken a commitment to act in accordance with Article 2 of the Charter.

1. Affirms that the fulfillment of Charter principles requires the establishment of a just and lasting peace in the Middle East which should include the application of both the following principles:

   (i) Withdrawal of Israeli armed forces from territories of recent conflict;

   (ii) Termination of all claims or states of belligerency and respect for and acknowledgment of the sovereignty, territorial integrity and political independence of every state in the area and their right to live in peace within secure and recognized boundaries free from threats or acts of force;

The Western, or "Wailing," Wall after 1967.

2. Affirms further the necessity

    (a) For guaranteeing freedom of navigation through International waterways in the area;

    (b) For achieving a just settlement of the refugee problem;

    (c) For guaranteeing the territorial inviolability and political independence of every state in the area, through measures including the establishment of demilitarized zones;

3. Requests the Secretary General to designate a special representative to proceed to the Middle East to establish and maintain contacts with the states concerned in order to promote agreement and assist efforts to achieve a peaceful and accepted settlement in accordance with the provisions and principles in this resolution.

4. Requests the Secretary General to report to the Security Council on the progress of the efforts of the special representative as soon as possible.

103. United Nations Security Council

[Resolution 338]

(October 22, 1973)

Source: United Nations Security Council. Official Records. Resolution 338. 1973.

[On October 6, 1973—during Yom Kippur, Judaism's holiest day—the Egyptians and Syrians launched a surprise attack against Israel. They sought to recapture Arab land lost to the Jewish state during the 1967 Six-Day War and restore Palestinian rights in those territories. The Egyptians crossed the Suez Canal and pushed into the Sinai. In the north, Syrian armies tried to seize the Golan Heights. The Israelis lost ground during the first few days, but then proceeded to rout the enemy.

The U.N. Security Council issued Resolution 338, which called for a cease-fire to this fourth Arab-Israeli war in 25 years. Once the cease-fire was in effect, both sides were to implement Resolution 242 by returning to pre-1967 borders while accepting the right of all parties to live in peace and security. Unlike 242, however, 338 mentioned the need for direct negotiations between Arabs and Jews to settle the problem finally as equitably as possible. Both sides agreed to the cease-fire, but the Arabs still refused face-to-face discussions.]

THE SECURITY COUNCIL

1. Calls upon all parties to the present fighting to cease all firing and terminate all military activity immediately, no later than 12 hours after the moment of the adoption of this decision, in the positions they now occupy;

2. Calls upon the parties concerned to start immediately after the cease-fire the implementation of Security Council Resolution 242, (1967) in all of its parts;

3. Decides that immediately and concurrently with the cease-fire, negotiations start between the parties concerned under appropriate auspices aimed at establishing a just and durable peace in the Middle East.

104. United Nations

Resolution Equating Zionism with Racism [Resolution 3379]

(November 10, 1975)

Source: United Nations General Assembly. Official Records. Resolution 3379. 1975.

[The Palestine Liberation Organization, born out of the seemingly hopeless Palestinian refugee situation, was one of several revolutionary groups intent on eliminating the State of Israel. The Arab nations and Palestinians, in general, and the liberation organizations, in particular, put forth their own interpretations of Middle East history vis-à-vis Zionism. To them, Zionism—the movement to establish a Jewish homeland in Palestine—was an imperialist, colonialist plot to replace a thriving Arab culture with a westernized Jewish one. The only answer for the liberation groups was the complete destruction of Zionist Israel. Along with this, they demanded the removal of all Jews and their descendants who had arrived in Palestine after 1881.

The Palestine Liberation Organization's battle to eliminate Israel and establish a Palestinian state in its stead won increasing support from developing African and Asian nations. Many of these countries accepted the PLO's thesis that Israel was one of the last outposts of repressive and rapacious European colonial rule. Having just thrown off imperialism's yoke and established their own independence, the "Third World" nations readily sided with the Arab cause. The fact that the PLO worked to achieve its ends by terrorist bombings, airline hijackings, and other attacks against defenseless civilians troubled them very little. At the same time, the emerging Third World began asserting itself against the developed, industrial west. Nowhere was this more evident than on the floor of the U.N. General Assembly.

In 1974, Yasir Arafat, the leader of the PLO, an avowedly terrorist organization which did not represent a member nation of the U.N., spoke before the General Assembly. Arafat entered the hall armed with a gun and proceeded to condemn Israel and Zionism as racist, militarily aggressive, and expansionist. In other words, the Jewish homeland was a threat to world peace.

Selective and myopic history not withstanding, Arafat's speech further polarized the Arab-Israeli impasse. It also deepened the clash between Arabs and Jews world wide and gave the impression that the United Nations supported—or refused to condemn—the PLO and its terrorist activities.

Arafat's General Assembly speech shocked and dismayed Diaspora and Israeli Jewry, but the U.N. vote on Zionism the next year absolutely stupefied them. On November 10, 1975, 72 members of the United Nations—including Arab and non-Arab Islamic states, the Communist countries, Brazil, Mexico, and numerous Third World nations in Asia and Africa—passed a resolution which condemned Zionism as a racist ideology that threatened world peace. Thirty-five member states opposed the resolution and thirty-two abstained. Jewish leaders and organizations in the U.S., Europe, Israel, and Latin America spoke against the U.N. vote. Zionism was not a form of racism, they argued, it was the reflection of the Jewish people's deeply felt desire for a homeland and a refuge from anti-Semitism.

The Zionism/racism resolution was ominous proof that, on the propaganda and popular support level, the Israelis were losing ground to the Arabs and the PLO.

Note: *On December 16, 1991, the United Nations General Assembly finally rescinded the Zionism-Equals-Racism Resolution.]*

THE GENERAL ASSEMBLY,

Recalling its Resolution 1904 (XVIII) of 20 November, 1963, proclaiming the United Nations declaration of the elimination of all forms of racial discrimination, and in particular its affirmation that "any doctrine of racial differentiation or superiority is scientifically false, morally condemnable and socially unjust and dangerous" and its expression of alarm at "the manifestations of racial discrimination still in evidence in some areas in the world, some of which are imposed by certain governments by means of legislative, administrative or other measures,"

Recalling also that, in its Resolution 3151 G (XXVIII) of 14 December, 1973, the General Assembly condemned, inter alia, the unholy alliance between South African racism and Zionism.

Taking note of the declaration of Mexico on the equality of women and their contribution to development and peace, proclaimed by the World Conference of the International Women's Year, held at Mexico City from 19 June to 2 July 1975, which promulgated the principle that "international co-operation and peace require the achievement of national liberation and independence, the elimination of colonialism and neocolonialism, foreign occupation, Zionism, apartheid, and racial discrimination in all its forms as well as the recognition of the dignity of peoples and their right to self-determination."

Taking note also of Resolution 77 (XII) adopted by the assembly of heads of state and Government of the Organization of African Unity at its 12th ordinary session, held in Kampala from 28 July to 1 Aug. 1975, which considered "that the racist regime in occupied Palestine and racist regimes in Zimbabwe and South Africa have a common imperialist origin, forming a whole and having the same racist structure and being organically linked in their policy aimed at repression of the dignity and integrity of the human being."

Taking note also of the political declaration and strategy to strengthen international peace and security and to intensify solidarity and mutual assistance among nonaligned countries, adopted at the Conference of Ministers for Foreign Affairs of nonaligned counties held at Lima from 25 to 30 Aug. 1975, which most severely condemned Zionism as a threat to world peace and security and called upon all countries to oppose this racist and imperialist ideology.

Determines that Zionism is a form of racism and racial discrimination.

105. World Council of Churches

Refuting Zionism Equals Racism Charge

(November 11, 1975)

Source: Edmund Jan Osmanczyk, *The Encyclopedia of the United Nations and International Agreements* (Philadelphia: Taylor and Francis, 1985), p. 956.

[Many American and western European groups, including the World Council of Churches representing numerous Protestant denominations, refuted the premise that Zionism was tantamount to racism. Jews everywhere welcomed this support as further evidence of Protestant Christianity's desire to narrow the gap which had previously separated Christians and Jews. The Vatican, however, made no effort to refute the racism charge. By still refusing to recognize the State of Israel and by giving audiences to Arafat and other Arab leaders, the pope offered clear evidence that the Catholic Church supported the Palestinian cause even when it involved armed attacks against innocent civilians.]

...there is no evidence that Zionism is racism, Zionism from the historical point of view was a movement connected with liberating the Jewish nation from racist oppression. Zionism is a complicated, involved historical process, an expression of many various aspirations of the Jewish nation and as such can be understood and interpreted in various ways, but no such interpretation allows one to unequivocally include it among forms of racism.

A synagogue in St. Petersburg, Russia, built in 1893 and still standing.

Chapter XVI

Jews in the Soviet Union after the
Second World War

Stalin's Non-Aggression Pact with Hitler in 1939 gave the Soviet Union Latvia, Lithuania, Estonia, eastern Poland, and sections of Bessarabia, along with their millions of devout, traditional Jews. When the German army later attacked the Soviet Union and overran these eastern possessions, the Soviets made no attempt to warn the Jews of the coming genocidal slaughter. With no foreknowledge of the Nazi atrocities, relatively few Jews felt compelled to flee deeper into Soviet territory for safety.

The Germans murdered entire Jewish populations of occupied villages, towns, and cities. The Soviets knew and said nothing. Jews volunteered and fought to save Mother Russia in much higher proportions than their percentage in the population. The Soviet leadership ignored this fact and even encouraged the people to believe that Jews were draft-dodgers, deserters, and generally disloyal to the nation. Russian, especially Ukrainian, partisans often turned Jewish partisans and refugees over to the Germans or murdered them themselves. The Soviets knew and remained silent.

During the war, the Kremlin did allow a small, rigidly controlled return of some Yiddish culture, mainly through the actions of the Jewish Anti-Fascist Committee. This group's purpose, in part, was to encourage Jewish patriotism at home. Stalin's main objective, however, was to win support of foreign Jewish communities—especially those in the United States—for the U.S.S.R.'s fight against Nazism.

The years following the end of the Great Patriotic War—as the Soviets called World War Two—saw a continuation of the same trends toward enforced assimilation and denial of separate Jewish cultural status. In addition, Soviet Jews became frequent scapegoats for the government's economic failures and for Stalin's xenophobic paranoia.

In 1947, the U.S.S.R. supported the Palestine Partition plan. It quickly recognized and established diplomatic relations with the new Jewish state in 1948. These moves did not imply a softening of Soviet condemnation of Zionism. Instead they represented support for a movement to dislodge the British from the Middle East. Jews in Moscow, perhaps misdiagnosing these actions as an official acceptance of the Jewish homeland, joyously thronged around Golda Meier as she took up her duties as the new Israeli Ambassador there. Stalin was furious and interpreted the Jews' enthusiasm as gross disloyalty.

From that moment on, Stalin waged an ever more fervent campaign against Soviet Jewry. The state's failure to deal with its economic problems was attributed to Jewish profiteering and embezzlement. Soviet propaganda agencies outdid themselves in inventing code phrases to slander Jews. In 1953, Soviet police arrested a group of doctors with names that obviously sounded Jewish. The state accused them of plotting to kill high Soviet officials in a conspiracy with the Jewish Joint Distribution Committee and U.S. intelligence. As a result of the "Doctors' Plot," all Jews, especially those in the medical profession, became suspect. Just before Stalin's death on March 4 of that year, rumors circulated through the country that he was planning the imminent evacuation of all Soviet Jews to Siberian areas. Many believed that only the dictator's demise prevented a new Holocaust.

With the close of the Stalin era, the official attitude toward Soviet Jews see-sawed between semi-tolerance and repression. How daily Jewish life fared depended on the leadership's perceived needs of the state and on the strength of foreign, mostly U.S. and Western European, opinion.

The Khrushchev years were ones of disillusionment. Even completely assimilated Jews lost their government, factory, and university jobs as the Soviet leader emphasized bringing traditionally under-represented minorities into positions of leadership. Jewish students faced declining acceptance to leading universities due to a newly enforced quota system. Many Jews began to seriously question what they had gained under the communist system at the expense of their religious and cultural identity. In the early 1960s, the government unleashed a series of vicious attacks against Judaism. These crudely anti-Semitic defamations reinforced the traditional fear and hatred of Jews which dated back to czarist times.

Israel's sweeping victory over the Soviet armed and trained Arabs in the 1967 Six-Day War was the final, and decisive, event which galvanized Soviet-Jewish consciousness. Pride in Israel's accomplishment stimulated a newfound pride in being Jewish. Unable to live as Jews within the Soviet Union, they began to demand the right to live as Jews in their national homeland, Israel. The Kremlin put every conceivable obstacle in the way of emigration. This was in spite of the fact that the U.S.S.R. had signed both the Universal Declaration of Human Rights and the Helsinki Accords, which guaranteed just such rights. In 1968, the Soviet Union finally began to issue exit visas, mostly to Jews in outlying republics. For the next two decades, the number of Jews allowed to emigrate fluctuated according to world pressure and the Soviet Union's need to win friends and trading partners in the West.

Mikhail Gorbachev's "glasnost" and "perestroika" were again double-edged swords for the nation's Jewish population. On the positive side, large numbers of Jews could go to Israel. Negatively, however, the new openness and freedom of expression in the U.S.S.R. and its successor, the Commonwealth of Independent States, brought a resurgence of reactionary anti-Semitic writings and threats. Which way Russia and the other former Soviet states will head as they approach the 21st century is an open question. The fate of its several million Jewish inhabitants rests on how that question is answered.

106. Nikita Khrushchev

Anti-Semitism in the Soviet Union

(May 1956)

Source: Kochan, pp. 36–37. As taken from S. Levenberg,"Soviet Jewry: Some Problems and Perspectives."

[Nikita Khrushchev became First Secretary of the Communist Party in 1953. He immediately began reversing many of Stalin's most undemocratic acts. During the February 1956 meeting of the 20th Party Congress, Khrushchev delivered a "secret speech" condemning Stalin's excesses, conveniently forgetting the fact that he had been one of Stalin's strongest supporters for three decades. When he exposed the Stalinist evils perpetrated against many different groups, not once did Khrushchev mention the former dictator's anti-Semitic actions.

Three months after the Party Congress, Khrushchev claimed anti-Semitism could not exist in the U.S.S.R. since assimilation had eliminated Russia's Jewish problem. At the same time, the First Secretary clearly depicted Jews as both strangers to Russian culture and aliens to the Soviet Union's various peoples. He dismissed jealousy and hatred toward Jews as "understandable," due to the Jewish tendency to support other Jews.]

They *[anti-Semitic feelings and actions]* are remnants of a reactionary past. This is a complicated problem because of the position of the Jews and their relations with other peoples. At the outset of the Revolution, we had many Jews in the leadership of the party and of the state. They were educated, maybe more revolutionary than the average Russian. In due course we have created new cadres. Should the Jews want to occupy the foremost positions in our republics now, it would naturally be taken amiss by the indigenous inhabitants. The latter would ill receive their pretensions, especially as they don't consider themselves less intelligent or less capable than the Jews. Or, for instance, when a Jew in the Ukraine is appointed to an important post and he surrounds himself with Jewish collaborators, it is understandable that this should create jealousy and hostility towards the Jews. But we are not antisemites...

107. Trofim Kichko

Judaism Unmasked

(1963)

Source: Gerard Israel, *The Jews in Russia* (New York: St. Martin's Press, 1975), pp. 229–230.

[Khrushchev's regime used Jews as convenient scapegoats to cover up deepening industrial, monetary, and agricultural difficulties caused by communism's failure to develop the country's economy. From 1961 to 1963, the Soviets tried and executed several hundred people for economic crimes against the state. A large majority of the defendants had recognizably Jewish names and many of the "crimes," such as money speculation and exchange, supposedly took place in synagogues with the complicity of rabbis. The Soviet media constantly emphasized these details. At the same time, the government stepped up its campaign against religion as a whole, with special emphasis on the Jewish "cult." While seeming to support atheism, its attacks on Judaism not only reflected a continuation of the long Russian tradition of hatred toward Jews, but also meshed neatly with its attack on Jews for alleged economic crimes.

Trofim Kichko's Judaism Unmasked, *published by the Ukrainian Academy of Sciences, was the most notorious of these anti-Semitic diatribes. Kichko borrowed heavily from 19th-century German anti-Semites, Nazi propaganda and all the old, traditional anti-Jewish defamations used in Christian Europe from the Middle Ages to modern times. By also adding anti-Israeli invective, Kichko and the Kremlin intended to stress the Jews' international connections with the West.*

Judaism Unmasked caused an international outcry, and the Kremlin, often sensitive to foreign opinion, halted this particular form of attack on Soviet Jewry. Later, under Brezhnev and Kosygin, anti-Zionist propaganda would thinly mask the Soviet Union's anti-Semitic programs.]

...An interpretation of the Decalogue...is particularly revealing: you shall not rob your neighbor, that is to say the Jews. But the Jews are free to rob the *goyim* because Judaism teaches that Jehovah has granted all of the wealth of non-Jews to the Jews. If the Jews have not taken everything, it is because they would not have wanted to deprive non-Jews of the many productive forces which help the Jews to profit from non-Jews without doing any of the work themselves.

The Jews very freely cite the commandment forbidding them to bear false witness. But when the interests of a Jew are at stake, false witness to commit perjury is licit... According to the Scriptures, it is enough to repudiate the perjury within one's own mind, and then it loses all meaning. But this must be done in such a way that "the glory of the God of Israel" and the honor and glory of the Jewish religion and its people do not suffer.

One of the commandments of Judaism is you shall not steal. But, according to the Talmud, it is only from other Jews that one ought not to steal anything. But one can steal all that one desires from others, because it is written in the Holy Scriptures that Jehovah gave all of the wealth of the non-Jews to the Hebrews. If the Jews have not taken it all by now, it is so as not to lose the non-Jewish labor force. Moreover, Judaism teaches its believers that the only true goal is to study the Torah and that if the Jews consecrate themselves exclusively to the study of the law of Moses, God will oblige other men to work for them.

Foreign Jews, together with the Zionists, use every means possible to spread their propaganda among the believers in our country...

[Israel's stunning success at the conclusion of the Six-Day War shocked the men in the Kremlin who had been supremely confident that Soviet armed and trained Arabs could easily destroy the Jewish state. They were humiliated by the Arab defeat and alarmed at the open Jewish celebration of Israel's victory. In order to save face, Soviet leaders conducted vicious propaganda attacks against Israel and Zionism.

In addition to shaking the Kremlin's complacency, the Six-Day War had a profound effect on Soviet Jews. It kindled a new pride in being Jewish and a renewed sense of solidarity with other Jews around the world. Knowing they would never be allowed to express their culture and heritage, thousands of Soviet Jews began to demand the right to leave the country. Brezhnev's and Kosygin's response was an organized anti-Zionist campaign which equated Israelis with Nazis and claimed Jews were part of an international Zionist conspiracy intent on destroying the Soviet Union.]

108. V. Bolchakov

Anti-Sovietism, the Profession of the Zionists

(*Pravda,* February 18–19, 1971)

Source: Israel, pp. 239–241.

[The following clearly documents the Kremlin's attempt to portray Jews—now referred to exclusively as "Zionists"—as the U.S.S.R.'s implacable enemies. Jews who sought to leave the Soviet Union were assailed as traitors. Anti-Zionism, with its barely concealed references to the Protocols of the Elders of Zion, became the new method of expressing anti-Semitism.]

Zionist circles play an increasingly active role in the fight waged by imperialism against socialism and the forces of progress. Zionism is an instrument of imperialism in its global battle and in its political and ideological subversion against the U.S.S.R. and world socialism. Its aim is to undermine socialist countries. Contemporary Zionism is an ideology, a system sustained by organizations of the Jewish upper bourgeoisie, which is tied in with the monopolistic circles in the United States and other imperialist powers.

The fundamental character of Zionist policy is militant chauvinism, anti-Communism and anti-Sovietism.

Zionist activities do not have the support of the State of Israel as their only goal. International Zionism, personified by the World Zionist Organization and its branch, the World Jewish Congress, encourages the activities of an international espionage center and a propaganda service which distributes erroneous information about the U.S.S.R.

It is characteristic that among those who systematically finance the activities of the Zionist organizations in the world, those who contribute to the arms race in Israel as well as to the military adventures of that state, we find the financial magnates of different nationalities...

On May 2, 1918, a secret congress was held by one of the clandestine Zionist organizations of the period. Its program was a concrete battle plan against communism. Here are its major points: "Socialism runs counter to Zionism, consequently Zionism and socialism are not only two poles which repel each other, but two elements which exclude one another."

Since the first days of its existence, Soviet power has waged a battle against the Zionist conspiracy which collaborated closely with the counterrevolution...

In 1905, Jabotinsky wrote: "Anti-Semitism above all considered as a principle, is very convenient and very useful as an argument in favor of Zionism..." The Zionists have not hesitated to ally themselves with the Nazis. During the war they were active in the countries of eastern and western Europe and in the occupied regions of the U.S.S.R. Numerous instances are well known when the Gestapo chose people from among the Zionists to be *kapos* in the death camps and recruited them for the special police force to watch over and maintain order in the ghettos.

During recent years, through the intermediary aid of tourists, Western journalists accredited in the U.S.S.R., traveling businessmen and temporary students, the international Zionist trust tried to organize the illegal entry into the U.S.S.R. of Zionist literature published in Russian and to organize a sort of clandestine Zionist organization in our country...

Zionist organizations are now feverishly engaged in building a world-wide Jewish Defense League. They are preparing for an international anti-Soviet drive...

My friends, the Zionists must know soon and for always that there is no place for Zionism in our country.

[Early in 1968, a group of Jewish professionals in Lithuania asked permission to emigrate to Israel. They cited the government's continued suppression of Yiddish culture, outright discrimination against Jews in positions of leadership and the fact that nothing in Soviet law prohibited leaving the country. Soon after, the government began issuing exit visas to some Jews, mostly in the Baltic republics. This took place at the beginning of détente and the Kremlin may have wished to create favorable opinion in the West. In addition, Soviet leaders felt the emigration movement was made up of a small, discontented minority of mostly traditional Jews from the outlying republics. They reasoned it was best to let them go in order to eliminate a source of unrest and to prevent the problem from spreading. Within a short time, however, the demand for exit visas climbed sharply. The leadership reacted with alarm. They developed one obstacle after another to discourage applications or simply refused permission to emigrate.

Soviet citizens, according to the country's laws, have the right to emigrate, especially if such emigration reunites families. The U.S.S.R. also signed the U.N. Universal Declaration of Human Rights which guaranteed unrestricted movement. Nevertheless, people who applied for exit visas were viewed as traitors. They lost their citizenship. They were dismissed from their jobs and were subject to constant surveillance and harassment. Every conceivable deterrent was put in the way of hopeful emigrants. They were arrested for "parasitism" because they no longer had "useful" employment. They were arrested for meeting with other would-be emigrants. They were arrested for teaching Hebrew or Jewish history. They were imprisoned for supposed ties to the zionist-imperialist West. They were exiled to Siberia and condemned to prison camps for agitating for the right to leave the country. Because of state pressure, friends, former co-workers, and family members, in some cases, deserted them. In the West, these people became known as "Prisoners of Conscience."

Through the whole difficult, dangerous, and frustrating process, Jews kept applying and demonstrating publicly. Many Refuseniks, *as the Jews who were denied visas were called, maintained contact with foreign Jews and news media, urging them to publicize the problem. Indeed, how many Jews received exit visas often depended on the degree of world interest and how sensitive the Kremlin was at any particular time to foreign protests.]*

109. Presidium of the Supreme Soviet

Emigration Taxes

(August 3, 1972)

Source: Israel, p. 302.

[The Soviet leadership used a variety of methods to discourage Jews from seeking to leave the U.S.S.R. In 1972, they authorized the formation of a Parasite Commission to review the cases of Jews who lost their jobs when they applied for emigration. Many of these Jews were scientists, computer specialists, doctors, or other professionals. When they asked for exit visas, they gave up their citizenship and/or their internal passports. The Commission would offer them jobs—most on the level of latrine cleaners or menial laborers. If the Jews refused, they were arrested and jailed as "parasites." Some Jewish men awaiting visa decisions found themselves drafted into the Soviet Army although they were well beyond the usual draft age.

Finally, the Presidium of the Supreme Soviet demanded exit fees. They claimed all citizens receive a free education in the Soviet Union and a Jew who wished to leave owed the government the cost of that education. Not mentioned was the fact that the Soviets generally considered that debt repaid after several years on the job. A Jewish man or woman with a Ph.D. could be assessed the equivalent of $30,000 in educational costs, in addition to a tax of approximately $500 for renouncing Soviet *citizenship and another $400 for the actual exit visa. Jewish groups and human rights advocates around the world saw the move as a cynical attempt to extort ransom from foreign Jewish communities since the emigrés themselves could never afford such exorbitant fees.]*

Citizens of the U.S.S.R. who want to establish indefinitely residence abroad, in countries other than socialist lands, are obliged to reimburse the state for the education which they have received in higher institutes of learning for the doctoral degree, for medical internship, for advanced military studies and for having been granted their respective university degrees.

[Signed:] Podgorny, President of the Supreme Soviet
Georgadze, Secretary

[In spite of a crackdown on dissidents, the Brezhnev regime authorized increasing Jewish emigration in response to continued pressure from the West. Then, in December 1979, the Soviets invaded Afghanistan. The United States and other western nations reacted to the threat to world peace by backing away from détente. With little to gain internationally, the Kremlin severely curtailed the number of Jews allowed to leave the country. The situation remained much the same until Mikhail Gorbachev took over the Soviet party leadership in March, 1985. Slowly, the conditions for Jews began to change. By 1987, most of the Prisoners of Conscience had been released and many emigrated to Israel. The Kremlin allowed a small, controlled return of synagogue worship and Yiddish cultural expression.

Gorbachev's reforms and the "opening up" of Soviet life, however, brought new troubles. Long repressed minorities in the outlying republics began attacking their neighbors, and the Baltic States tried to declare independence. The rise of right-wing nationalist groups revived fears of anti-Semitic pogroms. One such organization, Pamyat, *held an openly anti-Semitic demonstration in Red Square in 1989. Even in the Russian Republic's intellectual circles, some writers charged that Jews were always aliens and had been behind the worst excesses of the Stalinist era. Frightened by this resurgent hatred, record numbers of Soviet Jews applied for and received permission to leave the U.S.S.R.*

The failed coup attempt against Gorbachev in August, 1991 resulted in the almost unbelievably swift disintegration of the Soviet superstructure. The U.S.S.R. as a political entity ceased to exist. What type of political union will ultimately result and in what direction the former soviet republics' economies will head is a matter for world-wide speculation. How the new government(s) will respond to anti-Semitism is unclear. The future of Jews in that area of the world remains in doubt.]

Angelo Roncalli, Pope John XXIII.

Chapter XVII

Christian-Jewish Relations in the Second Half of the Twentieth Century

C hristianity's traditional teachings concerning Jews and Judaism in large part created the psychological climate for modern European anti-Semitism. This centuries-old animus saw its ultimate irrationality in the Nazi drive to destroy completely the Jewish people. While most churchmen did not condone or support the "Final Solution," Catholic, Orthodox, and Protestant religious education and liturgy endowed Christians with a firm belief that Jews were the perfidious and devilish people who killed Jesus. The Holocaust was the culminating expression of this hatred and fear that had made the Jews continuous targets of prejudice and persecution.

Following the Nazi defeat and the liberation of the concentration camps, many Jews and Christians of goodwill felt it was time for Christianity to reevaluate its teachings concerning Judaism and redefine its relationship with the Jewish people. This new look at the Jews had to include two major changes: a strong stand against anti-Semitism, including a rejection of the idea that all Jews—including those alive today—were responsible for murdering Jesus; and a relaxation of the pressure to convert Jews to Christianity. Clearly, part of this reform movement came from a deep-seated sense of guilt that churches in Europe did not speak out forcefully enough against the Nazis' brutal anti-Semitic policies. Many Protestant denominations searched their collective souls and found their humanity during the war sadly lacking.

The World Council of Churches (WCC), an ecumenical movement among Protestant and, later, Orthodox Christians, took the first tentative steps in Christian-Jewish rapprochement. At its First Assembly in Amsterdam in 1948, the WCC condemned anti-Semitism and urged understanding and goodwill between Christian and Jew. In calling for greater sympathy and kindness toward Jews, however, the WCC made clear these sentiments were meant to encourage Jewish conversion to Christianity. The Second Assembly held in Evanston, Illinois, in 1954, made no further progress on this issue. This was due to a division between those delegates who wanted to expand special efforts to convert Jews and those who felt such a move would antagonize Jewish friends and be counterproductive. In addition, representatives of Christian churches from the Arab Middle East wanted no specific mention of Jews at all for fear of Arab retaliation.

By 1957, Protestant and Orthodox Christians were beginning to accept a de-emphasis on converting the Jews. Finally, at the 1961 Third Assembly in New Delhi, the WCC not only repeated its condemnation of anti-Semitism, but also publicly acknowledged that the churches should not teach that Jews of today were guilty of killing Jesus. The Assembly also stated that the time of the ultimate conversion of the Jews should be left up to God.

The Catholic Church, although much more tradition-bound, also began to feel the need for a new approach to the "Jewish problem." In 1949, Pope Pius XII ordered the substitution of "unfaithful" or "unbelieving" for the word "perfidious" in the Good Friday Prayer for the Jews. Pius refused to go beyond that gesture. A number of Jewish leaders petitioned him to help deal with anti-Jewish Church teachings, but, swayed by Vatican conservatives, the pope set the problem aside, claiming it needed greater study.

His successor, Pope John XXIII, the former Angelo Roncalli who sent thousands of "baptism certificates" to Budapest Jews in 1944, began the Catholic Church's review of religious attitudes toward the Jews. He urged that a strong, positive statement on Judaism and the Jewish people be on the agenda of the Second Vatican Ecumenical Council. Pope John died before the beginning of the second session, but Augustin Cardinal Bea continued to pursue a new and positive attitude toward the Jewish people. In 1965, after three years of behind-the-scenes political fighting, numerous rewrites and strong Arab pressure to drop the Jewish statement, Vatican II issued a Declaration on the Jews as part of a Schema on the Relationship of the Church to Non-Christian Religions. Although the Declaration was not as strongly worded as Bea and the reformers had wanted, it denounced anti-Semitism and absolved the Jews of today from complicity in Jesus' death.

The Declaration was a definite breakthrough, which began to bear real fruit in 1974. That year the Vatican issued a set of Guidelines on how Jews and Judaism should be presented in liturgical interpretation and in religious education classes. The Guidelines also stressed the need for Catholic-Jewish dialogue and a lessening of the push for conversion. The Church issued further Guidelines in 1985, which showed an even greater sensitivity to the Jewish religion and people.

The two major divisions of Christianity shared common elements in their movements to establish friendly relations with the Jews. Both experienced internal conflicts between conservatives who saw no need to change Christianity's anti-Jewish teachings and reformers who realized that those teachings fostered anti-Semitism and ultimately led to the Holocaust. Both the WCC and Vatican II felt a great deal of Arab pressure not to regularize their relations with world Jewry. Finally, the Jewish statements of the WCC Assemblies and Vatican II were both compromise positions reached to keep a public appearance of unity.

The new Christian teachings concerning Jews and Judaism are really in their infancy. If they are adopted seriously by theologians and teachers, and passed on to the church faithful, perhaps religiously inspired hatred and fear of the Jews will begin to disappear in future generations.

---

110. The Provisional Committee of the World Council of Churches

Concerning Jewish Refugees

(1946)

Source: *World Council of Churches: Its Process of Formation* (Geneva, Switzerland: World Council of Churches, 1946), pp. 35–36.

[The Provisional Committee, during its session to plan the establishment of the World Council of Churches, took special cognizance of Jewish refugees and their terrible plight during the post-war era. The Committee urged Christians actively to counter anti-Semitism and take care of the Jews who still suffered because of the effects of the war and Nazi persecution. They asked the faithful to help find homes for these people and promote understanding and goodwill between Christians and Jews. This was a humane expression of concern from a large branch of Christianity, which also acknowledged that its failure to live up to its own beliefs contributed to anti-Semitic persecution.]

The Provisional Committee of the World Council of Churches records its deep sense of horror at the unprecedented tragedy which has befallen the Jewish people in consequence of the Nazi attempt to exterminate European Jewry… [it] recognizes with thankfulness the faithful witness of many Christians, who, at great peril to themselves, made their protest against Antisemitism and gave shelter to its victims. It also acknowledges with penitence the failure of the churches to overcome…those factors in human relationships which have created and now contribute to this evil which threatens both Jewish and Christian communities.

The Committee therefore urgently calls upon Christians throughout the world to combat this evil…

(a) by testifying against the…practices of Antisemitism as a denial of the spirit and teaching of our Lord;

(b) by ministering…to the needs of those who still suffer the consequences of Antisemitism…;

(c) by giving their support to efforts to find acceptable homes for Jews who have been displaced or who can no longer remain where they are;

(d) by co-operating with Jews in reciprocal attempts to remove causes of friction in personal and community relationships;

(e) by promoting understanding and goodwill between Christians and Jews, so that they may bear a common witness to the obligations of neighborliness…

111. World Council of Churches, Amsterdam Assembly

Christian Approach to the Jews

(1948)

Source: Allan Brockway, et al., commentators, *The Theology of the Churches and the Jewish People* (Geneva, Switzerland: World Council of Churches, 1988), pp 5–7.

*[The First Assembly of the World Council of Churches, consisting of representatives of 135 Protestant denominations from 44 countries, met in Amsterdam in 1948. (*Note: *Russian Orthodox, Greek Orthodox, and several non-Protestant, non-Roman Catholic Christian denominations joined the WCC in the following decades.) The Amsterdam Assembly gathered to discuss concerns common to Protestant Christianity, including the churches' relations with the Jewish people. The horrifying revelations of the Holocaust compelled the WCC to recognize officially and deal with the existence of Jews in the modern world.*

The Assembly handled this issue by first recognizing the special suffering of the Jews from early Christian times through the Holocaust and post-war era. They condemned anti-Semitism and urged Christians to treat Jews with equality and justice. The Assembly's statement, however, made it abundantly clear that such humane treatment was meant to break down the Jews' centuries-long resistance to conversion. Furthermore, the Assembly suggested that the Christians' mission to the Jews be made a normal part of parish work and be carried out by specially trained ministers. Nevertheless, the gathering did warn that no "unworthy pressures or inducements" be used to bring the Jews into the Christian fold.

The Amsterdam Assembly sent a clear message to world Jewry that Christianity was not yet ready to acknowledge its role in Jewish persecution, nor was it ready to accept Jews for what they were without attempting to missionize them.]

Introduction

No people in His one world have suffered more bitterly from the disorder of man than the Jewish people. We cannot forget that we meet in a land from which 110,000 Jews were taken to be murdered. Nor can we forget that we meet only five years after the extermination of 6 million Jews. To the Jews our God has bound us in a special solidarity linking our destinies together in His design...

2. The special meaning of the Jewish people for Christian faith

In the design of God, Israel has a unique position. It was Israel with whom God made His covenant by the call of Abraham. It was Israel to whom God revealed His name and gave His law. It was to Israel that He sent His Prophets with their message of judgment and grace. It was Israel to whom He promised the coming of His Messiah. By the history of Israel God prepared the manger in which in the fullness of time He put the Redeemer of all mankind, Jesus Christ. The Church has received this spiritual heritage from Israel and is therefore in honour bound to render it back in the light of the Cross. We have, therefore, in humble conviction to proclaim to the Jews, "The Messiah for Whom you wait has come." The promise has been fulfilled by the coming of Jesus Christ...

3. Barriers to overcome

...We must acknowledge in all humility that too often we have failed to manifest Christian love towards our Jewish neighbours, or even a resolute will for common social justice. We have failed to fight with all our strength the age-old disorder of man which anti-semitism represents. The churches in the past have helped to foster an image of the Jews as the sole enemies of Christ, which has contributed to anti-semitism in the secular world. In many lands virulent anti-semitism still threatens and in other lands the Jews are subjected to many indignities.

We call upon all the churches we represent to denounce anti-semitism, no matter what its origin, as absolutely irreconcilable with the profession and practice of the Christian faith. Anti-semitism is a sin against God and man.

Only as we give convincing evidence to our Jewish neighbors that we seek for them the common rights and dignities which God wills for His children, can we come to such a meeting with them as would make it possible to share with them the best which God has given us in Christ.

4. The Christian witness to the Jewish people

In spite of the universality of our Lord's commission and of the fact that the first mission of the Church was to the Jewish people, our churches have with rare exception failed to maintain that mission...

Owing to this failure our churches must consider the responsibility for missions to the Jews as a normal part of parish work...

...the churches should make provision for the education of ministers specially fitted for this task...

5. The emergence of Israel as a state

The establishment of the state "Israel" adds a political dimension to the Christian approach to the Jews and threatens to complicate anti-semitism with political fears and enmities...

112. Roman Catholic Church

Good Friday Prayer for Jews
Eliminating References to Jewish "Perfidy"

(1949)

Source: Arthur Gilbert, *The Vatican Council and the Jews* (Cleveland: the World Publishing Company, 1968), pp. 30–31.

[Pope Pius XII, perhaps recognizing a relationship between the Church portrayal of Jews and the existence of anti-Semitism, ordered the Latin phrase "pro perfidis Judaeis" to be translated into the vernacular as "for the unfaithful" or "unbelieving Jews." This was meant to eliminate the term "perfidious" from the traditional Good Friday intercessionary prayer.]

Let us pray also for the unbelieving Jews: That our God and Lord will remove the veil from their hearts so that they, too, may acknowledge our Lord, Jesus Christ.

Almighty, Eternal God, who does not withhold thy mercy, even from Jewish unbelief, heed the prayer we offer for the blindness of that people that they may acknowledge the light of thy truth which is Christ, and be delivered from their darkness.

[Pope John XXIII, in 1959, took the next step by deleting the words "pro perfidis Judaeis" from the original Latin text. Finally, following the Vatican II declaration concerning the Jews, Pope Paul VI eliminated all negative references to the Jewish people in the Good Friday Prayer.]

113. Report of the Ecumenical Institute to the Executive Committee of the World Council of Churches
"Attitudes in Relation to the Jewish People"
(1957)

Source: World Council of Churches Archives. Executive Committee Papers (1957), pp. 1–5

[The Ecumenical Institute was established in 1946 near Geneva, Switzerland, to train Christian leadership to deal with the realities of the post-war world. It stressed the need for understanding and communication among all peoples and worked to develop mutual respect between racial, ethnic, and national groups through a Christian perspective. In 1948, the Ecumenical Institute became a section of the World Council of Churches.

In 1957, after lengthy study, the Institute presented a report concerning "Attitudes in Relation to the Jewish People" to the WCC. It stated that conversion was the "true destiny" of the Jewish people, but only God could decide when that destiny would be fulfilled. In the meantime perhaps God kept the Jews separate to teach the world lessons about human diversity. With this in mind, the report recognized the Christian church's guilt—through presenting a distorted portrayal of Jews—in helping to create and nurture centuries of anti-Semitism. The Institute recommended that special missionary activity aimed specifically at the Jews should cease, since its continuation would only drive Jews and Christians farther apart.

The Christian attitude toward the State of Israel was not as favorable. The Ecumenical Institute accused the Israeli state of causing great Arab suffering. Furthermore, the Institute claimed that the Jewish people's calling was religious and ethical. The existence of Jewish nationalism (i.e., the existence of Israel itself) was a revolt against God's plan for the Jews. This part of the Institute's report could hardly have been seen by world Jewry as an attempt to increase understanding or better relations.]

The promise of the Kingdom of Christ is offered to all men, to Jew as to Gentile...

2. "Salvation is of the Jews" (John iv.22)

    a. ...the revelation of the living God is given through all Scripture, the Old Testament and the New... we must use the Old Testament in our worship, prayer and study, while seeing that the whole revelation of God finds its focus and fulfillment in Jesus Christ...

    b. ...the Jews had a unique role in the purpose of God as the bearers of His revelation...

    c. As Christians we owe a special debt to the Jewish people, and still have much to learn from them...

3. The Jewish People in Relation to the Christian Hope

    a. Since Christ is Lord over all the world, when He shall reign at His Second Coming, the fullness of both Jew and Gentile will have been brought into His Kingdom. In...the New Testament a "remnant" from the Jews accept Christ. A hardening has happened to other Jews, but God still holds out His promise for them, and their conversion is closely associated with the hope of the Second Coming...

    c. Our hope for the Jews does not mean that we can calculate the time or define the nature of the coming of Christ in his Kingdom...

    d. Of the fact of the hope for Jew and Gentile in Christ we are assured; as to the nature of its fulfillment we rightly keep an expectant mind, lest...we should be blinded by our...definitions, and so be unprepared when He comes to claim his own.

    e. For these reasons, we should maintain a certain caution in applying prophecies, whether from the Old Testament or the New...to contemporary events...

    f. One thing however we proclaim with absolute assurance. Christ will come. Christ will reign. God hath committed all things into His hands. His love embraces both Jew and Gentile. His Church must embrace both...

4. The Continued Existence of the Jewish People after the Coming of Christ...

    b. As Christians we affirm that the Jewish people will not find their true destiny until they turn and acknowledge Jesus Christ as Lord...at the same time, we acknowledge that the whole world is also guilty before God in its failure to acknowledge Christ as Lord; and further we acknowledge the sins of Christian people in their frequent failure to manifest the love and power of Christ to the people from whom He came. In addition to this, the Church has been guilty through the centuries in presenting a distorted picture of the Jew to the world, and this has been a major factor in anti-Semitism…

d. …we must ask whether the centuries' long preservation of the Jews as an ethnic as well as religious group…is not intended by God to teach both us and them new lessons concerning the problems of race and nationality, which so gravely vex the world…

f. …the setting up of the State of Israel, while it has relieved the sufferings of many Jews, has involved great suffering for many Arabs who have lost their land and…homes; and they also are a people under God's care. Moreover, while we understand the desire of many Jews to have a country of their own, we believe it is their calling to live as the people of God, and not to become merely a nation like others…

6. The Christian Responsibility Toward the Jewish People…

c. We shall not single out the Jewish people for particular attention in evangelism, where that would only emphasize the separation which we seek to overcome…

114. World Council of Churches Third Assembly, New Delhi

Resolution on Anti-Semitism

(November 1961)

Source: *The New Delhi Report: The Third Assembly of the World Council of Churches 1961* (New York: Association Press, 1962), p. 148.

[The World Council of Churches held its Third Assembly in New Delhi, India, in 1961. The delegates repeated the stirring denunciation of anti-Semitism made by the WCC First Assembly. They also publicly acknowledged the link between Christianity's claim that all Jews for all time were guilty of Jesus' death and the existence of anti-Semitic prejudice. The WCC reminded its member churches that the crucifixion came as a result of all people's sins, therefore, church teachings should not single out the Jews as "Christ killers."

The New Delhi resolution on anti-Semitism was a long-awaited breakthrough warmly welcomed by Jewish leaders. It also put pressure on the Roman Catholic Ecumenical Council (Vatican II), soon to meet in Rome, to reconsider its attitude toward the Jewish people.]

The Third Assembly recalls the following words which were addressed to the churches by the First Assembly of the World Council of Churches in 1948:

> We call upon all the churches we represent to denounce anti-semitism, no matter what its origin, as absolutely irreconcilable with the profession and practice of the Christian faith. Anti-semitism is sin against God and man. Only as we give convincing evidence to our Jewish neighbours that we seek for them the common rights and dignities which God wills for his children, can we come to such a meeting with them as would make it possible to share with them the best which God has given us in Christ.

The Assembly renews this plea in view of the fact that situations continue to exist in which Jews are subject to discrimination and even persecution. The Assembly urges its member churches to do all in their power to resist every form of anti-semitism. In Christian teaching the historic events which led to the Crucifixion should not be presented as to fasten upon the Jewish people of today responsibilities which belong to our corporate humanity and not to one race or community. Jews were the first to accept Jesus and Jews are not the only ones who do not yet recognize him.

115. Augustin Cardinal Bea

The Need for a Religious Statement by Vatican II on the Jews

(November 20, 1963)

Source: Henri Fesquet, *The Drama of Vatican II; the Ecumenical Council, June 1962–December 1965* (New York: Random House, 1967), pp. 243–244.

[In October 1958, Angelo Cardinal Roncalli ascended the Throne of St. Peter to become Pope John XXIII. The new pope dedicated himself to modernizing the Church and reaching out in friendship to non-Catholics. He wished to establish a dialogue with Protestant and Orthodox Christians as a preliminary to some sort of religious reconciliation. He also had a genuine interest, which dated back to World War Two, in Catholic-Jewish relations. In order to achieve the aims of his papacy, John called for a Second Ecumenical Council, later referred to as Vatican II, which would discuss all aspects of the Catholic faith and institute meaningful reforms.

John XXIII asked his friend and advisor Augustin Cardinal Bea, the head of the Secretariat for Promoting Christian Unity, to develop a declaration concerning the Jewish people. Both men felt the statement needed to denounce anti-Semitism and reform those Church teachings which could lead to anti-Jewish prejudice. Cardinal Bea, a German church leader who had witnessed Nazism and the Holocaust, approached the task with great zeal and determination. He believed misinterpreted sections of the New Testament and other early Christian writings had led to centuries of Jewish persecution. With Pope John's concurrence, he met with representatives of the major world Jewish organizations to form a sense of how Jews viewed the problem and what they felt needed to be done.

Almost from the beginning, the Declaration on the Jews ran into difficulties. As the opening of Vatican II approached, the World Jewish Congress announced it would send an unofficial observer. The Arab nations immediately protested and requested the same privilege. Fearful of creating open controversy and of offending the Arabs, the Declaration on the Jews was recalled to be rewritten. Nothing concerning relations with Jews was presented for discussion during the first session.

Pope John XXIII died before the second session began, and the College of Cardinals chose Giovanni Battista Cardinal Montini as his successor. The new Pope Paul VI was not strongly motivated concerning relations with the Jews, but he was greatly concerned with the safety of Catholics and the Church in the Arab Middle East. Nevertheless, Cardinal Bea and a group of liberal American Catholic leaders insisted that the newly drafted statement concerning the Jews be presented for consideration during the second session.

The following selection is part of Bea's official introduction to the Declaration on the Jews. It directly refutes the Church's claim that all the Jews were (and are) responsible for Jesus' crucifixion.]

Some decades ago, anti-Semitism, as it is called, was prevalent in various regions and in a particularly violent and criminal form, especially in Germany under the rule of National Socialism, which…committed frightful crimes, extirpating several millions of Jewish people… Moreover, accompanying and assisting this whole activity was a most powerful and effective "propaganda," as it is called, against the Jews. Now, it would have been almost impossible if some of the claims of that propaganda did not have an unfortunate effect even on faithful Catholics…

For the Jews of our times can hardly be accused of the crimes committed against Christ…actually, even in the time of Christ, the majority of the chosen people did not cooperate with the leaders of the people in condemning Christ…those among them who cried out to Pilate, "Crucify him," formed a very small part of the chosen people…

If therefore not even all the Jews in Palestine or in Jerusalem could be accused, how much less the Jews dispersed throughout the Roman Empire. And how much less again those who today after nineteen centuries live scattered in the whole world.

116. Vatican II

Declaration of the Relation of the Church to Non-Christian Religious, Nostra Aetate

(October, 1965)

Source: Walter M. Abbott, S.J., general editor, *The Documents of Vatican II* (New York: Herder and Herder Association Press, 1966.], pp. 660–661, 663–668.

[Cardinal Bea and those who supported changes in Catholic teachings concerning the Jews were particularly interested in combatting the charge that all Jews since the crucifixion to the end of time were guilty of deicide *(god-killing). They firmly believed that a large part of the rationale for Christian anti-Semitism would disappear when Christians no longer believed Jews to be Christ-killers.*

Not all of the 2,550 Council Fathers (official Church representatives to Vatican II) from more than 100 countries sought changes in Catholic-Jewish relations. The Patriarchs from Middle Eastern Armenian, Chaldean, Coptic, Maronite, and Syrian Churches were adamantly opposed to any specific statement mentioning Jews. Other prelates clung tenaciously to the traditional Gospel interpretations. Some outside groups tried to influence the Council by circulating anti-Semitic literature and crude accusations.

Over a period of two years, the wording of the Declaration on the Jews became more generalized. The final statement formally submitted to the Vatican Council II was a compromise, which, nevertheless, overturned centuries of beliefs and teachings concerning the Jewish people. On October 28, 1965, with 2,221 Council Fathers voting in favor and 88 voting against, Section 4 of Nostra Aetate *(Latin for "In our times...," the beginning words of this document) dealing directly with the Jews was officially adopted by Vatican II. Section 1 of this declaration served as an introduction. Sections 2 and 3 dealt with Hinduism, Buddhism, and Islam.*

The Declaration included a number of major points which opened the way to Catholic-Jewish dialogue and increased mutual understanding. Vatican II stated that God "does not repent of His gifts." He did not revoke his Covenant with the Jews nor did He repudiate or curse the Jewish people. The Catholic Church declared it wrong to blame Christ's death on all Jews living at the time of the crucifixion or upon Jews living today. The Declaration on the Jews also deplored anti-Semitism, no matter what its source. In this manner the Council Fathers tacitly admitted the Church's contribution to fifteen centuries of anti-Jewish persecution and prejudice. The real value of this declaration, however, depended on how vigorously the Church worked to bring religious education and liturgical interpretation into conformity with these newly stated beliefs.]

1. In our times, when every day men are being drawn closer together and the ties between various peoples are being multiplied, the Church is giving deeper study to her relationship with non-Christian religions. In her task of fostering unity and love among men, and even among nations, she gives primary consideration in this document to what human beings have in common and to what promotes fellowship among them.

For all peoples comprise a single community, and have a single origin, since God made the whole race of men dwell over the entire face of the earth (cf. Acts 17:26). One also is their final goal: God. His providence, His manifestations of goodness, and His saving designs extend to all men (cf. Wis. 8:1; Acts 14:17; Rom. 2:6–7; 1 Tim. 2:4) against the day when the elect will be united in that Holy City ablaze with the splendor of God, where the nations will walk in His light (cf. Apoc. 21:23 f.).

Men look to the various religions for answers to those profound mysteries of the human condition which, today even as in olden times, deeply stir the human heart: What is a man? What is the meaning and the purpose of our life? What is goodness and what is sin? What gives rise to our sorrows and to what intent? Where lies the path to true happiness? What is the truth about death, judgment, and retribution beyond the grave? What, finally, is that ultimate and unutterable mystery which engulfs our being, and whence we take our rise, and whither our journey leads us?...

4. *[Concerning Jews]* As this sacred Synod searches into the mystery of the Church, it recalls the spiritual bond linking the people of the New Covenant with Abraham's stock.

For the Church of Christ acknowledges that, according to the mystery of God's saving design, the beginnings of her faith and her election are already found among the patriarchs, Moses, and the prophets. She professes that all who believe in Christ, Abraham's sons according to the faith (cf. Gal. 3:7), are included in the same patriarch's call, and likewise that the salvation of the Church was mystically foreshadowed by the chosen people's exodus from the land of bondage.

The Church, therefore, cannot forget that she received the revelation of the Old Testament through the people whom God in his inexpressible mercy deigned to establish the Ancient Covenant. Nor can she forget that she draws sustenance from the root of that good olive tree onto which have been grafted the wild olive branches of the Gentiles (cf. Rom. 11:17–24). Indeed, the Church believes that by His cross Christ, our Peace, reconciled Jew and Gentile, making them both one in Himself (cf. Eph. 2:14–16).

Also, the Church ever keeps in mind the words of the Apostle about his kinsmen, "who have the adoption as sons, and the glory and the covenant and the legislation and the worship and the promises; who have the fathers, and from whom is Christ according to the flesh" (Rom. 9:4–5), the son of the Virgin Mary. The Church recalls too that from the Jewish people sprang the apostles, her foundation stones and pillars, as well as most of the early disciples who proclaimed Christ to the world.

As holy Scripture testifies, Jerusalem did not recognize the time of her visitation (cf. Lk. 19:44), nor did the Jews in large number accept the gospel; indeed, not a few opposed the spreading of it (cf. Rom. 11:28). Nevertheless, according to the Apostle, the Jews still remain most dear to God because of their fathers, for He does not repent of the gifts He makes nor of the calls He issues (cf. Rom. 11:28–29). In company with the prophets and the same Apostle, the Church awaits that day, known to God alone, on which all peoples will address the Lord in a single voice and "serve him with one accord" (Soph. 3:9, cf. Is. 66:23; Ps. 65:4; Rom. 11:11–32).

Since the spiritual patrimony common to Christians and Jews is thus so great, this sacred Synod wishes to foster and recommend that mutual understanding and respect which is the fruit above all of biblical and theological studies, and of brotherly dialogues.

True, authorities of the Jews and those who followed their lead pressed for the death of Christ (cf. Jn. 19:6), still, what happened in His passion cannot be blamed upon all the Jews then living, without distinction, nor upon the Jews of today. Although the Church is the new people of God, the Jews should not be presented as repudiated or cursed by God, as if such views followed from the holy Scriptures. All should take pains, then, lest in catechetical instruction and in the preaching of God's Word they teach anything out of harmony with the truth of the gospel and the spirit of Christ.

The Church repudiates all persecutions against any man. Moreover, mindful of the common patrimony with the Jews, and motivated by the gospel's spiritual love and by no political considerations, she deplores the hatred, persecutions, and displays of anti-Semitism directed against the Jews at any time and from any source.

Besides, as the Church has always held and continues to hold, Christ in His boundless love freely underwent His passion and death because of the sins of all men, so that all might attain salvation. It is, therefore, the duty of the Church's preaching to proclaim the cross of Christ as the sign of God's all-embracing love and as the fountain from which every grace flows.

Vatican Council II in session.

117. Vatican Commission for Religious Relations with the Jews

Guidelines on Religious Relations with the Jews
(December 1, 1974)

Source: Austin Flannery, O.P., general editor, *Vatican Council II; The Conciliar and Post Conciliar Documents* (Wilmington, Delaware: Scholarly Resources, Inc., 1975), pp. 743–749.

[In October 1974, the Vatican established the Commission for Religious Relations with the Jews. As part of the Secretariat for Promoting Christian Unity, the pope ordered the Commission to develop concrete ways to make the spirit of Vatican II's Nostra Aetate *a reality. Following the lead of the Catholic Church in such countries as the United States, the commission members drew up a series of "practical" guidelines which would be used by the Church in all nations to improve Catholic-Jewish understanding.*

The guidelines were very carefully worded and, although they again condemned anti-Semitism, they made no mention of the history of Christian anti-Jewish prejudice and persecution. Instead, the guidelines referred to "mutual intolerance" and an "unfortunate past." The document also took pains to stress that Christianity was the ultimate perfection of Old Testament religious tradition.

These issues notwithstanding, the Vatican guidelines were a true breakthrough which, if truly passed on to the faithful, could begin to reverse Christianity's traditional portrayal of Judaism as a cold, legalistic, moribund religion. The Commission told Catholics that the Jewish religion emphasized love of God and neighbor as much as Christianity did. Contrary to traditional teachings, Judaism in Christ's time was a complex mosaic enriched with deep religious and cultural values. Even after the destruction of Jerusalem, with the Jews scattered among the nations, the Jewish faith remained a living and vital religion. Precisely because of these truths, the Vatican Commission urged Christians to learn more about Judaism, not only to better understand the Jewish people, but also to gain a deeper knowledge of Christianity itself.]

...the spiritual bonds and historical links binding the Church to Judaism condemn (as opposed to the very spirit of Christianity) all forms of anti-semitism and discrimination... Further still, these links and relationships render obligatory a better mutual understanding and renewed mutual esteem...

With due respect for such matters of principle, we simply propose some first practical applications in different essential areas of the Church's life, with a view to launching or developing sound relations between Catholics and their Jewish brothers.

I. Dialogue

To tell the truth, such relations as there have been between Jew and Christian have scarcely ever risen above the level of monologue. From now on, real dialogue must be established.

...Dialogue demands respect for the other as he is; above all, respect for his faith and his religious convictions.

...Lest the witness of Catholics to Jesus Christ should give offence to Jews, they must take care to live and spread their Christian faith while maintaining the strictest respect for religious liberty in line with the teaching of the Second Vatican Council (Declaration *Dignitatis Humanae*)...

In addition to friendly talks, competent people will be encouraged to meet and to study together the many problems deriving from the fundamental convictions of Judaism and of Christianity...

II. Liturgy

The existing links between the Christian liturgy and the Jewish liturgy will be borne in mind. The idea of a living community in the service of God, and in the service of men for the love of God, such as it is realized in the liturgy, is just as characteristic of the Jewish liturgy as it is of the Christian one. To improve Jewish-Christian relations, it is important to take cognizance of those common elements of the liturgical life (formulas, feasts, rites, etc.) in which the Bible holds an essential place...

III. Teaching and Education

...Information concerning these questions [Judaism and its relationship to Christianity] is important at all levels of Christian instruction and education. Among sources of information, special attention should be paid to the following:

> catechisms and religious textbooks
> history books
> the mass-media (press, radio, cinema, television)

The effective use of these means presupposes the thorough formation of instructors and educators in training schools, seminaries and universities.

Research into the problems bearing on Judaism and Jewish-Christian relations will be encouraged among specialists, particularly in the fields of exegesis, theology, history and sociology. Higher institutions of Catholic research, in association if possible with other similar Christian institutions and experts, are invited to contribute to the solution of such problems. Wherever possible, chairs of Jewish studies will be created, and collaboration with Jewish scholars encouraged.

IV. Joint Social Action

...In the spirit of the prophets, Jews and Christians will work willingly together, seeking social justice and peace at every level—local, national and international.

At the same time, such collaboration can do much to foster mutual understanding and esteem.

Conclusion

The Second Vatican Council has pointed out the path to follow in promoting deep fellowship between Jews and Christians. *But there is still a long road ahead... [Italics mine—APR.]*

Bibliographies, Timeline, and Index

Documents Bibliography

Abbott, Walter M., S.J., gen. ed.
  The Documents of Vatican II: With Commentaries and Notes by Catholic, Protestant, and Orthodox Authorities. New York: Herder and Herder Association Press, 1966. Reprinted by permission of The Crossroad Publishing Company.

Ackerman, Walter.
  Out of Our People's Past: Sources for the Study of Jewish History. New York: The United Synagogue Commission on Jewish Education, 1977.

Bachrach, Bernard S.
  Early Medieval Jewish Policy in Western Europe. Minneapolis: University of Minnesota, 1977.

Baron, Salo Wittmayer.
  A Social and Religious History of the Jews. Vols. 11, 13, 17. New York: Columbia University Press, 1967, 1969, 1980.

Bernstein, Herman.
  The Truth About "The Protocols of Zion." New York: Covici, Friede, 1935.

Bible.
  The Bible. A New Translation of the Bible containing the Old and New Testaments. James Moffatt, trans. New York: Harper & Brothers, 1935.
  The Holy Bible. Douay-Rheims Version. Rockford, IL: Tan Books, 1899.

Borchsenius, Poul.
  Behind the Wall: the Story of the Ghetto. London: Allen & Unwin, 1964.

Brockway, Allan, et al., commentators.
  The Theology of the Churches and the Jewish People. Geneva, Switzerland: World Council of Churches Publications, 1988.

Chamberlain, Houston Stewart.
  Foundations of the Nineteenth Century. Vol. 1. Trans. John Lees. New York: John Lane, 1913.

Chazan, Robert.
    Church, State and Jew in the Middle Ages. New York: Behrman House, 1980.
    European Jewry and the First Crusade. Berkeley: University of California Press, 1987. Published by Behrman House, Inc., 235 Watchung Ave., W. Orange, NJ 07052. Used with permission.

Collections of the Public General Statutes. London, 1858.

Edwards, Mark, Jr.
    Luther's Last Battles: Politics and Polemics, 1531–46. Ithaca, NY: Cornell University Press, 1983.

Fesquet, Henri.
    The Drama of Vatican II: the Ecumenical Council, June 1962–December 1965. New York: Random House, 1967.

Flannery, Austin O.P., gen. ed.
    Vatican Council II: Conciliar and Post Conciliar Documents. Wilmington, DE: Scholarly Resources, 1975.

Flender, Harold.
    Rescue in Denmark. New York: Simon and Schuster, 1963.

Gersh, Harry.
    The Sacred Books of the Jews. New York: Stein and Day, 1968.

Gilbert, Arthur.
    The Vatican Council and the Jews. Cleveland: World Publishing, 1968.

Goebbels, P. Joseph.
    The Goebbels Diaries. Ed. and trans. Louis P. Lochner. Garden City, NY: Doubleday, 1948.

Grayzel, Solomon.
    The Church and the Jews in the XIII Century. New York: Hermon Press, 1966. Thanks to the Sepher-Hermon Press, Inc. for permission to use material from this work.

Hay, Malcolm.
    Europe and the Jews. New York: Beacon, 1961.

Hecht, Ingeborg.
    Invisible Walls: A German Family Under the Nuremberg Laws. San Diego: Harcourt Brace Jovanovich, 1985.

Hilberg, Raul.
    Documents of Destruction: Germany and Jewry, 1933–1945. Chicago: Quadrangle Books, 1971. Used with permission of Random House, Inc.

Hitler, Adolf.
    Mein Kampf. Trans. Ralph Manheim. Boston: Houghton Mifflin, 1943, renewed 1971; London: Hutchinson. Reprinted by permission of Houghton Mifflin Company and Hutchinson Publishers. All rights reserved.

Israel, Gerard.
    The Jews in Russia. Trans. from the French by Sanford L. Chernoff. New York: St. Martin's, 1975. Copyright © by Gerard Israel. Used with permission of St. Martin's Press, Inc.

Kochan, Lionel, ed.
    The Jews in Soviet Russia Since 1917. London: Oxford University Press, 1970.

Krey, August, ed.
    The First Crusade. Gloucester, MA: Peter Smith Publisher, Inc., 1958. Reprinted with permission of the publisher.

Laqueur, Walter.
    A History of Zionism. New York: Schocken, 1972.

Lindo, E. H.
    The History of the Jews of Spain and Portugal. New York: Burt Franklin, [1848] 1970).

Luther, Martin.
    Luther's Works. Ed. by Franklin Sherman. Philadelphia: Fortress Press, 1971. Used by permission of Augsburg Fortress.

Mahler, Raphael, ed. and trans.
    Jewish Emancipation. A Selection of Documents, Pamphlet Series, Jews and the Post War World, no. 1. New York: The American Jewish Committee, 1942. Reprinted with permission from the American Jewish Committee.

Marcus, Jacob R.
    The Jew in the Medieval World. Cleveland: World Publishing, [1938] 1961.

Maslin, Simeon.
    Selected Documents of Napoleonic Jewry. Cincinnati: Hebrew Union College–Jewish Institute of Religion, 1957.

Massing, Paul W.
    Rehearsal for Destruction: A Study of Political Anti-Semitism in Imperial Germany. New York: Harper & Brothers, 1949. Copyright 1949 by the American Jewish Committee. Reprinted by permission of Harper Collins Publishers.

Mendes-Flohr, Paul R. and Jehuda Reinharz, eds.
    The Jew in the Modern World: A Documentary History. New York: Oxford University Press, 1980. Used by permission.

The New Delhi Report. The Third Assembly of the World Council of Churches, 1961. New York: Association Press, 1962.

New York Times.
    "The Kishineff Outbreak." May 11, 1903, p. 3.
    "The Czar on Trial." October 9, 1913, p. 12.

Oberman, Heiko A.
    The Roots of Anti-Semitism in the Age of the Renaissance and Reformation. Philadelphia: Fortress Press, 1984. Used by permission of Augsburg Fortress.

Osmanczyk, Edmund Jan.
    The Encyclopedia of the United Nations and International Agreements. Philadelphia: Taylor and Francis, 1985.

Poliakov, Leon.
    The History of Anti-Semitism. Vol. 1, *From the Time of Christ to the Court Jews.* New York: Vanguard, 1965.

Schappes, Morris U.
    Documentary History of the Jews in the United States. New York: Schocken, 1971.

Synan, Edward A.
    The Popes and the Jews in the Middle Ages. New York: Macmillan, 1965.

Tama, M. Diogene.
    Transactions of the Paris Sanhedrin. Trans. F.D. Kirwan. London, 1807.

United Kingdom.
    British Parliamentary Papers. Cmd. 6019, Palestine, 1939.

United Nations. General Assembly.
    Official Records.

United Nations. Security Council.
    Official Records.

United States. Department of State.
    General Records, Consular Dispatches, National Archives.

Wannsee Conference.
    Protocols of the Wannsee Conference. International Military Tribunal. "Nuremberg Trials" Nuremberg document No. NG 2586.

War Refugee Board.
    Papers. Franklin D. Roosevelt Library, Hyde Park, New York.

Weinryb, Bernard Dov.
    Jewish Emancipation Under Attack. New York: American Jewish Committee, 1942. Reprinted with permission from the American Jewish Committee.

World Council of Churches.
    World Council of Churches: Its Process of Formation. Geneva: World Council of Churches, 1946.

World Council of Churches Archives.
    Executive Committee Papers (1957). Geneva.

Selected Bibliography for Notes and Comments

General Histories

Baron, Salo Wittmayer.
> *A Social and Religious History of the Jews*. Vols. 1–17. New York: Columbia University Press.

Dubnow, Simon.
> *Nationalism and History: Essays on Old and New Judaism*. New York: Antheneum, 1970.

Gilbert, Martin.
> *Jewish History Atlas*. New York: Macmillan, 1969.

Graetz, Heinrich.
> *History of the Jews*. Philadelphia: Jewish Publication Society, 1894.

Grayzel, Solomon.
> *A History of the Jews*. New York: Mentor, 1968.

Katz, Jacob.
> *Exclusiveness & Tolerance: Jewish–Gentile Relations in Medieval and Modern Times*. New York: Schocken, 1961.

Morais, Vamberto.
> *A Short History of Anti-Semitism*. New York: Norton, 1976.

Rivkin, Ellis.
> *The Shaping of Jewish History: A Radical New Interpretation*. New York: Scribner's, 1971.

Roth, Cecil.
> *History of the Jews*. New York: Schocken, 1961.

Sachar, Abram Leon.
> *A History of the Jews*. New York: Knopf, 1965.

Section One: The Genesis of Christian Attitudes Toward Jews

Bible.
> *The New Jerusalem Bible*. Garden City, NY: Doubleday, 1985.
>
> *The New Oxford Annotated Bible: The Holy Bible*. New York: Oxford University Press, 1973.

Grant, Michael.
> *Jews in the Roman World*. New York: Scribner's, 1973.

Josephus.
> *The Jewish War*. Trans. G.A. Williamson. Harmondsworth: Penguin, 1986.

Strong, H.
> "Jews as Seen Through Roman Spectacles," *Hibbert Journal*. 13: 300-13. January 1915.

Section Two: The Jewish Middle Ages

Bernard of Clairvaux.
> *The Works of Bernard of Clairvaux*. Vol. 1: *On the Song of Songs I*. Shannon, Ireland: Irish University Press, 1971.

Feuerbach, Ludwig.
> *The Essence of Faith According to Luther*. New York: Harper & Row, 1967.

Gritsch, Eric W.
> *Martin Luther, God's Court Jester: Luther in Retrospect*. Philadelphia: Fortress Press, 1983.

Lunt, W.E.
> *History of England*. New York: Harper & Brothers, 1957.

Mee, Charles L., Jr.
> *White Robe, Black Robe*. New York: Putnam's, 1972.

Roth, Cecil.
> *A History of the Marranos*. New York: Schocken, 1974.

Zuckerman, Arthur J.
> *A Jewish Princedom in Feudal France, 768–900*. New York: Columbia University Press, 1972.

Section Three: Ritual Murder Accusations and Other Charges

Beck, Fink, et al.
> *History of the Church.* Vol. 4. *From the Middle Ages to the Eve of Reformation.* New York: Seabury, 1980.

Chaucer, Geoffrey.
> *Geoffrey Chaucer: The Canterbury Tales.* A Prose Version in Modern English by David Wright. New York: Vintage, 1964.

Churchill, Winston.
> *History of the English Speaking Peoples.* Vol. 1. *Birth of Britain.* New York: Bantam Books, 1963.

Cohn, Norman.
> *Europe's Inner Demons: An Inquiry Inspired by the Great Witchhunt.* London: Chatto–Heinemann of Sussex University Press, 1975.

Waagenaar, Sam.
> *The Pope's Jews.* La Salle, IL: Open Court, 1974.

Section Four: Emancipation, Repression and the Growth of Organized Anti-Semitism

Bauer, Bruno.
> *The Jewish Problem.* 1843. Ed. Ellis Rivkin. Trans. Helen Lederer. Cincinnati: Hebrew Union College–Jewish Institute of Religion, 1958.

Borchsenius, Poul.
> *The Chains are Broken: the Story of Jewish Emancipation.* London: Allen & Unwin, 1964.

Kobler, Franz.
> *Napoleon and the Jews.* New York: Schocken, 1976.

Low, Alfred D.
> *Jews in the Eyes of the Germans: From the Enlightenment to Imperial Germany.* Philadelphia: Institute for the Study of Human Issues, 1979.

Meltzer, Milton.
> *World of Our Fathers.* New York: Dell, 1976.

Schorsch, Ismar.
> *Jewish Reactions to German Anti-Semitism, 1870–1914.* New York: Columbia University Press, 1972.

Schwarzfuchs, Simon.
> *Napoleon, the Jews and the Sanhedrin.* London: Routledge & Kegan Paul, 1979.

Treitschke, Heinrich von.
    A Word About Our Jewry. Ed. Ellis Rivkin. Trans. Helen Lederer. Cincinnati: Hebrew Union College–Jewish Institute of Religion, 1958.

Zimmerman, Moshe.
    Wilhelm Marr: The Patriarch of Anti-Semitism. New York: Oxford University Press, 1986.

Section Five: The Challenges of Communism, Zionism, and Nazism

Anger, Per.
    With Wallenberg in Budapest. New York: Holocaust Library, 1981.

Bolkosky, Sidney M.
    The Distorted Image: German-Jewish Perceptions of Germans and Germany, 1918-1935. New York: Elsevier, 1975.

Dawidowicz, Lucy S.
    The War Against the Jews, 1933–1945. Toronto: Bantam, 1981.

Elon, Amos.
    The Israelis: Founders and Sons. New York: Holt, Rinehart and Winston, 1971.

Feingold, Henry L.
    The Politics of Rescue. New Brunswick, NJ: Rutgers University Press, 1970.

Friedman, Saul S.
    No Haven for the Oppressed. Detroit: Wayne State University Press, 1973.

Gutman, Yisrael.
    The Jews of Warsaw, 1939–1943. Trans. Ina Friedman. Bloomington and Indianapolis: Indiana University Press, 1982.

Hirschmann, Ira A.
    Caution to the Winds. New York: David McKay, 1962.
    Life Line to a Promised Land. New York: Vanguard, 1946.

Levai, Jeno, ed.
    Eichmann in Hungary. New York: Howard Fertig, 1987.

Levin, N. Gordon, Jr.
    The Zionist Movement in Palestine and World Politics, 1880–1918. Lexington, MA: D.C. Heath, 1974.

Levin, Nora.
    The Holocaust: The Destruction of European Jewry, 1933–1945. New York: Schocken, 1973.

Mazour, Anatole G. *Russia: Tsarist and Communist*. Princeton, NJ: D. Van Nostrand, 1962.

Morse, Arthur D.
    While Six Million Died. New York: Hart, 1967.

Shirer, William L.
> *Berlin Diary*. New York: Popular Library, 1941.
> *The Rise and Fall of the Third Reich*. Greenwich, CT: Fawcett, 1967.

Stalin, Joseph.
> *The Works of Joseph Stalin*. Moscow: Foreign Languages Publishing House, 1953.

Stroop, Jürgen.
> *The Stroop Report: The Jewish Quarter of Warsaw is No More!* Trans. from the German and annotated by Sybil Milton. New York: Pantheon, 1979.

Suhl, Yuri, ed.
> *They Fought Back*. New York: Schocken, 1967.

Thalmann, Rita, and Emanuel Reinemann.
> *Crystal Night (Kristallnacht)*. London: Thames and Hudson, 1974.

Weizmann, Chaim.
> *Trial and Error*. New York: Harper & Brothers, 1949.

Wyman, David S.
> *The Abandonment of the Jews*. New York: Pantheon, 1984.

Zuccoti, Susan.
> *The Italians and the Holocaust: Persecution, Rescue and Survival*. New York: Basic Books, 1987.

Section Six: The Post-Holocaust World: Jewry in the Latter Half of the 20th Century

Cang, Joel.
> *The Silent Millions: A History of the Jews in the Soviet Union*. New York: Taplinger, 1970.

Collins, Larry, and Dominique Lapierre.
> *O Jerusalem!* New York: Simon and Schuster, 1972.

Foy, Felician, O.F.M., editor.
> *Catholic Almanac 1989*. Huntington, IN: Our Sunday Visitor Publishing, Division, Our Sunday Visitor, Inc., 1989.

Gaines, David P.
> *The World Council of Churches: A Study of its Background and History*. Peterborough: Richard R. Smith, 1966.

Gilbert, Martin.
> *The Jews of Hope*. New York: Viking, 1985.

Gitelman, Zvi.
> *A Century of Ambivalence: The Jews of Russia and the Soviet Union, 1881 to the Present*. New York: Schocken, 1977.

Grayzel, Solomon.
  A History of Contemporary Jews. New York: Antheneum, 1972.

Gutteridge, Richard.
  The German Evangelical Church and the Jews, 1879–1950. New York: Barnes and Noble, 1976.

Hardon, John A., S.J.
  The Catholic Catechism. Garden City, New York: Doubleday, 1975.

Laqueur, Walter, and Barry Rubin, eds.
  The Human Rights Reader. New York: New American Library, 1979.
  The Israel–Arab Reader. New York: Penguin, 1984.

Littell, Franklin H.
  The Crucifixion of the Jews: The Failure of Christians to Understand the Jewish Experience. New York: Harper & Row, 1975.
  The German Phoenix: Men and Movements in the Church in Germany. Garden City, NY: Doubleday, 1960.

Littell, Franklin H., and Hubert G. Locke, editors. *The German Church Struggle and the Holocaust*. Detroit: Wayne State University Press, 1974.

Maresca, John J.
  To Helsinki: The Conference on Security and Cooperation in Europe, 1973–1975. Durham, NC: Duke University Press, 1985.

New Catholic Encyclopedia. New York: McGraw–Hill, 1967.

Panish, Paul.
  Exit Visa: The Emigration of the Soviet Jews. New York: Coward, McCann and Geoghegan, 1981.

Sachar, Howard M.
  The Course of Modern Jewish History. Cleveland: World Publishing, 1958.
  Diaspora: An Inquiry into the Contemporary Jewish World. New York: Harper & Row, 1985.

Sharansky, Natan (Anatoly Shcharansky).
  Fear No Evil. New York: Random House, 1988.

United Nations.
  "Universal Declaration of Human Rights." December 10, 1948. United Nations Department of Public Information, 57–13951.

Timeline

Introduction: Foundations

Before the Common Era (B.C.E.)

2000	Abraham's Covenant with God
1500	Israelites enslaved in Egypt
1250	Exodus from Egypt
1000	Solomon builds the First Temple
950	Solomon's sons split the kingdom
722	Assyria conquers Kingdom of Israel
584	Babylonians conquer Kingdom of Judah, destroy Solomon's Temple and deport Jews to Babylon
583	Cyrus of Persia conquers Babylon, allows Jews to return to Judah
516	Second Temple dedication in Jerusalem
450	Torah (the Five Books of Moses) canonized
325	Alexander the Great conquers Kingdom of Judah
190	Maccabbean revolt against Antiochus Epiphanes
63	Rome conquers Judea

Common Era (C.E.)

66	Jewish revolts against Roman Empire begin

Section One: The Genesis of Christian Attitudes Toward Jews

C.E.

44	Traditional date given for Jesus' crucifixion and death
49	Paul's First Letter to the Thessalonians
66	Jewish revolts against Roman Empire begin
68	The Gospel According to Mark is written
73	Masada falls to the Romans
85-95	The Gospel According to Luke is written
100	The Gospel According to Matthew is written
100-125	The Gospel According to John is written
135	Bar Kochba Rebellion
140	New Testament compiled and edited
304	Council of Elvira sets religious guidelines for Christians and makes rules to separate Christians from Jews
311	Constantine converts to Christianity
313	Edict of Milan legalizes practice of Christianity in the Roman Empire
315	Beginning of Restrictions on Jews and the practice of their faith
379	Christianity becomes the official religion of Roman Empire
418	First forced conversions of Jews occurs in the Spanish Baleric Islands
600	Pope Gregory I confirms basic Jews "rights"
1090	Henry IV invites Jewish settlement in Holy Roman Empire

Section Two: Jewish Middle Ages

711	Moors conquer Spain
732	Battle of Tours halts Moorish expansion in western Europe
800	Charlemagne invites Jews to settle in his empire
843	Treaty of Verdun splits Charlemagne's empire
962	Otto I establishes the Holy Roman Empire
1066	Jews come to England with William the Conqueror
1095	Pope Urban II calls for First Crusade; Jews massacred by Crusaders on the way to the Holy Land

1182   First Explusion of French Jews

1215   Fourth Lateran Council adopts strict rules concerning Jews

1239   Church leaders begin denouncing the Talmud

1264   King Boleslaw invites Jews to settle in Poland

1270   End of Crusading era

1290   King Edward I expels Jews from England

1394   Final explusion of Jews from kingdom of France

1478   Pope Sixtus IV establishes holy inquisition in Spain

1492   Jews expelled from Spain

1516   Venetian Senate establishes official ghetto

1517   Martin Luther posts "95 Theses" beginning Protestant Reformation

1543   Luther denounces Jews in *On the Jews and Their Lies*

1555   Pope Paul IV orders all Jews confined to ghettos

Section Three: Ritual Murder Accusations

1144   First recorded ritual murder accusation appears in Norwich, England

1272   Pope Gregory X refutes validity of ritual murder charge

1348   Jews charged with causing "Black Death" plague

1543   Luther's *On the Jews and Their Lies* makes reference to ritual murder accusations

1840   Damascus Affair

1913   Mendel Beilis accused of ritual murder in Russia

1934   Nazi propaganda accuses Jews of ritual murder

1946   Jews in Kielce, Poland, accused of ritual murder

Section Four: Emancipation, Repression, and the Growth of Organized Anti-Semitism

1550   Ivan the Terrible refuses to allow Jews in Russia

1655   Oliver Cromwell invites Jews to return to England

1740   Jews become naturalized citizens in British colonies

1772   First Polish Partition; Pale of Settlement created

1789	French Revolution
1790	Sephardic Jews given French citizenship
1791	Citizenship extended to all French Jews
1797	Napoleon's forces abolish ghettos in Italy
1806	Napoleon calls for a Great Sanhedrin
1808	Napoleon restricts Jewish commerce
1812	Jews emancipated in Prussia
1827	Jewish children conscripted in Russia
1855	Aryan Myth first appears
1858	Jews may take seats as members of (British) Parliament
1869	Germany emancipates Jews, extends civil rights
1870	Italy's Jews achieve full civil rights
1879	Wilhelm Marr forms German Anti-Semitic League
1881	Karl Eugen Dühring popularizes "racial" anti-Semitism
1882	May Laws in Russia; pogroms begin
1889	Drumont founds French Anti-Semitic League
1895	Dreyfus Affair
1903	Kishinev Pogram
1905	*Protocols of the Elders of Zion* published in Russia

Section Five: The Challenges of Communism, Nazism, and Zionism

1882	Pogroms begin in Russia; First wave of Russian-Jewish pioneers settle in Palestine (First Aliyah)
1897	First Zionist Congress
1914	First World War begins
1917	Russian and Bolshevik Revolutions; Balfour Declaration
1922	British Mandate in Palestine established
1924	Hitler writes *Mein Kampf*
1933	Hitler becomes German chancellor
1935	First Nuremberg Laws passed
1938	Kristallnacht Pogrom; Evian-les-Bains Conference on refugees

1939	British White Paper limits Jewish immigration to Palestine; Nazis invade Poland beginning Second World War
1942	Wannsee Conference sets Nazi Germany on official course of genocide against Jews
1943	Danish people rescue their fellow Jews
1944	U.S. creates War Refugee Board
1945	Nazi Germany defeated; war ends in Europe

Section Six: The Post-Holocaust World: Jewry in the Latter Half of the 20th Century

1922	British Mandate in Palestine created
1939	British White Paper
1945	Nazi Germany defeated; war ends in Europe; illegal immigration to Palestine (Aliyah Bet) grows
1947	U.N. votes for Palestine Partition
1948	Israel becomes independent state; Arab armies attack Israel; World Council of Churches denounces anti-Semitism
1953	U.S.S.R. leaders claim to uncover "Doctor's Plot"
1956	Suez Canal Crisis
1959	Pope John XXIII eliminates references to "perfidious" Jews in Good Friday Prayer
1961	World Council of Churches proclaims Jews of today not responsible for Jesus' death
1964	Kichko's *Judaism Unmasked* published in U.S.S.R.
1965	Vatican Council II declares Jews living today not responsible for Jesus' death; condemns anti-Semitism
1971	*Pravda* articles continue anti-Semitic propaganda in U.S.S.R.; Soviet Jews ask permission to emigrate
1972	U.S.S.R. imposes emigration taxes; *Refuseniks* loose jobs, are jailed and sent into internal exile
1985	Gorbachev heads Soviet government; "glasnost"; more Jews allowed to emigrate
1989	Anti-Semitic *Pamyat* holds mass rally in Red Square
1991	Coup against Gorbachev fails

Index